Relativism and the
Social Sciences

Relativism and the Social Sciences

Ernest Gellner
Professor of Social Anthropology,
University of Cambridge

1985

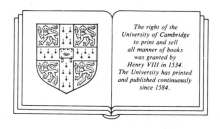

The right of the
University of Cambridge
to print and sell
all manner of books
was granted by
Henry VIII in 1534.
The University has printed
and published continuously
since 1584.

Cambridge University Press

Cambridge

London   New York   New Rochelle

Melbourne   Sydney

Published by the Press Syndicate of the University of Cambridge
The Pitt Building, Trumpington Street, Cambridge CB2 1RP
32 East 57th Street, New York, NY 10022, USA
10 Stamford Road, Oakleigh, Melbourne 3166, Australia

First published 1985
First paperback edition 1986

Printed in Great Britain at the University Press, Cambridge

Library of Congress catalogue card number: 84–17042

British Library Cataloguing in Publication Data

Gellner, Ernest
Relativism and the social sciences.
1. Social sciences–Philosophy
I. Title
300′.1   H61

ISBN 0 521 26530 4 hard covers
ISBN 0 521 33798 4 paperback

WV

Editorial preface

One of the surprises of editing several volumes of Gellner's essays has been the receipt of solicitous inquiries about when he died. Such inquiries would not be provoked before the mid nineteenth century, when the practice of one scholar's mediating the publication of the work of another was standard. With the professionalisation of the academy, mediation was ousted by patronage. Today a celebrity can write a foreword to a book by a lesser-known person, but not vice versa. This is clearly not the present case. Gellner is alive, well, and as productive as ever.

Less surprising was that our editorial work made us seem Gellner-cronies. We have indeed described ourselves as fans. This probably conjured up images of uncritical adoration of the Beatles. In the Popperian circles where we come from, being a fan does not exclude a critical attitude. How is it possible to be fans of, to value, ideas from which you dissent? Answer: ideas have to be challenging to provoke dissent: ideas, views, opinions, judgements, which we all endorse are usually trivial. The traditional rationalist view that every contribution to human knowledge, however minute, is very important, goes with the traditional view of the rational as the uncontestable – at least uncontestable in principle. Yet, being uncontestable-in-principle cannot be used as a criterion of significance.

Before we jump from the old rationalist criterion that the uncontestable is the intellectually and practically significant, to the new – Popperian – opposite criterion that the contestable is the (intellectually) significant, let us explore the grey area between the uncontestable and the contestable. There are two sides to it: firstly, exposing inconsistency; secondly, discovering new possibilities. Inconsistency is a matter of simple logic, but finding it in a person's ideas can be an intricate exercise in applied logic. Similarly with the discovery of new possibilities, e.g., destroying dichotomies. When we consider a set of ideas, theories, hypotheses, which satisfy certain conditions – certain desiderata – we seldom try to list them exhaustively, but often we have a short list. Adding to that short list is a discovery which is in a sense logical – we can prove it complies with the desiderata – it is applied logic. At times we can even complete the list of alternatives. For example, for the classical theory of rationality we have two and only two kinds of proof methods traditionally available – proof by observation and proof by contemplation – by the eye of the flesh and the eye of the mind. It is interesting to note that we do not know how to judge whether this list is complete or what conditions a newcomer must satisfy in order to enter it. Take divine revelation: is it a proof method? In a sense, of course, yes; in a sense, of course, no. Try to specify these senses. But do not be disheartened if you cannot. It takes a Gellner to do it.

So much for the grey area. As to the Popperian criterion that the contestable is (intellectually) the significant, one of Gellner's criticisms of it in this volume is that not all contestable ideas deserve to be contested. This brings us back to our relations to Gellner's ideas. Whether contestable or not, whether contested or not, Gellner's ideas are always valuable. They are sometimes so ordinary looking that one hardly feels like contesting them. He finds criticism which seems easy to patch up but which turns out on reflection to call for extensive overhaul. Or he discovers an alternative option which one wishes to dismiss out of hand, but which resists dismissal. In brief, Gellner's influence on his readers is as unavoidable as getting one's clothes wet while walking in the rain. If one gets soaked it is harder than expected to dry out: it turns out to have been no light April shower at all.

Gellner draws attention to inconsistencies and points out neglected workable options. How important are they, really? Gellner, charmingly, makes no claim, and humorously insinuates the claim to be moderate. His insinuations impinge on his style of writing to the point of interfering with the contents of his work: he eschews closely-knit, sustained arguments: preferring a sketch, a brief outline, a mere hint. This, we propose, is the strength and the weakness of his critical work.

It is the forte of a suggestive writer merely to hint. This leaves the working out to the reader. The writer can overlook a reply to his criticism when he thinks the overlooked reply has an overlooked rejoinder. He then seems disturbingly facile on a quick reading – but disturbingly astute on a careful one: Gellner's seeming facility is also garnished with corny polyglot–polycultural humour for accent. He skates fast over thin ice, while flapping his arms for lift. The requirement that he should be more careful and stand on solid ground amounts to insisting that he must not discover solid ground beyond the reach of the less facile and humorous among us. We therefore address readers disturbed by his levity with all due respect and suggest that they attempt to repeat his work more solidly with the aim of covering no less territory.

As to Gellner's positive ideas: some we endorse, some we reject. But we value these also. And, to repeat, one values the positive ideas of an author not necessarily when one agrees with them, much less when one deems them uncontestable, and not necessarily when one deems them contestable or contests them; rather, an author's significance stems from the questions he addresses being important and the answers he conjures to them being new, or from his defending old answers with new arguments or otherwise presenting them in a new light for reconsideration. All this Gellner does.

The agenda of this volume is not hidden, but may be worth rehearsing. Gellner's concern throughout is with understanding the nature of the modern world, partly by socio-historical contrast with the pre-modern world, partly by exegesis of the major attempts by philosophers to articulate explanations. Trained by the Oxford philosophy establishment, Gellner eventually came up with two criticisms of it: either it ignores the problem of the modern world or it offers facile attitudes towards it, or both. To understand a movement's ability to combine both, he turned to the study of society. Here the problem was addressed and so was the problem of addressing the problem. Hence, after expressing his utter exasperation with the philosophy of the Oxford establishment, he 'sociologised' that philosophy in his *Words and Things*. Indeed, he learns in due course to 'sociologise' all sorts of philosophies – which leads straight to philosophical relativism – except that he sociologises relativism itself as well.

His subsequent work can be broadly interpreted as his attempt to articulate a model to explain the modern world. This proceeds obliquely, as he criticises classical and contemporary rival models and attempts to elbow aside those who argue that the problem is a pseudo-problem: 'modern, pre-modern, what's the diff., its all relative, don't you see?' Between interpreting the whole of modern history (*Thought and Change*), carrying out concrete social scientific research to test the model (*Saints of the Atlas* and *Muslim Society*), and pondering the position of science in modernity (*Legitimation of Belief*), he had articulated his position only slowly and in fragments and, presumably, while grappling with continual corrections, modifications and new insights. His early volumes of essays were spin-offs and side-issues from this main project, the shape of which, we conjecture, may have revealed itself only piecemeal to Gellner himself. But by the time of *Spectacles and Predicaments* the pieces are no longer occasional, but rather integral building blocks of the whole edifice. In that volume and this we witness the appearance of two central themes which deserve future discussion.

The first is empiricism – Gellner's epistemological, sociological and moral commitment to empiricism. It is the matter, he states bluntly, of placing the wells of truth beyond the walls of the city, i.e., under the control of no group and of no interested party. Otherwise wells can be poisoned against truth, and involve the city fathers in personal and social corruption. Dare we hint that there are elements of the old shibboleth positivism here? Once more: we concur that the concern is central: the wells of truth must not be tainted, still less poisoned. Yet we would have to say that the only supplies of water we have are dammed into the social matrix and what has to be invented are not springs outside society, but, as Gellner well knows, social institutions and arrangements that make it hard to gain control of them, and which foster and reward vigilance.

The second is science; Gellner is deeply impressed by Kuhn's model of science. Kuhn may not join what Gellner has derisively called 'the pluralist chorus', but that is only because his mode of monism is deeply irrationalist and against the spirit of free inquiry that Gellner views as at the heart of science. Kuhn's model of science puts the wells of truth well within the walls, it puts them firmly under the control of the city fathers and even declares them bound by loyalty to their own edicts, whatever these be. The question whether these edicts are true is dismissed by Kuhn on the grounds that all talk of truth is pre-scientific anyway. Kuhn's radical break between pre-science and science is deceptive: it is not apposite to the problem of understanding the modern world as Gellner wishes to pose it. Less nakedly than positivism but with the same effect once more, it hands the keys of the city to the enemy. We still hope to see Gellner do a Gellnerite socioanalysis on Kuhn.

Joseph Agassi
I. C. Jarvie

Santa Monica–Toronto 1984

Contents

Introduction

These essays all circle around the problem of relativism, which is both simple and crucial. *We know better* – but how do we *know* that we know better? Others think the same with even greater confidence. There is a profound irony about the fact that this self-doubt has become most acute and anguished in the one civilisation which really does know better – namely, our own. Or rather, should this affirmation seem complacent and self-congratulatory and vainglorious, doubt seems most acute in the one civilisation which has persuaded, by the demonstration effect of superior economic and military technology, the rest of the world to emulate it. So, if its occasionally vacillating conviction of its own cognitive superiority is erroneous, it is an error which it has nevertheless, by fair means or foul, managed to foist upon others.

The claim to cognitive superiority is, however, accepted in only a limited sphere – that of natural science and related technology. This immediately raises the issue, pursued systematically by two of the essays (the second and the third), of the difference(s) between those areas and the regions in which rankings of cognitive excellence are far from consensual. Science and technology contain a fair degree of consensus internally, and receive fairly unanimous acclaim, within their sphere, from outside. But when it comes to explaining and appraising their performance, or accounting for their social roots, we find ourselves in disciplines (philosophy, sociology) where such convergence is largely absent.

It is no doubt significant that the culture heroes of the civilisation which has engendered cognitive breakthrough at least in some spheres should be Robinson Crusoe, Hamlet, and Don Quixote. They illustrate, firstly, the capacity to go it alone and reconstruct one's world from one's own personal resources, symbolised by Crusoe and exemplified in philosophy by Descartes; secondly, the tendency to fail to live up to standards of moral excellence owing to indulgence in sceptical trains of thought, and the capacity to view such weakness with sympathy, on the tacit assumption that well-founded doubt is to be preferred to brute confidence and firmness; and, finally, the pathetic capacity to leave the earthy certainties of one's own culture for a past or imaginary one. Each of these men highlights the failure of the cultural cocoon to encompass and smother the individual – or some individuals – within itself. It is of course tempting to speculate whether it is just because it is capable of engendering, tolerating, perhaps encouraging such doubts within itself, that it has become the most powerful and expansive tradition on earth.

Having thus both power and doubt thrust upon it, it has for some three centuries struggled with this question: in a world of competing dogmatisms and thought-styles, how on earth do you pick the right one? The story of this debate is largely the story of modern philosophy, in a broad sense. The answers offered have oscillated between two poles. At one extreme, there is the claim that the structure of our minds is merely the structure of *all* human minds, or even of all rational minds (Kant), and that, give or take a few built-in tendencies to error (the dialectic in Kant's, pejorative sense), valid cognition, and even a luminously self-sustaining morality, are our birthright. If this is so, why did the kind of science and morality which Kant admired, and legitimated as the inherent potential of human mind *an sich*, take quite a long time, historically speaking, to make its appearance? This question did not escape the generation of thinkers who followed Kant, and they answered it in ways which were no longer his.

At the other end of our polarity there are the romantics, who repudiate the seemingly vainglorious assumption that our reason is the norm of all humanity. They reject any claim of pre-eminence which has been made for *our* form of life, or the High Culture within it, partly perhaps from a kind of inter-cultural egalitarianism, and partly from a quite special masochistic distaste for their own culture. All cultures are equal, but one of them (their own) is a damn sight less equal than the rest. So they advise us to return to the cocoon-*Gemeinschaften* of the past, on the somewhat incoherent grounds that (a) they were much better, and (b) we never did or could leave them anyway. If this were true, it really would be rather difficult to make any sense of the transformation of the world in the past three centuries. One of the essays (the seventh) discusses in some detail an interesting recent exegesis of the philosopher who seems to be the most influential of the twentieth-century romantics.

Between these two extremes, other positions are available. There is the view that a wide diversity of cognitive styles and convictions does indeed exist, but that they can all be ranked as runners in a single race (cosmic, biological, or historical). Their difference of position is due in the end only to the fact that differential speeds have deposited them at diverse points along what, in the end, is but a single race-course. This solution, associated with the key word 'Progress', was probably the most pervasive idea in the nineteenth century, and in ours is still championed by thinkers as distinguished as Quine or (in one theme manifest in his thought) Popper. It certainly has the merit of not insisting on an unplausible universality of our own way of thinking, or of pretending, contrary to the manifest conviction of the participants in this alleged race, that each participant has his own finishing line and that *all* of them are winners. However, it still does claim that there is but one race, and that all participants are running in it. I am rather sceptical about either of these contentions.

The truth of the matter seems to me to be that diversity and radical change are indisputable realities, but that the solutions we have inherited from the nineteenth century to the problems called forth are no longer workable or even plausible. The romantic solutions are frauds. Nor is there a single-criterion perpetual endeavour, nor indeed is there perpetual change. Sustained and cumulative cognitive growth is neither a birthright nor the fulfilment of some age-old pervasive trend: it is an altogether singular predicament. So if the inherited solutions won't do, one must seek another. These essays explore the way towards it.

The comprehension of our singular situation, and of the chasm which separates it from other social orders, may well require an approach which is not the same as that formed within the successful, consensual, cumulative sciences. This brings us back to the problem of the difference between the natural and the social/human sciences, which is the theme underlying most of the book. One essay in particular (the fifth) is concerned with the discussion of one recent prominent style in the social sciences and humanities which has in fact had only partial success; and another (the sixth) with the type of half-historical, half-anthropological approach to the preconditions of our situation, which I believe to be fruitful. The work discussed in that essay is concerned with the emergence of the kind of High Culture which eventually becomes universalised in our type of society, and it is all the more illuminating by doing it through the seemingly trivial, but in fact very revealing, subject of gastronomy.

It is not the function of an introduction to summarise the arguments of a book. I only wish to say that, though the essays contained in the volume were written in diverse contexts, they possess a common core of problems and ideas. They play their part in a single, coherent, though as yet incomplete endeavour.

1 | Positivism against Hegelianism[1]

It is a curious but indisputable fact that every philosophical baby that is born alive is either a little positivist or a little Hegelian. It is also interesting that philosophically, Europe has remained in the eighteenth century, as it was prior to the diplomatic revolution: there is an Anglo-Austrian alliance, facing a Franco-Prussian one. Muscovy and the states and principalities of the Mediterranean area tend to be aligned with the Paris–Berlin axis, whilst the Scandinavians side with the opposing camp. Poles of distinction have fought on both sides.

A pattern which seems so deep, pervasive and persistent does require explanation and comment. It is possible, but improbable, that when so many men continue to be attracted by a given style of thought, there should be nothing whatever in it. Each side does of course have a very definite image of the other. If either of these images-of-the-enemy constituted the whole truth there would remain little to be said, other than dismissing one side or the other as unworthy of serious attention. There is even the possibility that both sides might deserve such dismissal. Professor J. O. Wisdom of York University, Toronto, once observed that he knew people who thought there was no philosophy after Hegel, and others who thought there was none before Wittgenstein, and that he was prepared to contemplate the possibility that both were right.

The image each side has of the other is simple and damning. In Hegelian eyes, positivists, by equating phenomena with their observable and isolated manifestations, are doomed to superficiality, a naive by-passing of the real problem of knowledge, and the endorsement of the political status quo: *chiens de garde*, jackals of the established order. They are doomed to such conceptual and political one-dimensionality by the fact that they cannot ask deep questions or consider radical alternatives, and they have willingly, nay eagerly, imposed such shackles or blinkers

[1] I am indebted to many people for helpful criticism of this paper, but especially to John Watkins, who read it in typescript, and to Hans Albert, who commented on it at a conference devoted to the thought of Karl Popper, in July 1980. Needless to say they cannot be held responsible for my views.

upon themselves. They revere observable facts, and these are but the surfaces of things. Truth is deeper.

By contrast, look at the members of the other movement, as seen by the most distinguished living representative of the Anglo-Austrian alliance, Sir Karl Popper:[2]

Many years ago I used to warn my students against the widespread idea that one goes to university in order to learn how to talk, and to write, impressively and incomprehensibly. At the time many students came to university with this ridiculous aim in mind, especially in Germany . . . most of those . . . who . . . enter into an intellectual climate which accepts this kind of valuation . . . are lost.

Thus arose the cult of un-understandability, the cult of impressive and high-sounding language . . . I suggest that in some of the more ambitious social sciences and philosophies, especially in Germany, the traditional game, which has largely become the unconscious and unquestioned standard, is to state the utmost trivialities in high-sounding languages.

Some of the famous leaders of German sociology . . . are . . . simply talking trivialities in high-sounding language . . . They teach this to their students . . . who do the same . . . the genuine and general feeling of dissatisfaction which is manifest in their hostility to the society in which they live is, I think, a reflection of their unconscious dissatisfaction with the sterility of their own activities.

There you have it. Victims of their own humbug: their self-deception leads them into social dissent. Presumably they would learn to accept their environment more graciously if only they knew how to think, talk and write clearly.

The counter-image is as brutal. The late T. W. Adorno writes:

Society is one . . . Sociology, which disregards this and remains content with such weak and inadequate concepts as induction and deduction, *supports what exists* in the over-zealous attempt to *say* what exists. Such sociology becomes ideology in the strict sense – a necessary illusion. It is illusion since the diversity of method does not encompass the unity of the object and conceals it behind so-called factors into which the object is broken up . . . it is necessary since the object, society, fears nothing more than to be called by name, and therefore it automatically encourages and tolerates only such knowledge of itself that slides off its back without any impact.

This quotation comes from the same volume as the one from Popper, namely *The Positivist Dispute in German Sociology* (p. 76; italics mine). Other observations by Adorno also deserve citation:

Positivism internalizes the constraint exercised upon thought in a totally socialised society in order that thought shall function in society. It internalizes

---

[2] *The Positivist Dispute in German Sociology*, by T. W. Adorno, Hans Albert, Ralf Dahrendorf, Jürgen Habermas, Harald Pilot and Karl Popper, London, 1976, pp. 294 and 296. This volume constitutes the starting-point of the present discussion.

these constraints so that they become an intellectual outlook. Positivism is the puritanism of knowledge. What puritanism achieves in the moral sphere is, under positivism, sublimated to the norms of knowledge . . . knowledge denies what it seeks; what it ardently desires, since this is denied by the desideratum of socially useful labour. Knowledge then projects the taboo which it has imposed on itself onto its goal, and proscribes what it cannot attain. . . The felicity of knowledge is not to be . . . positivism grants a logical form to the sexual taboos which were converted into prohibitions on thought some time ago . . . Knowledge resigns itself to being a mere repetitive reconstruction. It becomes impoverished just as life is impoverished under work discipline.

(pp. 55–6)

Or again:

As a social phenomenon, positivism is geared to the human type that is devoid of experience and continuity, and it encourages the latter – like Babbitt – to see himself as the crown of creation. The appeal of positivism must surely be sought in its a priori adaptation to this type . . . Positivism is the spirit of the age, analogous to the mentality of jazz-fans. Similar too, is the attraction it holds for young people . . . Perhaps objective emptiness holds a special attraction for the emergent anthropological type of the empty being lacking experience. The affective realization of an instrumental thought alienated from its object is mediated through its technification. The latter presents such thought as if it were avant-garde.

(pp. 58–9)

These are fighting words. A pseudo-radicalism which in fact serves the established order, emasculates those who use it (literally or figuratively), fit for Babbitts, jazz-fans, and empty minds. (The cultural downgrading of jazz has a certain period flavour, dating from Adorno's youth rather than the 1980s.) So we have an army of verbiage-intoxicated, pseudo-rebellious windbags, meeting a horde of inwardly vacuous, conformist, impotent Babbitts, presumably led into battle by its own jazz-band. One assumes that the other side fights to the strains of Wagner. This should be quite some encounter.

The volume under discussion presents such a confrontation. It must be said right at the start, firmly if with regret, that it is a damp squib. It is a little like that last battle at which Muscovy secured its freedom from the Tartar yoke – when the Russian and Mongol armies took a good look at each other and both wisely decided to retreat, though no doubt abusing each other in the process. A contributor to the volume, Ralf Dahrendorf, records the disappointment:

the discussion generally lacked the intensity that would have been appropriate to the actual differences in view . . . the underlying moral and political positions were not expressed very clearly . . . At times, it could indeed have appeared, astonishingly enough, as if Popper and Adorno were in agreement . . . For many participants, the Tübingen discussion left a keen feeling of disappointment.

(pp. 123–30)

Moreover, Dahrendorf noted that the battle was not only disappointing, but also strangely triangular:

the discussion was dominated neither by Popper nor Adorno, but instead by a 'third man', conjured up by almost all participants . . . against whom the two symposiasts unreservedly adopted a common stance. This 'third man' was given several names by his friends and enemies alike – 'positive method', 'unmetaphysical positivism', 'empiricism', 'empirical research', and so on.

(p. 125)

The plot thickens.

Perhaps it is necessary to bring out the underlying issues between Hegelian windbags and positivist Babbitts, whilst at least temporarily suspending the contempt they feel for each other, and at the same time bringing back that Third Man, the *jointly* disavowed character, on to the scene. Paraphrasing Oscar Wilde, when Popper and Adorno damn a position in unison, there really must be a great deal in it. The mediaeval Frederick II was said to have a Christian view of Islam and a Muslim view of Christianity. Perhaps we can achieve a similar kind of objectivity.

Battle lines

What are the features of the intellectual life of mankind, if one takes modern scientific knowledge as its paradigm? This sketch is meant to be provisional, and as expository and as unprejudicial as it is possible to make it. If, inevitably, it will be prejudicial, I hope it wears its prejudices on its sleeve, so that issues prejudged can be examined afresh. The picture presented manifestly owes a good deal to Popper, though obviously he cannot be blamed for any particular defects in this particular presentation.

Knowledge is cumulative and progressive. The cognitive capital of mankind *grows*. There are occasional cases of the reopening of issues which had been supposedly closed, of a reversal of a past consensus; but nevertheless, by and large, *later* means *better*. This is so notwithstanding the fact that it is difficult to express formally the criteria in terms of which such progress is achieved.

Knowledge is also technical and often genuinely difficult. It is articulated in a specialised idiom which is not continuous with ordinary speech and which can be acquired only by sustained effort and training (in most cases, fairly early in life); and the idiom is of the essence of the knowledge formulated in it. This is true notwithstanding the fact that *some* technicality may be redundant, spurious, or possess no real function other than the protection of the monopoly of the guild of its users. In most cases, however, the technicality is genuine: the ideas formulated in it cannot genuinely be translated into non-technical terms. When they are so translated, they lose the precision, or whatever quality it is, which makes them so genuinely operational and cumulative.

The joint consequence of the first two traits is that there is genuine innovation in these fields. Hence it is possible to write intellectual history in terms of the first occurrence of a given idea. It is possible to locate the point in time when it was first put on the ledger. Once it is firmly formulated and publicly available, there is a strong and natural presumption that other formulations of it are cases of repetition, of diffusion. Conversely, it follows that it is not very likely that earlier formulations will be found: had they occurred, they would have been diffused and been known from the start.

Connected with these traits is the fact that there is an infinite reservoir of possible ideas and theories.

From this in turn there follows the well-known consequence that the finding of a true theory, or even one true-so-far, is something of a miracle, the location of a needle in an infinitely large haystack. But as there is also an infinity of ever-accumulating data, no theory can be known to be definitely established, even if it should be wholly compatible with all currently available data.

Both theories and data are *relatively* isolable, both generically from each other, and, so to speak, laterally, from fellow-theories and fellow-data. *Problems*, above all, are relatively separable from each other. One issue can be dealt with at a time. Orderly procedure, step by step, is feasible, and does not appear to vitiate the activity as a whole. Bulk purchase, total package-deals, are not generally mandatory. It is possible to implement Descartes's Second Rule of Method:

Divide each . . . difficulty . . . into as many parts as possible, and as might be necessary to resolve them.

Apart from being separable from each other, problems, data, and ideas are also separable from their human carriers or agents. Scientific truth falls upon the just and the unjust alike. It is uninterested in their private lives.

In rough and provisional outline, the world of intellectual endeavour and cognitive advance, in the natural sciences, seems to have these traits. Contrast this with the realm of social and moral ideas, which after all also constitute part of our intellectual life.

The number of available ideas seems limited rather than infinite. If there is one well-established law in the field known as the History of Ideas, it is that whatever has been said has also been said by someone else on an earlier occasion. Although a certain relative originality is possible, it is largely a matter of the combination of primary ideas and of context. The ledger *already* seems to contain very nearly all possible ideas, and the unsatisfactoriness of that tacit sociology which is half incapsulated in the history of social ideas lies in the fact that it seems to explain what people do in terms of what some thinker said or wrote. But, as all the ideas are in effect ever-present, the problem is rather why some of them acquire a powerful appeal at a given time. The History of Ideas becomes a pseudo-sociology when it pretends to explain historical events in terms of the thinkers of the age. The pool of ideas being ever-present, conduct cannot be explained in terms of the sheer presence of an idea. One has to explain why *it*, rather than its rivals, came to be effective on that occasion.

The pool of basic ideas seems limited. Moreover, they are not technical. Admittedly, some of those who articulate social ideas occasionally do so in difficult language, which strikes terror and awe in the hearts of the non-initiate, and is presumably meant to do so. But the genuineness of this technicality is generally open to doubt. It cannot be a pre-condition of cumulativeness (because there *is no* cumulativeness), and it is by no means obvious that the ideas in question cannot be successfully and without essential loss translated into an ordinary idiom, continuous with common speech.

The insulation of ideas from each other and from the data also seems far more difficult to implement. Problems seem curiously inter-dependent, not to say intertwined. Answers to one question seem inescapably cross-linked to answers to other questions. Even if we do not know what the answers are, we seem to know that they stand and fall together. . .

More particularly, the insulation of theories or ideas from data and facts seems much harder to ensure. This holistic quality of both social ideas and facts used to be called the Principle of Internal Relations: everything is what it is in virtue of its relations to everything else, and thus in the end there is but One Big Thing. In contemporary idiom, this reappears as the contention that the data are concept-saturated, and the concepts in turn theory-saturated. This may in some measure be true generally, but it is doubly and especially so in the human and social sphere, for the following reason: the conceptual saturation occurs not merely in the mind of the observer, but equally in that of the person *observed*. He too has ideas which guide, pervade, and constitute his actions. Ideas pervade the action itself and not merely its interpretation. This leads to the well-known variant of the idealistic solution to the problem of knowledge: the knower and the known are the same, and it is for this reason that the former can know the latter. For such idealism, knowledge is self-knowledge; thereby it overcomes that otherwise terrifying barrier between Subject and Object. (Not only is knowledge self-knowledge, but morality becomes self-recovery, and the problem of why one should be moral at all finds its solution in the identity of true self and of moral command.) Giambattista Vico is celebrated as the man who most clearly articulated the view that we can understand the human and social world best, because *we made it*. (The successful history of modern science suggests that it is nature which we understand better, because we did *not* make it.)

Moreover, whereas scientific theories are relatively insulated from the identities of their propounders, or critics, social theories tend to be identity-involving. The social identity of the person holding a crucial view concerning the legitimacy of this or that type of social order changes in accordance with the belief. The ability to use the very concepts required to characterise, and indeed to act out, a given social role or a given social relationship may depend on the prior comprehension and endorsement of a given social vision. In other words, social ideas frequently produce what may be called the Pirandello effect. That is, they resemble the theatrical devices characteristic of the playwright Luigi Pirandello, who causes his characters to converse with the author, the actors with the audience, and so forth, in a deliberate attempt to break down the barriers between author, character, actor, audience – between subject and object, in effect. In the theatre, this only happens as the result of a deliberate ploy on the part of the author and/or producer; in modern philosophy, it happens persistently.

Moreover, these ideas are not just intimately involved with their carriers and their social identities; they are intimately involved with *each other* too. The affirmation of one idea tends surreptitiously to refer back to the alternative view which it replaces, in a way which suggests the modern associations of the word 'dialectic'.

Finite in number, ever-present and doomed or destined to an eternal return, wedded to each other in intertwined holistic tribal groups, incapable of observing the decencies of separation of subject and object – such are, by and large, our social ideas.

But there's worse to come, if we look at the decision procedures, the manner of settling disputes amongst them. The strangeness of these procedures is of course a corollary of their peculiar traits. Their decision procedures are identity-involving, where those of natural science are identity-abstracting. The manner in which one's identity is involved in the choice of social ideas is both weird (if measured against the standards of the conventional models of the theory of knowledge) and yet also most familiar and human. It resembles not so much the matching of theory and fact, of subjecting a general idea to an experiment, but rather the way in which a man struggles in inner conflict, with the inward confrontation of rival and incompatible moods, each of which claims sovereignty over the entire and persisting self, and in the end settles for one of them; or the way in which an emotionally absorbing interpersonal conflict, a *row*, finds its resolution (if indeed it does).

In such situations, no hypothesis is tested against a crucial experiment. There are no such: generally speaking, both sides have access to the same range of facts (whether the contestants are two moods within one individual or two persons). Nothing really hinged in *Othello* on the availability of the handkerchief. Two total interpretations of Desdemona are locked in conflict within Othello's breast, and each of them can cope with all the facts. (The manner in which the rival interpretation can and does cope with all the facts is, precisely, infuriating. The recognition that facts can be *so* brazenly distorted, that a blatant truth is so cynically flouted, when seen from the rival stance, raises the temperature of the dispute. But it feeds a sense of doubt as well as a feeling of anger, and facilitates the eventual switch-back.) In genuine inner conflict, a man tries on each of the conflicting moods for size; generally, he is not wholly happy with either (if he were, there'd be no conflict). Each of the moods tries to grip and tie him to itself, to make itself permanent; he may indeed swear to himself that this time, no, he will not weaken and let himself be seduced by the rival one . . . but the weakness becomes reclassified as deliverance when the vision switches again.

If the problem is resolved, in the sense that a stable inner peace is re-established, it seems that eventually one of the two moods finds a strong and permanent anchorage and support in both external and internal 'facts', and an identity is 'found'; but one might equally say that an identity is chosen and selects its facts and interpretation. There simply is no outside, 'objective' view.

The manner in which the rival moods/vision feed on each other, are parasitical on each other, eventually generate each other's emergence, claim but do not really possess outer vindication – all this strongly suggests those abstract philosophy-invented nouns which haunt one school of socio-epistemological thought: nouns such as 'dialectic', 'negation', 'positing', 'transcendence', 'mediation', 'totality'. Vacuous verbiage for the positivists – yet it seems at least to be an idiom for conveying, perhaps with excessive deference and solemnity, this particular kind of intellectual experience.

It is worthwhile putting down this impressionistic binary opposition, the alignment of two loose syndromes, in tabular form:

Natural Science	*Social Thought*
infinite reservoir of possible ideas	a limited, possibly a finite and not too large pool of ideas
Technical formulation, i.e., the dependendence of the ideas on a prior erection of a complex conceptual scaffolding whose mastering is a prolonged and arduous business, is of the essence of the enterprise.	Technicality, though it exists, is suspect and questionably relevant. It is not seen to lead to superior performance, and is, with disproportionate frequency, part of the window-dressing.
markedly cumulative	rather given to Eternal Return
issues are separable from each other and can be dealt with one at a time, without prejudice to other issues	strong tendency to mutual interdependence of issues, so that a revision of one reopens many or all others
is predominently transcultural	deeply culture-involved
specific issues (if not the style as a whole) dissociated from the personality and social role of investigator	Pirandellian: issues involve choices of identity, morality, total vision
testable with relative finality	'deep' and ever inconclusive
incommensurateness relatively rare	choices between viewpoints that are often 'incommensurate' and involve a 'leap'
new ideas can be discontinuous from old ones	innovations tend to retain an intimate link with their predecessors, being their 'dialectical negations'

Note that I have attempted to use relatively neutral, ironic and hence unprejudicial terms to characterise the right-hand syndrome. But the holistic, 'jumpy', incommensurate and identity-involving traits found there are what, it seems to me, gives some sense to the terminology favoured by the neo-idealists (words such as 'totality', 'mediation', 'dialectic', 'transcendence'). They are of course wrong in supposing that these terms either explain, or even characterise with much precision, the phenomena which concern them. But then, the presentation of words in lieu of explanations is a sin which can be found in many quarters.

The Third Man

So far, I have not attempted to pass any judgement on these two models or approaches. But the fact that I have attempted such a provisional neutrality must not be interpreted as implying that I think that there is nothing much to choose between them, that they are equally good, each in its own sphere, or something of the kind. The resolution, if it comes, will not be that facile. In the mean time, we can just note how concentrating on one sphere or the other may naturally lead us to one of the two favoured models of the cognitive life of mankind. The comportment of social ideas – relatively few in number, human in idiom, tending to merry-go-round, interlocking, emotive, reduplicating the subject in the object, and identity-linked – easily leads us to a holistic and idealistic theory of knowledge. Natural science, with an endless reservoir of discrete, impersonal and technical ideas, cumulative and seldom step-retracing, naturally leads us to another. There is an elective affinity rather than a compulsion about this alignment: sometimes, features may be reversed and found in the opposing camp. (Marxism is a curious conflation of a materialist sociology with an idealist epistemology and ethic.)

The Positivist Dispute in German Sociology was intended to bring about a confrontation between these trends for the edification or enlightenment of all, but, as Dahrendorf noted, conspicuously failed to do so. The mysterious Third Man, whose haunting presence he also noted, may be part of the clue to what went wrong. *Is* there a Third Man? He certainly pervaded the discussion. But was perhaps one of the official participants impersonating him, casting his shadow?

Perhaps part of the explanation of the failure of the confrontation lies in the excessive contempt for each other of the main combatants. In his second and interestingly autobiographical contribution to the volume, Popper observes (p. 289):

... I did not go out of my way to attack Adorno and the 'dialectical' school of Frankfurt (Adorno, Horkheimer, Habermas, *et al.*) which I never regarded as important, unless perhaps from a political point of view; ... I could never take their methodology (whatever that may mean) seriously from either an intellectual or a scholarly point of view.

Then he turns to the sub-plot of the volume, to the Third Man. Now the curious thing is that whilst the main plot – empiricist v. Hegelians – never takes off, the sub-plot *does*. This issue concerns 'positivism' (the name given to the haunting Third Man), and in particular, the question whether Popper himself is a positivist. Popper hotly denies it. His opponents, on the other hand, use the term to describe his position. The issue is far more than a verbal one, and it is highly interesting. It also feeds back into the main issue, and throws a great deal of light on it.

Is he or isn't he?

There are at least two quite distinct criteria for what a man believes, or for his doctrinal classification: (*a*) self-characterisation, and (*b*) interpretation of his centre of gravity. As far as criterion (*a*) is concerned, what a man says about himself is final. He ought to know. Excluding untruthfulness (which is not contemplated here), this method gives interesting results on the assumption that the thinker questioned is tolerably coherent, is familiar with the terminology for classifying beliefs, and has a reasonable measure of intellectual self-knowledge. All these assumptions may be granted. As far as *this* criterion is concerned, the answer is simple and final: Popper is not a positivist.

Criterion (*b*) is more complex and less conclusive. The work of a significant thinker can never be simply a list of atomised, isolable ideas. What makes a thinker significant, amongst other things, is that his work possesses some measure of unity, and that it contains some central ideas which pervade and inspire the corpus as a whole. Just what those ideas are, and the manner in which they pervade the rest (or on occasion fail to do so) must in the nature of things be in greater or lesser measure a matter of interpretation, depending on emphasis, on one's interests, and so forth.

If, in the case of Popper, I were asked to identify one idea only which is at the centre of his vision, I should unhesitatingly name *falsifiability*: the supreme requirement that our convictions should earn their keep by being occasionally, or indeed as much as possible, at risk; that they should make plain what they say about this world by indicating the conditions or considerations which would make them false. There is no safety in safety, you might say: the central doctrine of Popper's is in effect a condemnation of those ideas or systems of ideas which attain safety by being so constructed as to evade all danger.

One of the considerations invoked by Popper to rebut the suggestion that he is a positivist is that he warmly embraces various overtly metaphysical views. There are at least three such: realism (in the sense of the objective existence of an external reality); libertarianism (doctrine of the freedom of the will); and Platonism, in the sense of belief in the independent existence of 'thinkables'. Such views are no doubt incompatible with positivism; he does hold them, on the evidence not merely of his say-so, but also of interesting and supporting observations he makes about them. *Ergo*, he is no positivist. QED. As far as criterion (*a*) goes, there the matter rests.

In terms of criterion (*b*), the matter is more complex. The main objection one may raise against these various beliefs is, *precisely*, that they sin against the requirement of falsifiability. Take, for instance, realism, in the sense of a belief in the objective existence of an external world. The contrary view consists of asserting that the 'external world' is simply a way of referring indirectly to our experience. Many people find this view repellent and paradoxical. Things *explain* the occurrence of appearances; they are not exhausted by appearances. They are not just code words for clusters of possible experiences.

However, what induces some of us at least to be hesitant about objectivisim is the following consideration: what piece of *evidence* could ever turn up which would show that the external world is something *more* than just experience? Whatever piece of evidence turned up would be, precisely, just one *further experience*. So, with a sigh, perhaps, we acknowledge that the difference between realism (the outer world is *more* than experience) and phenomenalism (the outer world is *nothing but* experience) simply isn't one which can be settled in the way in which we settle differences about more specific matters of fact *within* the world.

The difference between the two positions, realism and idealism, apart from the verbal one, may be found in the suggestiveness of each vision for further inquiry; but neither vision, in its dispute with its rival, seems susceptible to testing. It is just this reflection – which of course is very old, but which can be formulated in highly Popperian terms, and which must spring naturally in the mind of anyone deeply imbued with a good Popperian sense of the importance of testability, of the obligation of cognitive risk – which makes one somewhat lukewarm about asserting the 'reality of the external world' – *precisely* because one cannot quite imagine what risk this contention can run. At best, I am inclined to say that the phenomenalist reduction of external things cannot do justice to the manner in which theoretical objects and scientific constructs are fertile in leading to further problems and discoveries: if these 'con-structs' were merely convenient abbreviations, notational devices, as phenomenalism requires, then one would expect them to be, as it were, inert, and not heuristically pregnant. The invention of shorthand was after all no landmark in the history of science. The fact that they seem to be *active* agents, not passive notational conveniences, can be *conveyed* by 'realism', if you wish: but it doesn't really *explain* this 'lively' quality of our 'constructs'.

This makes me allergic to assertions of realism with emphasis: emphasis and joy, it seems to me, should be reserved for theories which contain genuine explanations, models which *really* throw light on that which is to be explained, and which are really testable by application to data other than those initially suggesting the problem. Realism about the existence of the external world does not seem to me a theory satisfying these requirements, and for this reason I accept or reject it with a shrug. And it seems to me that one must never forget that phenomenalistic reductionists do have a point in reminding us that no data can ever show that there is something in the world over and above our data.

The active nature of our inquiry, the denial of the passive receptacle theory of mind, is central to Popper's views, of course. It seems to me entirely correct. Knowledge is the exploration of something Outside, *not* the stock-taking of his possessions by a person locked into a solitary cell. But epistemological realism seems to me more a way of highlighting this than of explaining it. To be a genuine explanation of this independent life and penetrative power of our theories, realism would have to be testable by some *other* consequence; and there seems to be no such independent testing-ground. This being so, realism seems to me a pseudo-explanation.

The dangers of realism

Popper likes to stress the active nature of mind. He believes this to be linked to his epistemological realism as follows: the commonsense (realist) view of the world can be retained, if one abandons the commonsense (passive, receptacle) theory of mind. Thus the active theory of mind is a kind of Enabling Act of realism: it makes it possible to hold realism.

The situation seems to me more complex. In a sense, what matters for realism is not the active theory of mind, but the active theory of *concepts*. Concepts are more than a shorthand code, more than abbreviations for patterns of experiences: our concepts, when they are good ones, enable us to handle experiences which we had never noticed before, and which, consequently, we had previously not needed to subject to any abbreviating notation. It is this active aspect of concepts which inspires realism: what the concepts refer to, what they name, must really be there, must it not, if quite new manifestations of it turn up? Abbreviations are inert and only lead back to what they abbreviate.

But beware: does realism say any more than that concepts have this active, creative capacity? Does it in any way *explain* it? I fear that it does not, and that is why I am chary of treating such 'realism' very seriously.

But there is even more to it than this. Realism carries certain dangers with it. The big danger is that this or that concept is explained by assuming that what it refers to must be 'out there', that some of our concepts are absolutised, and not seen for what they are, *our* tools, or as Popper would have it, *our* conjectures. It is for this kind of reason that R. G. Collingwood, whom Popper is otherwise inclined to admire, insisted that realism has its base in human stupidity. The stupidity is twofold: the human-conceptual element in knowledge is ignored, being replaced by a naive echo theory of knowledge, where knowledge echoes what is 'really' out there; and some specific version of what is conjectured to be 'out there' is absolutised.

Realism would be harmless if indeed it remained totally unspecific (which is of course what Popper intends), insisting merely that there is *something* independent of us which in the end decides whether our conjectures are valid. (Kant conveyed this unspecificity when he said that the Thing in Itself was a kind of X, a limiting or contrasting notion.) Unfortunately, realists in this imperfect, dogmatism-addicted world tend to be a bit more specific, surreptitiously or otherwise, and tend to absolutise this or that interpretation of the real, making it mind-independent and turning it into something *more* than mere conjecture. The paradox of Popper's position is that he wants everything to remain for ever conjectural, non-absolutised, man-made, but at the same time wishes to affirm a realism (which is, in these circumstances and with these reservations, totally unspecific and harmless). Its only important content is that it conveys that the truth of conjectures (which *we* make) depends on something we do *not* make or control. This is an admirable view which I endorse totally. What is objectionable in such a form of realism is only that firstly, it can hardly avoid giving the impression that it explains the situation (by invoking the 'real') when it merely characterises a situation; and secondly, in the hands of careless and potentially dogmatic people, it becomes specific and exempts some concept or doctrine from conjectural, man-made status.

There are further ironies in this situation. The first-person orientated subjectivists to whom he objects are in fact fellow-realists: their insistence on the primacy of private data arose precisely from the fact that only by concentrating on the *given* data could one escape the often dogmatically imposed interpretations of this or that world-view. The point about the absolution of sensory data by the empiricist tradition was not that they were private, but that they were *given*, out of reach of the manipulation and control of any social thought-system. They were an escape route to objectivity: and, indeed, the only one.

They can only be spurned by those who naively and complacently assume that a basically sound intellectual tradition is our ever-present birthright. Then, of course, there is no need to escape and we do not need pure data to help us to do it. Then one can firmly opt for a third-person language and the current aggregate of science, as Quine[3] has it, or construct an epistemology without an individual subject, trusting the Third World of collectively erected thinkables (Popper). It amounts to much the same. Both thinkers believe that taking it all in all, all's well with the world, and in particular without cognitive tradition, and has been so ever since the amoeba. Quine seems to think so all the time, Popper only seems to think so most of the time: he has his qualms when he remembers the Dark Age, between the establishment of the Closed Society by early tribal man and its erosion by the Ionian proto-Popper. (He has never properly integrated this Dark Detour into his pan-evolutionary, amoeba-to-Einstein cognitive optimism.)

The facts of the matter are different, and rather sadder, alas, than either Quine or Popper realises. All is not at all well with most cognitive traditions. Most are stagnant. The Cosmic Exile, or subjectivist empiricism, which both these thinkers spurn, was probably essential for the establishment, or at any rate the philosophical ratification, of that healthy, cumulative cognitive tradition which both of them take far too much for granted. It is *not* our birthright. Its emergence was a miracle. It had a historic start, emerged in specific conditions, and is much beholden to the empiricist–'subjectivist' tradition which codified its rule and philosophically ratified it.

Quine's version of this objectivism, the denial of a first-person, data-orientated epistemology, is well argued in the aptly named 'Epistemology Naturalized'.[4] Here as elsewhere, he advocates the shift from the first- to the third-person idiom, the abandonment of the search for the ego-centred data base. What is wrong with this position is highlighted by a very significant pun which Quine allows himself (p. 72):

The Humean predicament is the human predicament.

In a very important sense, the Humean predicament is *not* the human predicament. Hume and the tradition to which he belongs are highly untypical of the human condition. Most men and traditions make individual observations (e.g., about the vagaries of the weather) only

---

[3] Willard Van Orman Quine, *Word and Object*, Cambridge (Mass.), 1960, p. 24.
[4] In his *Ontological Relativity and Other Essays*, New York, 1969, ch. 3.

within the framework of a fairly rigid vision, an aggregate, not of science, but of something else (dogma, assumption, myth, what have you). The problem of validating scientific inference and extrapolation, i.e., Hume's problem, arose only in the idiosyncratic tradition which happened to become endowed with cumulative science. The problem needed to be posed in the first-person, ego-centred manner, as indeed epistemology from Descartes to Kant formulated it: for initially, this tradition was established and codified by Crusoe-like individual refugees from an earlier, cognitively stagnant culture. The Cartesian myth of Cosmic Exile, so well named, and also derided, by Quine, was important because it provided the tools for thinking about *cultural* exile. Science, cognitive accumulation, was not a birthright dating back to the amoeba; it began as a cultural aberration. One might put it like this: later Popper clearly is aware of the importance of World Three, culturally created. But he has not given sufficient thought to the fact that historically, there is a plurality of such worlds, erected by diverse societies. Only one has engendered cumulative science. How does one identify its secret? Was not individualism an important ingredient in it? And was not the subjectivist–empiricist tradition in philosophy the epistemological charter of that individualism?

This aspiration for an epistemology without a knowing subject (Popper), or a naturalised epistemology, without Cosmic Exile or a 'prior philosophy' (Quine), can also be criticised in the following terms: it is all very well, if you assume, tacitly or otherwise, a unilineal vision of the history of mankind or of all life. If we are all safely on the right rails, there is no need to pull the emergency cord and endeavour to get off. Quine obviously does believe that, all in all, we are on the right lines. Popper also believes it – trial and error is all the secret of cognitive advancement, and it has always been with us – though with the not quite coherently worked out qualification about a dead-end branch-line, known as the Closed Society. But what if, in fact, unilinealism is radically wrong? What if most lines lead to cognitive perdition, and only a minority, perhaps only a single one, lead forward? And what if the only way to find out whether or not one is in a dead-end is to get off and look at one's line from the outside, and what if the Cartesian Cosmic Exile strategy, subsequently refined by the ego-centred empiricist tradition, happens to be the only way of doing this?

Historicist philosophies which openly espoused unilinealism and articulated it explicitly were conducive to a subsequent perception of its falsehood. The trouble with Popper's and Quine's philosophies is that the unilinealism, whilst essential and presupposed by their positions, is so tangential and peripheral to their central and clearly formulated interests that it is barely noticed, or not noticed at all. Hence its falsehood does not lead to a rethinking of the position.

One can in some measure empathise with the allergy which Popper evidently feels towards subjectivism, towards the reduction of the whole scientific enterprise to a mere tabulation, codification and manipulation of one's private experience: this seems to devalue the spirit of the whole thing. Science is reduced to the pursuit of a shorthand code for tabulating one's own sensations, with a view to manipulating their future occurrences for one's own advantage – Narcissus doubling up as accountant and profiteer – ugh![5] The elegance of any simple but far-ranging theory is demoted to the status of a mere convenience. This crass instrumentalism seems somehow to fail to do justice to the drive behind inquiry, which is to know something true independently of ourselves. (The fact that the theory devalues something we hold dear does not automatically make it false, but it does help explain why some of us so ardently wish it to be false.)

But the situation is complex and deceptive: is it not possible that the repugnant-seeming subjectivism is in fact really an objectivism? The empiricist–positivist tradition tends towards the position that in the end, knowledge is and can only be about *my* experience, *my* data – because if it were about anything else, it would be about that which I do not experience, about the transcendent, and that is metaphysics. But it all depends on how you read this. Is knowledge about *my* data, or about my *data*? The reason why empiricism clings so to experience is not because it is mine (experience presumably has to be *someone's*), but because it is *outside my control*, because it is *given* to me, and there is little or nothing I can do about it. It is its imposition *on* me, without my consent, not its imposition on *me*, that makes it so valuable as the ultimate arbiter of cognitive claims.

This is the real root of the marked empiricist predilection for the first person singular, and against the third person singular, as the ultimate idiom of knowledge. Of course, the third person idiom is inherently 'realist' in that it places the knowing self in the context of a wider world and treats them both alike, thus presupposing or prejudging the reality of that world outside the agent. It does not favour the agent or observer as against the world, but treats both of them alike. By contrast, the first person singular gives priority to the observing self, and suspends the world, treating its existence as *sub judice*. A third-person language is

---

[5] The positively religious quality of Popper's epistemological realism, and the manner in which its denial is a kind of *lèse majesté* of science, is well and sympathetically conveyed by Bryan Magee, *Popper*, London, 1973, pp. 37 and 38.

articulated in terms of *things*, a first-person language in terms of *evidence*. In a first-person language, everything is on trial; the world and everything in it, to use Popper's favourite term, becomes a *conjecture*.

The point of the alleged 'subjectivism' is not that this or that self becomes the judge, but that there *is* a judge at all, some judge, for everything, that everything becomes subject to judgement, to conjecture. The self is introduced not in order to introduce private caprice, but for the opposite reason, to curb it: a *judge* is required to reduce all other participants to the status of mere witnesses, allowed to present evidence which is then assessed, but *not* allowed, as is their wont in the traditional order, to demand credence by virtue of their status (which is then, in time-honoured circular fashion, confirmed by the picture which they are presenting in their testimony). The epistemic subject of the empiricist proscribes such behaviour: he coldly inspects the data and finds they do not warrant the attribution of authority to the theories accompanying them.

It is difficult and perhaps impossible to achieve this in third-person language, which has an in-built bias towards 'realism', in the bad sense of dogmatism, of projecting our concepts on to reality as if they were inherent, immovable aspects of it. It neglects the human, optional element in the conceptualisation of things: it attributes reality, and a very solid, immovable reality at that, to the shadows which our own intellectual activity has cast. It is in this sense that R. G. Collingwood equated realism with 'dogmatism or error in general'.[6] Realist third-person language can of course doubt of *some* things, it can render *some* ideas conjectural; but it is very difficult for it to doubt a very great deal, for its very articulation depends on using a kind of referential language, indicating and presupposing this or that kind of object, and insinuating their existence in its own terms of procedure. This is all very well in a healthy, cumulative cognitive tradition; but hopeless in a stifling, dogmatic one. *Then* only a first-person idiom, which, as it were, conjecturalises everything, can help one break out of it. This is what the Cartesian epistemological tradition did. The seemingly subjectivist ego-judge contemplating its own 'data' looks at everything as evidence, and thus minimises prejudgement. Third-person language is realist–dogmatic: first-person language is conjecturalist.

The highly familiar counter-argument is of course that the procedure which transforms all (prejudicial) things into (supposedly quite neutral, unprejudicial) evidence, is illusory. All data, all evidence, are interpretation-saturated, even when articulated in first-person language. Even to

[6] *Speculum Mentis*, Oxford, 1924, p. 281.

identify and characterise them as this or that kind of data invariably presupposes classifying and interpreting them. Not all interpretations can be queried at the same time – so some prejudgement survives even in the subjectivist trial, in which the observing ego contemplates its evidence in its *forum internum*. Recently, it has been fashionable to assert that a first-person language is in principle impossible and that playing at it is covertly parasitic on a presupposed third-person, public language. This was the significance of the assault on the idea of a 'private language'.

No doubt freedom from interpretation is not fully achieved even in a first-person idiom: but the amount of prejudgement is far less. The very act of looking at data as *data*, as evidence for or against theories or interpretations which are inherently conjectural, *rather than as examples of theories seen as inherently parts of the very nature of things* (which was the old way), completely transforms the situation. It signals and highlights that everything is conjectural, that there is no fundamental indubitable furniture of the world; there can at most be a fundamental form of *evidence*, but not of *things*.

We may of course indulge in conjectures of which we aren't even aware and which we consequently do not query; but the subjectivist twist ensures that whatever is properly articulated can then no longer be absolutised, cannot be treated as a kind of guaranteed echo or part of reality, in the old naive realist manner. First-person language may not be able to pick out automatically each and every theoretical interpretation which pervades this or that piece of 'data'. But, by the very fact of being first person, of speaking about 'evidence before me' rather than 'the world', it automatically and mercilessly ensures that no interpretations can be sacrosanct. If articulated, they can also be queried. They are the fruits of *our* theoretical activity, and cannot be hallowed, absolutised by 'reality'. Thus everything is bracketed in doubt.

It seems to be eminently doubtful, historically and logically, whether this bracketing, the vision of world-as-conjecture, could have been achieved without empiricist subjectivism, without the use of personal experience as a 'prior philosophy', as a device of attaining Cosmic Exile. Historically, the ego-centred epistemology of Cosmic Exile did of course flourish in an individualist age in which private inquiry for once refused to honour public, shared, collective, 'realist' orthodoxy. But over and above this manifest historical association, it seems to me doubtful whether a well-entrenched dogmatism, well equipped with self-maintaining circular devices, can ever be budged, as long as it is allowed to insist on 'realist', third-person language. It is only the switch to a first-person language, which suspends the authority of the language in which the dogmatism is articulated, and insists on bringing it before a first-person court, which can break through a well-fortified, well-entrenched dogmatism. It is the atomism (which calls for one issue and one fact at a time, no self-maintaining packages please) and the seeming subjectivism of the empiricist–positivist tradition which alone achieved this, and I doubt whether it could have been done in any other way.

Popper of course wants to make everything conjectural, but without subjectivism, doing epistemology 'without a knowing subject'. This is strictly parallel to Quine's eagerness for a 'naturalised', third-person epistemology.[7] The paradox of Quine's pragmatism is that it is realist, third-person-addicted, whilst at the same time throwing away the great aesthetic benefit of realism (which one suspects to be very important in Popper's philosophical motivation), namely, a non-instrumental view of science. Quine's realism appears to remain in service of a view of knowledge which in the end is concerned primarily with predicting the flow of *our* data . . .

Popper's and Quine's mistakes here seem to me to be identical, and to have the same root: excessive, insufficiently troubled confidence in that third person, realist language or system of ideas which we happen to use. Most significantly, both invoke its historical-evolutionary record. If the cognitive practice of humanity, indeed of all life since the amoeba, is all in all sound, well, that's just fine. There is no need for a total re-examination of our conceptual equipment from a private-judge viewpoint, which is just as well, given that this operation of cognitive Inner Emigration is fraught with notorious difficulties. The establishment of a genuine, effective private conceptual quarantine is difficult, if not impossible. So it is just as well that it is not necessary.

But isn't it? Popper's evolutionary optimism is less unqualified than Quine's, in so far as Popper also has a theory of a tendency of a certain important part of life, namely of all early and of much later humanity, towards Closed thinking and a Closed Society, in which scientific method, or learning from experience, is suspended, in the interests of a social and conceptual system-maintenance. Progress then requires that this deadlock be broken, which may not be easy. Popper unfortunately rather vacillates between saying that the break-out is very easy and presents no problem, and holding that it is very difficult and requires heroic intellectual qualities. I fear that the latter view is closer to the truth.

Nevertheless, the effort made in this direction, the inadmissibility of

[7] 'Epistemology Naturalised', in *Ontological Relativity and Other Essays*.

invoking evidence other than that allowed by the private court, does make for greater justice. Above all, it excludes the prejudgement of issues which are *sub judice*. By contrast, the great dogmatisms of human history do exactly the opposite: they endeavour to proscribe and castigate any attempts at treating their doctrines as *sub judice* as blasphemous. The empiricist court-like procedure, which is subjectivist only in the sense that it invites each individual to act as a solitary juror, has broken this device, and I doubt whether it could have been done in any other way.

The Popperian injunction to treat all ideas as conjectural is ineffective against well-constructed self-maintaining intellectual systems, which can easily go through the motions of examining objections but can be relied upon to come out with the right answer in the end.[8] Philosophers nowadays are a little easy with claims that certain jumps or leaps involve transitions between two incommensurate banks. But the leap from a substantive-realist world in which basic features were rightly entrenched to an epistemic world-as-conjecture where everything is, in the end, for grabs, and where only evidence is king, really was a qualitative transformation.

It is doubtful whether it could have been accomplished without the realisation that our data are but *our* data, that we cannot go beyond them, and that what is out of reach is indeed out of reach, and cannot be rigid and prescribe to us what our data may be. We may still use the limiting or contrast-notion of the other as an unspecified X, as Kant said about the Thing in Itself. Such a minimal and apologetic realism may be allowed, and formally speaking, it could be claimed for Popper that his realism is of this kind, given his insistence on the conjectural nature of all, but *all* ideas. But somehow his realism, given its enthusiastic exposition and the lack of sympathy shown for the considerations underlying the empiricist 'subjectivism' and epistemological Machismo, is more substantial.[9]

---

[8] I wonder whether some enthusiastic Popperite will develop a legal philosophy recommending the abrogation of the fiction of inadmissible evidence, and advise courts to allow juries to bring in and above all to avow any prior impressions, provided they are willing to submit them to test. The trouble is that, whereas the court of natural science can remain ever open and refrain from any final positive verdict, ordinary courts must reach conclusions, one way or the other, within a finite time limit. So must we all in facing the issues of daily life. This is of course the simplest way of formulating the well-known objection to Popper's claim to have solved the problem of induction, if that problem is interpreted as requiring that we should explain why it is that some as-yet-unfalsified theories are treated as much better bases for action than others.

[9] There is also the interesting question as to whether realism or Machismo is more suggestive for the working scientist. It seems to me that it can work both ways. Sometimes a 'sense of reality', as opposed to a 'sense of data', can suggest hypotheses; but at other times, a sense of how *we* assemble or construct our data

The seemingly subjectivist empiricist or positivist tradition, insisting that all theories be judged by isolated data contemplated by isolated individuals, who are cognitively sovereign and not obliged, or allowed, to consider anything other than the evidence brought before *them* – so that all the great visions and theories can only enter as well-behaved, deferential witnesses, and not as authoritative Higher Courts, as was their wont – *that* story is a beautiful and important parable and confirmation of the manner in which the sway of dogmatism was broken. This achievement might not matter, if it were the case that we did not and do not have much to fear from dogmatic stalemates, forcibly imposed. But in a world in which this danger is an important reality, the repudiation of the empiricist private-court theory seems to me to have a touch of ingratitude and complacency about it. It underrates the great discontinuity in the cognitive history of mankind, and the role of empiricist, 'subjectivist' thought in our liberation. Historically speaking, individualism can be assumed to have been crucial in our liberation; philosophically, ego-centric epistemology was its ratification and confirmation. The myth of Cosmic Exile, like the Robinson Crusoe story with which it is patently linked, marked and symbolised historic rupture, a great *coupure*.

The case of Platonism, the doctrine of the independent reality of thinkables, seems to me similar. It is plainly an important fact that we think in abstract concepts, that the terms we use have a one–many relationship to things, and the classes of objects delimited by them are often open and infinite – all of which suggests that the meanings of these terms cannot be equated with classes of concrete, denumerable objects. It also seems obvious that systems of concepts are inter-personally sustained and not built up by individual minds. Moreover, attempts to explain this capacity of ours in terms of homely human things such as custom and decision, which would shift the responsibility for the application of concepts to new cases to our habits and choices and thus dissolve the mystery, do not seem to work. All this is indeed so: and if the assertion of Platonism is a way of reminding us of this, and of the fact that it is a *problem*, that we do not understand how this works, well, that's fine, and in that sense I am a Platonist too.

But in that sense only. The offensive thing about this kind of

can lead to a fruitful shift of vision. However, the claim that this factor was at work in Einstein, and that his ideas were rooted in Hume–Mach operationalism, has been interestingly criticised by Elie Zahar. See 'Mach, Einstein and the Rise of Modern Science', *British Journal for the Philosophy of Science*, 28, 1977, and 'Second Thoughts About Machian Positivism', *British Journal for the Philosophy of Science*, 32, 1981.

Platonism seems to me precisely that it seems to offer an untestable pseudo-explanation. To say that 'abstract entities exist' doesn't even remotely offer a model of how we come to have this mysterious power, or of the manner in which our thought is constrained by concepts. The differences between his and Plato's Platonism which Popper lists[10] do not seem to me to affect this objection.

In the physical world, the existence of an object often does constitute a genuine explanation and is of course testable; but the generic 'existence' of Ideas as such explains nothing whatever. (Popper's insistence on the entirely human manufacture of the Third World makes it difficult to understand how such an all-too-human version of the transcendent can do the job traditionally assigned to it – to explain logical and moral compulsion.) The existence of concrete things is contingent, and genuinely explains certain situations. The existence of an American continent explains why Columbus *could not* reach the East Indies by sailing west from Spain. But the assertion of the 'existence' of abstract objects does not, to my mind, explain the phenomena it is intended to explain – such as the validity of moral ideals, or the possibility of mathematical inference, or the possibility of abstract thought. (Popper admittedly puts a lesser load on this theory than Plato did; how *much* smaller, I am not clear.) The existence of abstract entities *seems* to explain these phenomena, but as the alleged existence cannot be independently tested and checked, its assertion amounts to little more than a reaffirmation of those phenomena, falsely masquerading as an explanation.

Popper explicitly asserts[11] that realism is not refutable, but he also unambiguously characterises realism as a 'conjecture'. It is precisely my Popperism which makes me feel ill at ease with a conjecture that runs no fatal risks. Popper seems to allow these risk-free conjectures a special kind of status as a type of metaphysical auxiliary service to real, testable science. (This is an amusing form of inverse Platonism, in which the Transcendent serves the Immanent rather than vice versa.) His account of the situation seems convincing. But why should one prefer realist to instrumentalist language to describe it?

The affirmation of 'free will' seems to me to suffer from the analogous defect.

An interesting argument in favour of the doctrine of free will is found in Popper: could anyone have predicted, for instance, Mozart's next composition?[12] Intuitively, we feel that the answer must be *no*. So was it

---

10   Karl Popper, *Objective Knowledge*, Oxford, 1972, pp. 102ff.
11   *Objective Knowledge*, pp. 38, 100, 115.
12   *Objective Knowledge*, p. 223.

not a free creative act? It is particularly heartwarming to demonstrate libertarianism from the greatest flights of human creativity. But is the argument cogent?

It seems to me that on closer examination, the argument from Mozart breaks up into three distinct but conflated or confused subsidiary arguments, each of which is rather questionable:

(i) In our cultural tradition, works of art are, by definition, *original*. If someone called Bloggs had predicted, ahead of time, a sonata of Mozart's, it would then be Bloggs' sonata, and Mozart would promptly become a plagiarist. The notion of predicting, ahead of time, a work ascribed to a given person, in all its details, is in a covert way a contradiction. The notion of originality, i.e., the absence of a full prior specification, is tacitly incorporated in the notion of authorship. (This is particularly true of musical compositions, which in a sense are not 'things' at all – unlike, say, paintings or sculptures – but *are* the specifications, the recipe, for a repeatable *performance*.) So one reason why we cannot predict a composition of Mozart's is that to do so is simply a contradiction.

But this purely logical and in a way quite vacuous consideration in no way excludes, so far as originality goes, the possibility of predicting a given composition, provided it is not *defined* in the prejudicial and question-begging way as being the work of a given man at a later date. Such a description already entails that no one else had previously constructed the specification of that particular work – and 'prediction' would of course have to be just such an earlier specification.[13]

The sense of contradiction is further reinforced by another thought. Great achievements, which are remembered and attached to the name of those who attained them, are generally at the limits of human powers. That is what makes them great. They are very, very difficult. Predicting complex events is also very difficult. It is hardly imaginable that someone should bring off *two* such supreme achievements simultaneously – to compose as well as Mozart, *and* to predict such complex achievements (which in fact has seldom, or perhaps never, been done). It would all be a bit like the cartoon joke about the reporter waiting on the peak of Everest for the first climbers to reach the summit. What made that worthy of a laugh was that it suggested that a man could achieve *en passant*, alongside another job (reporting) a feat which was at the limits of the powers of the best climbers of the day. Predicting a Mozart composition is strictly

---

[13] This alleged proof of the unpredictability of works of art, and hence of human free will, is also found elsewhere. See, for instance, Maurice Cranston, *Freedom: A New Analysis*, London, 1953, p. 166, or Peter Winch, *The Idea of a Social Science and its Relation to Philosophy*, London, 1958, p. 93.

analogous. But once again, it does *not* follow from the fact that some achievements (notably such a simultaneous 'double') are patently beyond us that determinism is false.

(ii) Extremely complex phenomena are generally unpredictable. This, however, in no way implies that they are undetermined. Complex physical phenomena, in which the end result is the consequence of the interplay of a large number of small and subtle factors, are unpredictable, but we do not therefore conclude that they are undetermined. It is very easy to make use of this fact to construct artefacts producing unpredictable, random results. The roulette wheel is one such artefact; but we do not invoke the roulette wheel to prove the possibility of freedom.

Works of art are clearly complex and, in virtue of their complexity, unpredictable. But this consideration, on its own, in no way justifies our invocation of works of art as demonstrations of human liberty.

(iii) Aesthetic excellence has certain unusual characteristics. In other fields, where problems sometimes have unique solutions, great performances can on occasion be predicted. If, say, a mountaineering problem has only one solution, then someone who knows the facts of the case may be able to predict its solution, *because he knows the criteria of what is to count as its solution.* Those criteria, jointly with the facts of the case, determine the solution and make it predictable in principle for someone in possession of the facts of the case *and* of the criterion of a solution. Note that the second condition is indispensable. But in aesthetics, the criteria of excellence, if they exist, remain undiscovered. It also follows from this that we can never have good grounds for believing that a given artistic problem has a unique solution.

In the argument from Mozart to human liberty, 'Mozart' is evidently a code name for excellence. But someone assigned the task of predicting how Mozart will construct his next composition of a given type does not have the advantages given to a man predicting how a superb chess player, mountaineer, or engineer, will solve a given problem. Solutions in chess, mountain climbing or bridge construction at least quite often seem uniquely determined, partly because the criteria of success are reasonably clear (in chess, almost totally clear). Not so in music and art generally, especially within a tradition such as ours which values originality and incorporates it within the norms of excellence. So prediction is *also* precluded because the person attempting to predict is deprived of one of the absolutely crucial pieces of information relevant to his task, i.e., the criterion of its accomplishment. It is impossible to predict the course of a ship if you are not told its intended destination.

Predicting a work of art in an originality-stressing culture is like predicting the course of a ship which is forever changing its destination. But volatile destinations could exist in a determined world, and thus the argument fails once again. Volatile or unidentified destinations cannot automatically confer freedom on the world in which they happen to occur.

So the fact that those in pursuit of beauty cannot define their objective, and thus deprive those who would chart and monitor their progress in advance of one of the pre-conditions of doing so, does *not* seem to me to exclude the possibility that their conduct is nevertheless determined. Predictability and determination are not so closely linked, and when predictability is excluded by these extraneous considerations, the issue of determination remains open.

Thus three quite distinct arguments lie hidden and conflated in the appeal to Mozart. No one of them seems to me remotely cogent. The failure to separate these arguments may have given them an entirely spurious air of persuasiveness. But linking very weak arguments in a chain does not result in a strong chain.

Of course, we do have powerful motives for feeling drawn towards the notion of free will. We seem to have an intimate (though not necessarily veridical) experience of it; and the assumption that we are endowed with free will seems to be the basis of moral reasoning, which we are loth to abandon. But the problem is not advanced by the sheer assertion that we are indeed endowed with free will (still less when the assertion is buttressed by very feeble arguments). The reason why the mere assertion does not advance matters – whereas the affirmation of the existence of specific physical objects or classes thereof often does provide genuine explanations – is precisely that this affirmation does not seem open to independent testing, and in the end it amounts to little more than a somewhat mystifying, prejudicial, and perhaps cheaply optimistic reformulation of original problems. In other words, it is Popperian reasons – the penchant for testable, non-vacuous, genuine explanations – which make me feel so ill at ease with bland and bare assertions of libertarianism. I hope libertarianism is true, but I'd prefer it to be a genuine theory with some cutting edge, before giving it full attention.

This attitude of distrust towards the untestable is one which I learnt partly from Popper's work and its pervasive spirit. The ironic conse-quence is, however, that when Popper upholds positions which seem to violate this central attitude, I have some difficulty in treating them seriously.

Meaning and science

The issue of *meaning* can also be invoked as a means of product differentiation between Popperism and positivism. If Popper is not distinguished from latter-day positivists by his objectivism, realism and libertarianism, perhaps the dissociation can be established by means of their divergence on this point. The logical positivists practised philosophy above all by circumscribing *meaning*. Popper insists that he never did anything of the kind. His falsifiability principle demarcated not meaning, but *science*. Thus, he insists, it is a grave mistake, committed by many, to contrast his falsifiability principle with the Verifiability Principle as two rival theories of the limits of meaning. I have in fact heard a distinguished professor of philosophy castigated by another well-known professor of philosophy of Popperian persuasion for committing a *howler* in making precisely this contrast, and thus attributing a falsifiability theory of *meaning* to Popper.

Is it a howler? It seems to me not merely no howler, but not a mistake at all – rather a perfectly reasonable and plausible interpretation. Once again, if we go by criterion (*a*), there is of course no question about it: Popper has not endorsed a falsifiability criterion of meaning, but on the contrary repudiated such a theory, and thus, by this criterion, it may not be attributed to him, and that's that. By criterion (*b*), the answer is again much more complex, and criterion (*b*) is to my mind at least as significant as (*a*), and perfectly legitimate as long as one does not confuse or conflate the two criteria.

The logical positivist definition of meaning was inevitably somewhat confused. Clearly, though, it could not define 'meaning' in the sense used by working linguists as the classes of sound patterns which are emitted, recognised and socially accepted in a given speech community. By such a criterion, 'metaphysical' statements patently would be meaningful. The anti-Platonism of paradigmatic logical positivists equally prevents us from interpreting the delimitation of meaning as the characterisation of a given essence of 'meaning', as for them there are no such essences (though in some semi-conscious manner, and in disharmony with their nominal anti-Platonism, I strongly suspect that this was precisely what many of them *did* mean).

The only thing which in effect they could mean, plausibly and in harmony with their other principles, was this: the definition circumscribed, not the *de facto* custom of any one or every linguistic community, but the limits of the kind of use of speech which deserves respect and commendation. It was a definition not of meaningful speech, but of commendable, *good* speech. Their verificationism was a covert piece of

ethics. Meaninglessness was a condemnation, and meaning a commendation. The valuation conveyed was underpinned by an important
and plausible background model of language and the world, a model
which stressed the importance of interaction between the two. Such a
model highlights the uselessness of parts of language which in no way
interact with non-linguistic reality, i.e., the world, or provide services for
other parts of language which do. One can characterise and stigmatise
this uselessness as 'meaninglessness', nonsense, which of course is
precisely what the logical positivists did.

But what precisely did Popper's demarcation of *science* amount to?
Science is defined in terms of falsifiability. Popper's early work is a
paean in praise of falsifiability, and a condemnation of *un*falsifiability.
Science is not merely circumscribed, but held up as a model for
knowledge. Falsification-evading systems such as Marxism or
psychoanalysis are held up to derision not merely because, as a matter of
academic interest, they happen not to satisfy a given criterion, but
because it is *wrong* to violate that criterion; because theories which
satisfy it advance knowledge, while those which systematically evade it
not merely fail to advance it, but actually hamper its advancement.
Those who present unfalsifiable claims as *Knowledge* are guilty of
passing counterfeit currency.

The only thing which gives bite and interest to the demarcation of
'science' is precisely this evaluative content, and its linkage to an
important and plausible background model for the world and knowledge. Without all this, the demarcation of science would constitute a
fairly pointless lexicographical exercise. One might as well say that X is
definable by falsifiability plus perhaps other traits, and then go on to add
that X corresponds more or less to what in a given language or culture is
called 'science'. (As a piece of descriptive linguistic sociology, this claim
would probably need an awful lot of qualification.) But it is quite plain
that the young Popper was not working on linguistic sociology, or
compiling dictionaries; less obviously, he probably was not an essentialist either, and hence it ought not to be supposed, at least not without
further evidence, that he was on that occasion describing an essence, an
independent thinkable, called 'science'. What he was really doing was
identifying science in order to hold it up as the beau ideal of *good*
cognitive practice. (Einstein good, Marx, Freud, Adler bad.) He was
proposing a covert ethical principle, to be applied to our cognitive
comportment.

So, on interpretation (and I hold these interpretations to be correct),
we do get two entirely comparable ethical principles, eminently suitable
for mutual confrontation: one articulated in terms of verification, and

the other, of falsification. The bit about 'meaning' in the case of the logical positivists was just part of the rhetoric, in fact a rather effective way of conveying the evaluative charge of the principle. Likewise, the significance of the definition of *science* on the other side was not a sociological delimitation of one cultural activity amongst others, comparable to the demarcation which an anthropologist might be anxious to make between, say, magic and religion. The real point of it was that science was to be taken as a model and an ideal. So the model has to be defined with precision. And so the alleged incomparability between Popper on science, and logical positivism on meaning, also evaporates.

But *The Logic of Scientific Discovery*[14] was not merely a paean to testability and to its proud carrier or champion, science. It was also a putative solution of the problem of induction, and thereby a legitimation of science, or of the cognitive mode it exemplifies or spearheads. The scandal of the unfounded and dubious base of scientific inference was thereby to be cleared up at long last. Popper's solution is well known: induction does not exist. Science does not proceed by inference from facts to theories or to other facts. It proceeds by postulating theories, *deductively* inferring their consequences, and checking those consequences against the facts. This process of elimination of theories employs only steps whose logical status is deductive. The celebrated consequence, warmly welcomed by Popper, is of course that whilst science eliminates falsehood, it does not definitively and finally establish any truths. There is an ever-growing area of eliminated falsehood; but although its recruits were previously inhabitants of the other pool, containing the as-yet-unfalsified, yet this second pool, though supplying the members of the *growing* rival one, cannot itself be said to shrink – for its membership is infinite. There is an infinite reservoir of possible theories.

The major and most pervasive logical operation in science, conceived in this manner, is the *modus tollens*. Its general form is: suppose p; if p entails q, and if q is false, then p is false. In this schema, p is a theory, p *implies* q conveys the relationship of the theory to any one of its consequences, and q is the consequence which, through its experimental falsification, brings down the entire theory.

All this is of course utterly familiar. But it itself has a consequence which must be valid if it is not to bring down the entire argument, whether or not it stands up to *other* objections. That consequence is: the world must contain what might be called falsifiers, reasonably hard, self-sustaining facts which can establish, with reasonable confidence, the

[14] London, 1959.

truth of *not-q*, which can then bring down some *p*. Perhaps, indeed the world must ultimately consist of nothing but such hard falsifiers; as the late Imre Lakatos once observed, for us Popperians, facts are basically falsifications. But in any case, whether or not this is also required, what is certainly needed is that it should at least contain a good supply of them. If theories are to be shot down, there must be some bullets with which this is to be done. If the world were to contain nothing but mushy, soft material, unsuitable for bullets, nothing could ever be shot down.

But that is of course *precisely* what holistic idealists maintain is the case. They live in a world of the tropical jungle, in whose thick undergrowth everything is so tangled with everything else that you can never isolate any one single thing, or can do it only by the ruthless use of a machete which kills that which it separates. 'Abstraction' was once for them a term of philosophical abuse. By contrast, empiricists/atomists live in a desert consisting of hard, discrete, isolable pebbles, each one of which can easily be separated from the others. This is of course the background metaphysics of classical empiricism, and it is mirrored in logic by the calculus of propositions, whose first rule is that every atomic proposition is totally independent of all others.

Now my point here is this: elimination by *modus tollens can only work* in a world which is at least closer to the metaphysics of the empiricists than to that of the holistic idealists, to the sand/pebble desert rather than to the intertwined flora of the Amazon jungle. It need not perhaps be absolutely like the granular vision, but it must not be too much unlike it. Even if grains are not absolutely hard, they must not be too mushy; in the viscous mud of the tropical swamp, we should flounder helplessly. To put it in unmetaphorical language: there must be at least reasonably unambiguous and certain facts, which can serve to eliminate theories. Even if they are not endowed with absolute bedrock status, and even if it be admitted that they themselves are also theories when looked at from the viewpoint of micro-evidence, yet they must be more certain, more reliable than the theories which they are eliminating. The regress of argument which terminates in these eliminations must go from the more abstract, more general, more speculative, to the more concrete, specific, and the better established. If the argumentation by which a given theory is eliminated loops back and *up* again to other theories of equal or greater generality and abstractness, without which it cannot be eliminated, then we are back in that conceptual interdependence and intertwining which finds its expression in the coherence theory of truth and holistic idealism. Progress by elimination cannot function in such a world. It can only aspire to All or Nothing, or, in some characteristic Hegelian ecstasy, to both at once. But not to sober cognitive progress.

In fact, *The Logic of Scientific Discovery* is indeed pervaded by a sense of such a granular world, which it shares with the logical positivists and of course with classical empiricism. But whether or not it is so pervaded (I think it is), it is logically compelled to presuppose it because without it, the *modus tollens*, the hypothetico-deductive model of science, simply cannot work.

Popper's development

It is customary to distinguish between the young and the old Karl Marx, the young and the old Wittgenstein. An important difference of stress or focus also exists between the early and the late work of Popper, and it is closely connected with the issues under discussion.[15]

In my view, epistemological principles are basically normative or ethical: they are prescriptions for the conduct of cognitive life. The pseudo-psychological, pseudo-logical or pseudo-linguistic forms in which they are often formulated obscure that. I have of course made use of this in attempting to show that the cutting edge both of the Verifiability theory of *meaning*, and the Falsifiability theory of *science*, are in fact entirely comparable. They are both covert pieces of cognitive ethics. The rest is rhetoric or mystification.

But moralists, in any field, seldom castigate sins which do not tempt their clientèle. The conduct of an age can generally be reconstructed from seeing what its preachers denounce. And so it is in the sphere of knowledge. Moralists have to be *agin* something. An epistemologist is a species of moralist. The real problem of knowledge, however, is a differential problem: it is important to show why some have it and why others don't, and to explain both success and failure, to commend the one and to reprove the other.

The young Popper fits in well with this schema. The early work is plainly normative; it distinguishes between Good and Evil (the falsifiable and the falsification-evading, though the matter is complicated by his leniency towards metaphysics, which is unfalsifiable but tolerated,

---

[15] An important precedent for a stratigraphical approach to Popper was of course set by the late Imre Lakatos in 'Criticism and the Methodology of Scientific Research Programmes', *Proceedings of the Aristotelian Society*, 69, 1968–9. My own identification of strata in the thought of Popper is particularly indebted to W. W. Bartley III's 'Theories of Demarcation Between Science and Metaphysics', in I. Lakatos and A. Musgrave, eds., *Problems in the Philosophy of Science*, Amsterdam, 1968. However, Bartley's paper seems to be more of a recommendation of the way in which Popper's thought or its interpretation should go than an account of a development which had already occurred. I am inclined to think that the change of stress had already taken place (I'm not clear whether or not Bartley shares this view); though this historical claim is not essential for my overall argument.

thanks to providing auxiliary services to science). The principle of segregation of the sheep from the goats involves above all the *modus tollens*, and that, in turn, presupposes the granular picture of the world.

The normativeness is strongly marked in the Young Popper (hereafter YP); its differentiating principle between Good and Bad cognition is *science*, defined as the practice of subjecting guesses to tests of their consequences. The use of science for this end presupposes the granularity of the world, and a well-defined, sharply outlined picture of the method of science. Though this account of method differs from the alleged Baconian version of empiricism by its stress on elimination rather than verification, it nevertheless overlaps with it at another point: whether we verify or falsify, on either account we do it with the help of two tools, and two only – logic, and the confrontation with fact. Theories are judged by two judges – logical consistency, and conformity with facts. (The difference between the two models lies only in whether the facts damn sinners, or canonise saints. For YP, there were some properly certificated sinners, but never any definitively canonised saints.)

These two judges exhaust the panel; no others are available. This doctrine of two-and-two-only is tied in with the granularity and the enormous stress on the *modus tollens*. Within these terms of reference there is indeed no room for anything else. It is this stress which accounts for the widespread, natural, and to my mind justified identification of YP with positivism, notwithstanding the protests of Popper himself. It is true that in YP, the granular world-picture, presupposed by the centrality of the *modus tollens*, is not also egocentric and subjectivist, as it is in classical empiricism. (I have never understood how this is consistently possible. Physicalist language, after all, is a theory, which only some men have elaborated and learnt to use; so it cannot be the ultimate idiom for all the grains available to all men. Commonsense language likewise embodies theories which deserve testing. If the idiom in which the grains are described is itself subject to doubt and query, we are back in the circular world of interminable debate; and away from the factterminated world of the *modus tollens* with its definitive eliminations. But if physicalist or commonsensical language is not so subject to test, with what right do we so absolutise it? And if we do not, what is there other than the data of private experience, by which we could test it?)

The general philosophical spirit of *The Logic of Scientific Discovery* overlaps with positivism not merely in its use of a background granular metaphysic which resembles the positivist one (in being granular, even if not in being articulated in the first person singular, but impersonally, 'physicalistically'), but also in the *status* of this picture. It is a kind of ante-world, prior to inquiry, a 'prior philosophy' in Quine's sense. The defining property of positivism seems to me the use of such an ante-world, together with the fact that it is granular, and that the grains are seen as independent of each other, and of man and culture.

The Later Popper (hereafter LP) is different. In summary one might say that whereas YP held up science as the model for knowledge, LP holds up knowledge as the model of science. More explicitly, one might say that the crypto-positivist ante-world withers away, and is replaced by an unpruned *Lebenswelt*, roughly. The normativeness is toned down, the interest in defining science is replaced by an interest in defining the broader notion of rationality (which turns out to be the use of trial and error), and the positivist two-judges doctrine is replaced by a much less specific injunction to *criticise*, without any delimitation of the number of or type of methods to be used in criticism. In *The Positivist Dispute in German Sociology*, the closest Popper comes to making this issue clear is in this statement on p. 98:

I consider it important to identify scientific method, at least in first approximation, with the critical method.

Unfortunately, I know of no place where the second, third or *n*th approximations are discussed or specified. Until that is done, I shall remain inclined to conclude that a deliberately uncircumscribed 'spirit of criticism' is being commended as the essence of science and the secret of cognitive growth, and thus has replaced the earlier stress on elimination by the *modus tollens*, with its presupposition of a granular world.

At the same time, he seems also to stress with emphasis that learning by trial and error (with error initially punishable by death) has gone on in the natural (not specifically granular) world ever since the beginnings of life. Science merely perpetuates this old tradition, perhaps with a little more speed and method, and with mercy to the carriers of eliminated ideas.

This shift of stress in Popper's thought is curiously parallel (though less extreme) to the more familiar transformation of the Young Wittgenstein into the Old one, though of course wholly independent of it. Wittgenstein too moved from a granular and two-stroke world, a 'prior philosophy', with delimited, circumscribed modes of thought, to a pluralistic *Lebenswelt* within which thought fulfilled an undelimited set of quite diverse purposes, instead of being restricted to mirroring facts and to providing a scaffolding for all the mini-mirrors.

Relative evaluation

The difference between YP and LP is one of emphasis rather than sharp divergence. Nevertheless, it seems interesting to try to evaluate this difference. What seems crucial to me is not so much that YP is superior to LP, but that LP is parasitic on YP and presupposes him; and, moreover, that YP is a positivist. And so we return to the Third Man, felt to be present in the discussion and yet disavowed by both sides. The truth of the matter seems to me to be that Popper is and ought to be a positivist, and that this is in fact an excellent position. (I refrain from saying that it is also a true one, for the matter is somewhat more complex, as will emerge.)

The central theme in LP is the stress on rationality (not science), the definition of rationality in terms of criticism (not falsifiability), the willingness to indulge in trial and error, the recognition of falsifiability, and finally, the lack of any theory of criticism, of any circumscribing or enumerating of the *kinds* of criticisms which are relevant, permissible or conclusive. In other words, the positivistic two-kinds-only theory of knowledge, which was present in YP through the stress on the *modus tollens* quietly leaves the scene. One seems to be told instead that criticism is the thing – never mind how it is done, or of what kind it is.

Willingness to change and to criticise and be criticised may indeed lead to tolerance and permissiveness, and be to that extent laudable, but I doubt whether they generally lead to knowledge and its cumulation. Consider David Hume's laudatory comments on the practitioners of ancient traditional religion:

> The tolerating spirit of idolators, both in ancient and modern times, is very obvious to anyone, who is in the least conversant in the writings of historians and travellers ... The Romans commonly adopted the gods of the conquered people, and never disputed the attributes of the local and national deities, in whose territories they resided.
>
> (*The Natural History of Religion*)

Tolerant they may have been, but they were not the founders of science, and partly perhaps for that very reason. One may suspect that, on the contrary, it was the exclusiveness of jealous Jehovah, together with a Greek mathematisation of nature, leading eventually to the puritan refusal to see God as stooping to impress his creation with petty conjuring tricks, which led to the surprisingly successful search for a law-bound natural order.[16] Popper himself has pointed out in another

---

[16] On the theological origins of the notion of an orderly class-bound nature, see John R. Milton, 'The Origin and Development of the Concept of "Law of Nature"', *Archives Européennes de Sociologie*, 22, no. 2, 1982.

context[17] that contradiction only promotes cognitive advance if it is *not tolerated*, and creates a tension, a need to eliminate the conflict. Allowing *anything*, any attack, to count as 'criticism' must have something of the same debilitating effect as *tolerated* contradictions. The positivist two-kinds-only theory of knowledge served precisely to make the game relatively determinate, for it defined and circumscribed legitimate types of criticism. It lays down the ground-rules for what is incompatible with what, thereby leading to a rational, rather than haphazard and accidental, process of elimination. It ensures that everything is not compatible with everything else. Without some such decision procedure, 'criticism' cannot but cover, quite indiscriminately, both what we should call criticism proper and *any* kind of instability of opinion under the influence of *any* inner or outer stimulus (including threats, suggestion, emotive rhetoric, anything). Instability as such is not equivalent to criticism and openness: change is rational only if based on *good reasons*. Allowing *any kind* of criticism is a bit like tolerating contradictions.

What is a good reason? The great merit of the positivist two-kinds-only theory of knowledge is, precisely, that it gives us a good clear model and answer to this question. Perhaps, who knows, there are other and better models. If they are presented, we shall have to think about their merits and compare them with the positivist version. But all we seem to be presented with now, by way of an alternative, is not any kind of genuine and specific alternative, but a quite unspecific, totally nebulous and uncircumscribed notion of criticism-in-general (never mind by what methods and never mind about the criteria which are to decide its adequacy), which in effect tacitly presupposes the positivist rules and is liable surreptitiously to fall back on them when in difficulties. This will not do.

Where YP contained a paean of the *modus tollens* (and thereby implicitly of the two-kinds-only theory and thus of positivism), and hence also of a well-demarcated science, well demarcated so as to be able to serve as shining norm and model to less reputable forms of knowledge, LP moves on to praise the ill-defined critical spirit. The shining – and severe – norm-reminder becomes shadowy; LP is not merely much less scientistic, and less given to an ante-world with its two clearly defined moves, but he also seems far more at home in a *Lebenswelt* with its indenumerably plentiful moves, critical and other. But the prescriptiveness does not evaporate altogether. If there were nothing at all to reprove, what would thought be about?

---

[17] 'What is Dialectic', in Karl Popper, *Conjectures and Refutations*, London, 1963, ch. 15.

Hence we must look at the manner in which LP now separates the sheep from the goats in his debate with the Hegelianising opponents of the Frankfurt school, the principles by which good and evil are separated, and which replace YP's stress on falsifiability as the prime sheep–goat sorter. In *The Positivist Dispute in German Sociology*, we find three such principles. I suspect that Popper's contributions to the book, from which these three principles are drawn, are in this respect representative of LP. The three principles are

(1) Clarity v. obscurity
(2) Reason or violence
(3) The perenniality of trial and error, or Albert and the amoeba.

Each of these corresponds to themes in LP's thought (possibly also in YP), and deserve discussion.

Clarity v. obscurity

Some of Popper's abuse in the volume of the so to speak institutional, traditional, normative obscurity of German sociology professors was quoted at the beginning of this chapter. It is well in the tradition of what Popper has said earlier about Hegel, and indeed what Schopenhauer had said about Hegel. It is high-quality abuse, as abuse goes. But what is of importance here is not its rating for elegance, wit, or whatever qualities one may look for in literary abuse: what does matter here is its precise role in the overall argument.

Now it is virtually the sum of what Popper has to say about his opponents here. He does not bother much with their specific doctrines. On the contrary, he observes contemptuously that much of what they say is only too trivially true. It is the use of pretentious, pompous obscurity to mask triviality of content which is virtually the whole of his charge against them. It is *this* which serves to exclude them from serious consideration.

What it amounts to, however, is this: obscurity/pretentiousness now assumes some of the role which *untestability* had played in the YP. Then it was the presence or absence of testability which had served to distinguish praiseworthy from unpraiseworthy contributions to the cognitive life of mankind. Now it is the presence or absence of clarity which appears to do this job.

Rightly or wrongly, I feel I understand the notion of testability, but alas, I am not at all clear about clarity. Testability had its problems: can one easily distinguish that which is untestable in principle from that which, whilst testable, requires great ingenuity and imagination for the devising of the test? I'm not so sure. But this does not matter quite so much here. What does matter is the status of clarity. Clarity is a *very* suspect notion.

One of Popper's important insights is that *truth is not manifest*. This insight quite transforms our view of the human situation. For one thing, it shows that error is not culpable. We may no longer condemn those who err by reproaching them (as the clergyman shouted at the football match) – *thou hast eyes but thou seest not*. The trouble is that Popper talks, certainly throughout his contributions to this volume, as if clarity were manifest. But it is not.

There are some poignant testimonies to this inside the book:

Albert's strategy . . . I could characterise, with a certain symmetry to his accusation of obscurantism, as one of pretending to be stupid. One refuses to understand what the other person is saying. This strategy, intended to force the opponent to accept one's own language, is several centuries old. . .

(Jürgen Habermas, p. 224)

And again:

The accusation of unintelligibility belongs to this context . . . in so far as it is aimed at a structure of thought and expression, it requires explanation. Understanding is a two-sided relationship. Whilst carrying out my required reading of ingenious positivistic studies, I have had the painful experience of not, or not immediately understanding a great deal. I attributed the difficulty to my defective learning processes and not to the unintelligibility of the texts. I would not venture to exclude altogether the impression that the same thing could happen the other way round . . .

(Jürgen Habermas, p. 225)

In an extremely interesting and generous footnote (p. 256), Hans Albert comments:

I firmly reject the wish to bind an opponent to my language, particularly as I was neither born a positivist nor have remained such . . . I only became acquainted with the philosophy of the Vienna circle after I had previously had 'acquaintance' with almost all philosophical traditions within my reach . . . I too have more recently had the experience of which Habermas speaks . . . in my reading of positivistic studies.

Earlier, Hans Albert also quoted (p. 251, n. 72) an interesting remark of Adorno's about Hegel, who apparently is a philosopher

with whom at times one literally does not know and cannot conclusively decide, what in fact is being talked about, and with whom even the possibility of such a decision is not guaranteed . . .

It seems to me obvious that clarity is to a considerable extent culture-bound, that what people find clear depends on their training and so forth. Over and above this, I would like to believe (but with a touch of despair about being able to show or justify this) that there is also a kind of absolute clarity which transcends local taste, and to which local styles of clarity approximate when they are at their best, and which they ought not to (but do) often violate. How one would identify and defend this notion is a big and difficult subject, and it can hardly be broached here.

But it is relevant and possible to indicate some of the difficulties. 'Clear' has some connection with the notion of the 'intuitive' as used by mathematicians. It is also evident from their use of it that some truths are *counter*-intuitive, so that intuition, a 'nose', though perhaps quite a good guide, is by no means a reliable one. The same is true of the more general notion of clarity (of which 'intuitiveness' is a part or species). Secondly, clarity overlaps with simplicity. But simplicity in handling any topic or problem can best be attained by taking over as much of the current and local background assumptions as possible: the matter to hand can *then* be treated with simplicity and clarity, because one is not obliged to introduce new conceptual machinery, and explain its rules. But what if the background assumptions are themselves obscure, questionable, or inconsistent? This may well happen. Then one must build one's own background structure. But having so much more to do, simplicity may no longer be attainable. But is the man who questions more, and therefore needs to re-erect so much more, really less clear than the one who questions little and can therefore allow himself stylistic elegance? Voltaire is certainly a clearer stylist than Kant; is he therefore *necessarily* a clearer thinker? Or is his ability to stay close to the intuitions of the average educated reader simply due to his challenging fewer background assumptions, to his probing less deep?

Bluntly, one must add that clarity has by now justifiably acquired a bit of a bad name. Whether or not Habermas is justified in his complaints of Albert, there is no doubt whatever in my mind that alleged invocations of clarity have been used to bamboozle, to silence without convincing (or advancing the argument) in as dreadful a form as the bamboozling by Elevated Depth which so rightly incenses Popper. For instance, the game of playing-stupid mentioned by Habermas, intended to force the opponent to adopt one's own language, which language is then so designed as to ensure that he cannot win, was brought to a dreadful perfection by the late Wittgenstein and some of his followers.

Having made all these caveats about the identification of clarity and its use in philosophy, I should like to say that nevertheless, my heart is on the side of clarity rather than depth, when one has to choose; and that I should grant licence to indulge in depth-without-clarity, like some therapeutic but very dangerous and addictive drug, only very rarely, with reluctance, and with great precautions: adults only, keep out of the reach of children, and references will be required and scrutinised; and to be administered only when medical personnel is to hand. As the publicity for American Express Cards says, frankly this is not for everyone.

So my values on this issue are in fact not so different from Popper's, or perhaps not different at all. My objection is rather different: can a notion so unclear and so tricky as *clarity* do the job of distinguishing between healthy, fertile promising styles of thought, and those which are self-indulgent, mind-befuddling, and sterile? I was (and I continue to be) willing to entrust the notion of *testability* with this important role of censor – and particularly so in the refined form in which YP presented it, so richly orchestrated with an awareness of its implications both in sciences and in society. I am simply not willing to entrust the notion of clarity with so weighty a task. I have witnessed far too much misuse of that drug. Popper has not said in so many words that he intends this, but alas his handling of his opponents in *The Positivist Dispute in German Sociology* does seem to thrust such a weighty burden on this notion. *If* that was intended, and I imagine the question was not clearly posed, then I for one would refuse to follow him in such a move.

Reason or violence

Critical reason is the only alternative to violence so far discovered.

> (Karl Popper, *The Positivist Dispute in German Sociology*, p. 292)

The above statement, italicised in the original for emphasis, is actually asserted, and asserted with emphasis, by Popper. I hold it to be a truly dreadful argument. Consequently I have some difficulty in believing that a thinker of very great distinction and brilliance has actually perpetrated it. The evidence is, alas, conclusive. Popper goes on to link this argument to the clarity consideration discussed above:

It seems to me clear that it is the obvious duty of all intellectuals to work for *this* revolution – for the replacement of the eliminative function of violence by the eliminative function of rational criticism. But in order to work for this end, one has to train oneself constantly to write and to speak in clear and simple language. Every thought should be formulated as clearly and as simply as possible. This can only be achieved by hard work.

(p. 292)

The problem of identifying, defining or characterising rationality has bothered and perplexed many thinkers. Had they but known it could be solved with such stunning simplicity! It appears that rationality and violence between them exhaust human activity or relations (at least, until some new as yet undiscovered – *sic* – third activity or relationship turns up). So, rationality is defined as a residue: everything that isn't violence, is reason. It is a definition of rationality which at least seems clear, whatever other merits it may lack.

This breathtakingly simple and apparently clear, not to say conclusive definition or theory of rationality also performs, with a similar economy of means, the important task of *legitimating* reason. It only takes one additional, and fairly uncontentious, value premiss – a repudiation of violence, or even less contentiously, a repudiation of unnecessary violence – and we are home. Reason is not merely identified and circumscribed, it is also convincingly vindicated!

In the face of an argument of this quality, one can only feel embarrassment. There is in fact an enormous wealth of human styles of influencing each other, all lying between violence and rational persuasion, and not identical with either of these roles. Even if we do so restrict our discussion to the realm of methods available for inducing men to change their opinions, the wealth of choices which are guided by neither reason nor violence is enormous and probably boundless. Actual physical violence or the threat thereof is relatively rare in human affairs; in well-centralised political units, such as are now common, it is very rare indeed, which is attested by the fact that most citizens of such states go about unarmed and have little training or aptitude for either exercising or resisting violence. Conditions such as those prevailing in the Wild West or amongst feuding clans are now fairly untypical. But even if one notes the fact that the central state itself exercises violence or the threat thereof on its citizens, this leaves the equally significant class of situations in centralised but liberal societies, in which neither the state nor other citizens normally employ violence in persuasion. Can Popper seriously maintain even for one second that everything which happens in these societies, when men induce others to change opinions (barring those very infrequent irruptions of violence), are instances of rationality? I remember a film about consciousness-enhancing groups in California, in which the organiser explained to the participants that everything other than physical violence was allowed in the therapeutic sessions. The participants did indeed refrain from such physical violence, but proceeded to tear each other to shreds psychologically. Would Popper say that all they said, as they savaged each other's psyches, was an example of *reason*?

I leave this rhetorical question unanswered.

I suppose that what slight – very slight – plausibility the argument possesses, it owes to the following consideration: of course men use a wide variety of methods to induce others to change their opinions: but in so far as they use methods other than the right reason, those methods, whatever they be, are illegitimate; and hence, even though they do not involve force or the threat of it, they are a kind of violence-by-extension; they might be said to do violence to our rationality, even if they do not commit it against our bodies. An argument of this kind is a standard ingredient in Leftist denunciation of liberal societies.

The formula is simple: take ethical objectivism and sociological functionalism, and the conclusion follows. If you take a given moral position (e.g., socialism) to be objectively true, then anyone deprived of the opportunity of either seeing its truth, or living in a social order embodying it, is in a way deprived. But this liberal society is one which does not practise full socialism; nor does it lead its citizens, in general, to perceive the truth of socialist doctrine. Yet at the same time (like any surviving society) it perpetuates itself, and is sustained by its own institutions and values. But these deprive its citizens both of the ability to see the truth, and to live in an order based on truth! And this is done in the interest of preserving the present order! Clearly this does violence to the true nature and interests of its citizens, and thus is a kind of violence, albeit camouflaged. And if a minority endeavour to subvert the institutions which perpetuate this deplorable state of affairs, are they are not impeded by spacious appeals to legality and democracy? As if these concepts could legitimately be used in an order actually designed to prevent those living under it from seeing the truth and living under justice![18]

Such reasoning extends the notion of 'violence' to any institutional support for views deplored by the speaker. But whether it is the notion of violence or the notion of reason which is expanded to absorb all the truly enormous territory between them, either way it is disastrous to make these two jointly exhaustive.

For just this is the problem. If reason is defined in the narrowest possible way, say as coextensive with argument which has the form sanctioned by strict deductive logic (a sphere about which there is considerable, though not complete consensus), then notoriously most human activities become *ir*rational, inasmuch as decisions and priorities within them cannot be selected or justified deductively, any more than

---

[18]   The application of this formula can be found in R. Miliband, *The State in Capitalist Society*, London, 1969. A sympathetic analysis of this style of thought can be found in S. Lukes, *Power, A Radical View*, London, 1974. Both books are good examples of Leftist devotional literature.

the background empirical assumptions on which the decisions are based. So we need a broader definition of reason. But what is it? Answer comes there none – other than the repudiation of positivism which, for better or for worse, did at least offer an answer, in terms of the two-kinds-only theory, of the judges fact and logic. It may not be an adequate answer. There are numerous objections to it, such as the ambiguity of 'facts', or the consideration that this answer too, though not quite as narrow as the logic-only answer, is still far too narrow to cover many spheres in which we do and must make decisions.

But before we repudiate this important model, we'd better have another one. The job which needs to be done most certainly cannot be done by a travesty of 'reason', equated with anything-that-is-not-violence. This is a realm which in fact contains all the irrational, illegitimate but pervasive deceptions practised by societies on their members and by men on each other, which do not go as far as actual and real violence or its immediate threat. This is a very wide realm indeed, and its omnibus, indiscriminate incorporation in 'reason' seems to me absurd.

The tables are turned. Normally, thinkers such as Popper are rightly admired for upholding a fairly strict, discriminating idea of reason, whereas their Hegelian opponents indulgently extend reason to include the operation of political and historical forces, the Cunning of Reason, using earthly passionate and violent means, the Dialectic, the knowledge incarnate in social situation, blood, and what have you. Reason is virtually anything that goes on historically, except for the bits they don't like.[19] We now see Popper rather absurdly incorporating all the historically operating forces of intellectual change – other than actual direct violence – in reason. If this be reason, I want no truck with her.

The manner in which Popper makes an honest woman of such Reason without effectively defining the lady is also regrettable. It implies, by claiming that only two options are available, that any opponent of his viewpoint is *ipso facto* a partisan of violence. This is somewhat in the spirit of his regrettable dedication of *The Poverty of Historicism*,[20] which implies that anyone not endorsing his views on the philosophy of history is an accessory after the fact of the crimes of Hitler and Stalin. Ironically, *just this* seems to me an example of a form of persuasion which is so disastrously omitted by the dichotomy employed by Popper to delimit reason: clearly Popper uses no violence – but, by Jove, this is not reason either!

[19] Cf. H. Marcuse, *Reason and Revolution*, 2nd edn, London, 1964, p. 11.
[20] London, 1957.

The perennity of trial and error, or Albert and the amoeba

The third argument or principle employed by Popper to do some of the work once done by testability and science-demarcation is the perennity of sound cognitive method.

But although it does the same job, it is not entirely commensurate with the other two: it endeavours to achieve the same end, but by quite different means. The clarity–obscurity and reason–violence distinctions were *distinctions*, sifters, principles of selection (though in my view quite inadequate for the important and difficult purpose for which they were intended); but the idea of the perennity of the fundamental cognitive method is not a sifter at all. On the contrary, it is something inherently all-embracing, one of those characteristically expansive philosophical categories which may defeat their own purpose by creating a night in which all cows are the same shade of grey.

Popper reasserts this idea in the volume under discussion (pp. 291–2):

We may start from Darwinian evolution. Organisms evolve by trial and error, and their erroneous trials . . . are eliminated, as a rule, by the elimination of the organism which is the 'carrier' of the error. It is part of my epistemology that, in man, through the evolution of a descriptive and argumentative language, all this has changed radically. Man has achieved the possibility of being *critical of his own tentative trials, of his own theories*. These theories are no longer incorporated in his organism . . . they may be formulated in books, or in journals; and they can be critically discussed . . . without destroying the 'carriers'.

In this way we arrive at a fundamental new possibility: our trials, our tentative hypotheses, may be critically eliminated by rational discussion, without eliminating ourselves. This indeed is the purpose of rational critical discussion.

(Popper's italics)

The argument is visibly linked to the preposterous thesis or assumption that violence and rational criticism between them exhaust the relevant universe (at least so far, till some third method of elimination be discovered). The above passage in particular highlights the weirdness of this assumption, for it could only be cogent if everything which was eliminated in the course of human history, since the discovery of language, had been eliminated either by the violent extinction of the carriers, or by reason! But the cultural options adopted by the limited number of currently existing societies must be a very small sub-set of the cultural possibilities which have emerged (and in most cases, disappeared again) in the course of history. Can anyone believe that all those eliminated options were either excluded because they were irrational, or because their carriers were killed off? I do not think Popper himself can possibly believe this: it contradicts his oft-asserted thesis about the importance of unintended effects in social life.[21] On the assumption which is here criticised, all eliminations of cultural options which were not violent had to be rational. But this is absurd. But what we need is a principle of discrimination between rational and other non-violent (or not directly violent) procedures of human societies. It is ironic to find Popper led by the logic of his argument to a variant (admittedly, a *pacifist* variant) of the Hegelian doctrine of the Cunning of Reason.

Let us, however, turn to the third device which is here under discussion. It must be said that the view with which I am crediting Popper here is not asserted unambiguously: he does not altogether practise the virtue of clarity which he preaches with such vehemence. If it is said, however, that the view may not be credited to him at all, one can only reply that it is a natural interpretation of the passages in question, and does do the job which the overall argument seems to require. The ambiguity is twofold. We are told that both biological organisms and human theories progress by trial and error. We are told that a radical change separates the two stages (biological and human) of this elimina-tive process, and that this change consists of the replacement of the elimination of carriers by the more humane elimination of ideas only. The carriers may now live to reformulate their hypotheses another day.

The two ambiguities are: is trial and error the whole, or only part, of the eliminative process? Is the separation of carrier and idea, making possible the survival of the former even in cases of elimination of the latter, the whole of the radical change as between nature and man, or nature and culture?

It must be stressed that nothing in this text (or any other I know of) enables one to convict Popper of endorsing clearly the affirmative answer to either of these questions. Nevertheless, I tentatively credit LP with such a view, because (*a*) there is no evidence of *other* elements; if they existed, surely they should be at least indicated; (*b*) the point he makes here can play its role in the overall argument on such an assumption, but hardly otherwise; and (*c*) it is natural (though not obligatory) to interpret the passage in this way. The distinguishing of YP and LP hinges on this: if I am shown to be wrong in these attributions, LP may turn out to be a construction identical with no living thinker – though I doubt whether one could claim that this similarity to any living thinker is, as the phrase goes, accidental. At the very least, we have received much encouragement for erecting this construct. It doesn't really matter too much for the present argument. YP pre-supposes

---

[21] For instance, in *The Positivist Dispute in German Sociology*, p. 102.

granularism; and LP presupposes YP. If the two thinkers are identical, the first half of the preceding sentence still provides the premiss required for the argument.

Problems of the Continuity thesis

First of all one must look at the role of the Continuity thesis. It obviates the need for any severely normative and sharply demarcated theory of *good* knowledge (whether this be conceived as science or in any other way). If, all in all, we always have been, are and will be on the right lines, there is no need to identify and validate a unique and arduous path which alone leads to salvation. If salvation is and was ever-available and everywhere, this difficult philosophical task – the singling out and justification of its stigmata – becomes redundant. The general air pervading the work of LP does indeed suggest that this is so. (The work of YP and of the positivists, on the other hand, is pervaded by a sense of the uniqueness and exiguity of sound cognitive method, surrounded by the endless temptations and enticements of false paths leading to cognitive perdition.)

The point of the Continuity thesis is, so to speak, the perennity and ubiquity of salvation. If we have it – it is everywhere, we need not identify, locate or justify it. Note that this does not mean, of course, that all our ideas, all our individual concrete trials, are good: on the contrary, the method of trial and error works by the elimination of misguided trials, and presumably works on the assumption that such erroneous tries will vastly outnumber successful ones. Salvation is not to be had at that level. But it does seem to be ever ready and available at the higher level, the level of method rather than substance: we make countless errors, but the method of learning from errors (the *only* method, it would seem) is and was ever with us.

But even at this second level, we confront a problem. If, methodologically speaking, all's well and always has been, what need to preach sound views on method? What do we need to be protected from, if no danger lurks? Well, apparently salvation is not *absolutely* perennial and ubiquitous. Somehow or other, methodological error has crept into the Garden of Eden, at least for a time. Presumably it could not creep in during the biological period, for animals, though on Popper's view they are unwitting carriers of theories, are not also carriers of meta-substantive, methodological views about how ideas they carry are to be located and judged. Presumably Darwinian nature had its own harsh way with any Baconians who strayed into the jungle. (Better avert your gaze if you are squeamish.)

So the philosophical error can only enter after we have eaten of the tree of knowledge. Popper's theodicy at this point clearly resembles the biblical story. There are at least two known forms of error which enter with the snake: inductivism, the recipe for sticking to the facts and avoiding perilous guesses; and Closed thought which is seduced by the snares of certainty, and attains it by conceptual devices which evade the possibility of falsification.

Note that this is a rather pleasingly optimistic philosophy of history. Seen *sub specie aeternitatis*, the Age of Error is brief indeed, stretching merely from, at worst, the first cases of philosophical speculation about method (as opposed to the practice of the in-built and inherently sound universal method of trial and error), till the publication of the *Logik der Forschung*. In the state of nature, one could hardly avoid using the sound method; so that at this point, one could, rather ironically, class Popper's vision with those romantic philosophies which wish to restore a healthy pristine innocence, threatened by an error which can only enter with cerebral sophistication. Such is not normally the spirit in which he reasons, but his enthusiasm for the Popperian methodological views of Mother Nature lead him to a variant of this view.

This has a certain affinity both with pragmatism and with the views on morality of the Austrian school of economists. The affinity with pragmatism lies in the same principle being seen as underlying both biological history, and that very recent past in the history of mankind, which has clearly been a story of sustained growth, in knowledge and elsewhere. This came naturally to nineteenth-century thought, looking at its own age and at Darwinism. The intervening, often stagnant or regressive period of human history is rather ignored or played down. Nevertheless, it is not ignored altogether, for the principles which underlie *it*, or which are held to have done so, are precisely that which is being combated. They are a kind of brief temporary excursion into evil, a short-term banning of mankind from the Garden of Eden. Pragmatism and Popperism alike seem to be a curious sub-species of Manicheanism in which the Evil Principle has a very short run in the world, a mere three or four millennia . . .

The vision also has much in common with the moral philosophy implicit in Austrian neo-classical economics, and here of course the overlap is not accidental. That kind of economics looks at pursuit of individual advantage as both natural and beneficial, and at collectivism, the yearning for submersion in a community, as a regrettable aberration, economically harmful and somehow contrary to human nature and the general interest. Still, there is the puzzle of where we picked up this habit, which in the eyes of its adherents actually constitutes a *morality*!

The answer, to be found in writers such as F. A. von Hayek,[22] is that this collectivism is a bad habit mankind had picked up during the tribal stage of its development, and which it had better shed as quickly as possible, in the interest of returning to its own best nature as well as of economic advance. From the viewpoint of this kind of normative (or crypto-normative) individualism, such strong social morality itself is an ethically deplorable weakness, absent in the jungle and again in a post-Enlightenment world, but holding a temporary and deplorable sway in the intervening Dark Age.

Perhaps this was a natural reaction of an economic individualist looking at the world from the vantage point of the Viennese melting pot, and noting with distaste the obstacles presented to liberalism – of various kinds – by the surge of ethnic communalisms from the more backward parts of the Hapsburg empire. A Viennese reaction of the *zadruga* and the *staetl*, perhaps. Popper's historical epistemology is evidently similar: trial and error ruled in the jungle and will rule again now, but there was a bit of a lapse in between. The Closed Society, rooted in the collectivist yearning of the human heart (which had evidently been engendered by tribalism) is the social base of closed, untestable thinking, which Plato and Hegel endeavour to keep going[23] even after the re-emergence of trial and error in the new form of science.

This *temporary* emergence of a Manichean dualistic world with a powerful Principle of Evil (Collectivism, Closed thinking, inductivism) in an originally healthy world is a problem facing this outlook, and we must leave its adherents with it. It resembles other forms of theodicy – why did an angel fall, why is there evil at all in a basically good world? – but it is perhaps somewhat aggravated by a certain inelegance and asymmetry, in so far as the Fallen Angel is given such a relatively short run, a few millennia only. Some of us like doing things in style, and if we have to tackle the Problem of Evil at all, we prefer to deal with evil which is well and truly entrenched in the universe (its deep roots will then also serve as an explanation of why it had to exist at all), rather than a form of it which, with seeming arbitrariness, makes its appearance on the world's stage for a mere fragment of its total duration. But I leave this problem to Austrian neo-classical economists, pragmatists and Popperians, whom it concerns. Pragmatists, rooted in the American

---

[22] A brilliant formulation is found in his 'Three Sources of Human Values', L. T. Hobhouse Memorial Trust Lecture no. 77, London School of Economics, 1978, esp. p. 20. See also his *Studies in Philosophy, Politics and Economics*, London, 1967, esp. ch. 6.

[23] Cf. Karl Popper, *The Open Society and its Enemies*, 3 vols., London, 1962, *passim*.

experience which barely notices the lapse between jungle and market (linking the two in one continuous story) hardly even notice this problem.[24]

What concerns me more are the reasons for which I find the entire Continuity thesis unacceptable. If these reasons are cogent, as they seem to me, then the little internal problem of a short-term theodicy within that vision hardly arises.

General objections to Continuity

The Continuity thesis seems to me open to various fundamental objections. One of them is the *deep* discontinuity between natural selection and selection of ideas. The other is the deep discontinuity between science and pre-science. Both these *coupures* are erroneously obscured or under-estimated by the Continuity thesis.

Natural selection tests organisms in quite a different sense from the sense in which science tests a hypothesis. A hypothesis can contain or constitute a generalisation which is simply false. By contrast, an organism, a 'carrier', cannot literally embody a falsehood: no living creature itself literally *defies* a law of nature. A *theory* can contradict a valid law of nature, an organism cannot. The laws of nature are not literally contradicted by organisms due for extinction. The sense in which an organism 'carries' an idea due to be tested and failed is somewhat indirect: it 'carries' the idea that the particular combination of elements of which it is composed, plus the manner of their composition, are more suited to survive in the conditions which are about to prevail than other organisms, other carriers, which happen also to be available at the time. There is of course not the slightest presumption that nature has tried out all available combinations. But more significant, what is being tested is not hypotheses in isolation, but hypotheses in combination with others. It is not the viability of the isolated elements which is being tested: it is the relative viability of each particular combination, so to speak, of these ideas/elements in given organisms.

Hence nature, in its operation of natural selection, cannot be compared to science. It could only at best perhaps be compared to a special kind of science, truncated as follows: imagine a community in which scientists can formulate hypotheses, but are not allowed to perform experiments to test them. The only other thing they *are* allowed to do is to devise technologies which follow from these hypotheses, and flood the market with products based on them. The truth of rival hypotheses

---

[24] Willard Van Orman Quine, *From a Logical Point of View: Nine Logico-Philosophical Essays*, Cambridge (Mass.), 1953, pp. 42–6.

would then be judged, not by their ability to survive well-designed crucial experiments, but by the market success of the products, based on the technologies derived from those hypotheses . . . I hazard the guess that the science of such a society would bear little resemblance to ours. The abstract theories receiving its Nobel Prizes would not be the ones which are so honoured in our world. The laurels would go to those science–technology clusters which had the best technologists and designers, and who knew how best to combine the abstract elements supplied them into viable and attractive combinations/products.

It is only in this, profoundly *un*-scientific, way that nature can 'test' ideas by testing their 'carriers'. *Perhaps*, in our imaginary society, if the technologists–designers were supplied with very mistaken theoretical premises, their designing skill might not save them. I suspect that, on the contrary, skilful designers could build viable products from theoretically defective elements, and often in fact do so, and I am certain that theoretically impeccable elements, incarnated by bad design work in defective combinations, do fall by the wayside.

The point about science seems to me not simply that it *tests*, but that it tests suitably *isolated* elements – where the proper definition of this notion of suitable isolation may be very difficult. I am of course aware of the fact that the isolation of the element (ideas, hypotheses, what have you) is not and presumably cannot be 'pure' in science either; that the presence, overt or hidden, of background hypotheses ensures that crucial experiments need not be final and that questions can be reopened.

There is of course the notorious problem of the allocation of blame: which part of a theoretical system is at fault, when a consequence of it is falsified? But science at least *tries* to identify the faulty element, to localise the defect. Natural selection, on the other hand, operates on the complexes, or incarnated organisms, and has no way at all of dealing with, so to speak, technologically non-incarnated, pure theories. So there seems to me an enormous, gaping, qualitative difference between the admittedly incomplete 'purity' of theoretical testing of relatively isolated hypotheses, and the testing by nature of an organism which 'carries' a large conflated, uninsulated package of such ideas (or even, in my analogy, the testing by a market of the technological products which are the spin-off of this or that theoretical background).

Science and pre-science

Similar objections can be raised to the assimilation of science to pre-scientific cognition, which is also implicit in the doctrine that it is all trial and error, no more. There are of course general and very cogent objections to applying the idea of natural selection or trial and error to the development of human ideas, institutions and societies. Firstly, the number of participants in the selection game is too small (when the contestants are cultures, civilisations, institutions) to create a presumption of the selection of the fittest. History is like the football cup, not the league: a single encounter between two teams really proves little – yet in history it can be decisive. Secondly, the environment in which the game is played, and indeed the game itself, changes so rapidly, that there is little presumption that those successful in one round are also those most fitted for the quite new set of rules operative in the next one. The teams themselves change radically between rounds, which further undermines any significance of the result . . .

But these are general considerations against interpreting history as the application of trial and error, *even if we subtract the role of violence* as Popper would have us do, and thus turn world-history into *Weltgericht* (how often Popper's later views seem to approach Hegelian ones!). Even with violence abstracted away, history seems to me nothing of the kind. *Weltgeschichte* is a Moscow trial. But there are more specific objections.

The normal course of social or historical selection operates not on isolated or insulated theories or ideas, but on complex institutional package deals, analogous in this respect (though not in others) to the organisms which submit to natural selection, or to the technological products which are tested in the market. 'Ideas', 'solutions' to 'problems', adaptive devices of all kinds, are normally complex, many-stranded and multi-purpose things. Their survival depends on their satisfaction of a wide variety of human and social requirements, amongst which theoretical truth is not very prominent. This is of course the central fallacy of pragmatism: the failure to see that truth cannot be assimilated to usefulness (or some circumlocution thereof), because things are useful for a wide variety of reasons other than their 'truth', and may indeed be useful because they are *not* true.

The emergence of science – of that transcultural, cumulative, and qualitatively superior form of knowledge which has so totally transformed the modern world – is somehow connected with the capacity for insulating ideas from their practical enmeshment and testing them by a simplified criterion. To put this in Popperian terms, though ideas were born testable, they are nevertheless everywhere in chains. Something has to be done to restore them their birthright of freedom, of testability. Whatever it was that rendered them *falsifikationsfähig* was achieved at the beginning of the Scientific Revolution, and did *not* come easily, naturally and generally. (It did not happen in the same place and at the same time for all sciences, of course.)

The LP doctrine that science is but trial and error leads to a terribly simplified view of science. Imagine a distinguished and enlightened scientist whose young son wants to follow in his footsteps. 'Dad, I want to become a scientist, like you. What shall I do, where shall I go to learn?' 'Sonny, don't you see I'm busy? Anyway, this business about learning first is just antiquated inductivist nonsense. Look, just go out into the garden and falsify something, there's a good boy. When you have falsified a few things, you'll be a scientist. That's all there is to it. Trial and error. Now beat it before I lose my temper and falsify your hypothesis about my patience.'

The lad who followed this advice of his Late-Popperian father would not, one fears, become a scientist – or at any rate, not just by following this advice. What else need he do? On an LP view, all he would risk by going out into the garden and falsifying a few things would be that he would be repeating someone else's work. But in fact, he would be failing in a more important way than that. Obviously he wouldn't even be repeating someone else's science. He would not be doing science at all.

It seems to me useless to improve on Dad's advice by telling the boy to find and then seek to solve a *problem*, as a follower of Popper has argued to me. Problem-solving can only be equated with science if certain criteria of what counts as a solution are assumed. These criteria must contain some separation of 'practical' solutions from genuine theoretical ones. In *praxis*, a problem is solved when the damned thing works. But knowledge is only genuinely advanced when we know *why* it works, even if it doesn't. The trouble with the Popperian Continuity thesis (and its equivalent, presupposed or asserted by pragmatists such as Quine) is that it wrongly assumed that men were, throughout history, engaged in solving intellectual or cognitive problems; so that natural selection could operate on their success or failure in this field. In fact, men were dealing simultaneously with a number of problems, most of them not cognitive, and success or failure of their package-deal solutions seldom advanced *knowledge*. This erroneous intellectualist view of history has a curious affinity with Frazer's theory of development of the human mind, progressing from magic via religion to science by (allegedly) noticing the intellectual, cognitive deficiencies of abandoned options!

In the ordinary idiom and the ordinary social context, ideas are not really falsification-liable at all. Their failure leads to no elimination. They live a life of Eternal Return. Alternatively, they perish without justice, without having failed, or at any rate, without having failed more than their fellows. What is the extra quality they need before they become falsification-worthy? How must they be anointed before being fit for the supreme sacrifice of being *scientifically* falsified, as opposed to perishing without honour or glory, as is the fate of ordinary ideas?

In defence of positivism

Ideas must be clothed in a proper idiom before they become usefully falsifiable, before their death can be a fertile sacrifice on the altar of genuinely cumulative knowledge. Unhallowed, raw, unpurified propositions are ineligible for immolation. Somehow or other the idiom which fitted them for this ultimate sacrifice was found, and its discovery, adoption and diffusion constitutes the Scientific Revolution. What is it?

The significance of positivism, which by common consent itself grew out of the empiricist tradition, is that it attempts to codify and justify the general and distinguishing traits of this crucial idiom. A particular merit of positivism, especially in its classical, Comtian form, seems to me that it perceives how and why this needs to be done: it is imbued with the sense that this is indeed a new idiom, not just more of the same, not just a perpetuation of something practised since the Stone Age or since the amoeba, something which also has social preconditions and implications. (In the ahistorical atmosphere of local philosophy, this crucial and valuable element is lacking, and it is virtually non-existent in recent formulations of so-called 'logical positivism'.)

How has positivism codified the falsification-capability-conferring idiom?

(1) Exclusion of the transcendent, the stress on the observable world.

(2) Insistence on intelligibility and logical consistency.

(3) Insistence on maximum separation of questions, and indeed of everything else. Whatever can be separated in thought should be thought of as separable. A strong tendency towards a kind of atomisation, a granular vision.

(4) Exclusion of idiosyncratic explanation. The same type of explanation applies to all. There are no sacred, exceptional events or elements.

Is the world such that it can best be known and understood by a vision operating on these principles? Reasons can be invoked for doubting so. For instance, there is the well-known and important objection arising from the fact that science evidently cannot restrict itself, in its explanatory schemata, to observables, and that there seems to be no effective way of treating the unobservables which it does use as mere shorthand for observables. There are the objections relating specially to knowledge of human and social matters: to understand men and societies, it is said, we must invoke their meanings, and this involves interpretation, not just observation. Or again, it has been claimed that some or all human events and hence also their explanations are unique.

But I do not wish at this stage to attempt an assessment of whether the positivist vision is correct. What really arises at this stage is whether or not this vision is presupposed by a 'criticalist' position, the view that the path of virtue in the cognitive life of mankind consists of the 'critical attitude', the sustained application of the method of trial and error, and no more. I believe that the positivist vision *is* presupposed, if the 'critical spirit' is to have any teeth at all.

Let us assume that the critical spirit and its injunction to criticise and allow oneself to be criticised is obeyed, but with no other restrictions (other than the eschewing of violence); would this really lead to science, to a cumulative, progressive elimination of false guesses and their replacement by as-yet-unfalsified ones? In an ordinary world, where people were free to use any idiom, it might lead to a kind of agreeable permissive chaos, something like Plato's conception of democracy, a tapestry of all hues and patterns . . . but without order, rigour, progress. Progressive elimination is conditional on a certain discipline, on orderly unambiguous articulation, and the eschewing of conceptual package deals, which evade falsification without seeming to forbid criticism; their concepts are just so constructed and interrelated that all criticisms pass them by. (They can be so constructed as not merely to evade criticism, but to guarantee conversion of all listeners who agree to speak their language. Not merely preservation, but expansion too can be internally guaranteed.) The culture of highly affluent, fully industrialised society may indeed assume such a form, if 'California' trends are harbingers of the future. On the basis of technological wealth, a plethora of sloppy, self-indulgent styles of belief succeed each other in a liberal atmosphere in which criticism, voluntary change, are certainly not proscribed or inhibited. But that does *not* amount to any kind of accumulation, of an intellectual or cognitive progression.

Can this kind of self-preservation be excluded merely by the injunction that everything be subject to criticism, to trial and error? Can the critical spirit, if required to be *pervasive*, and to allow no exceptions, as it were flush out the self-maintaining, protective devices which enable belief-systems to *pretend* to indulge in genuine discussion, whilst remaining immune to any real risk? If so, then the 'critical spirit' would indeed be sufficient for the definition of rationality, and we might dispense with the empiricist/positivist metaphysic.[25] But I do not think it is in fact sufficient. As long as the closed minds, the closed conceptual circuits, stay within the idiom they have (consciously or otherwise) constructed, they can be as sweetly receptive of criticism as you may wish, and yet no one can touch them. They are like the hero of the fairy tale who, as long as he remains within the circle he has traced with holy water, cannot be touched by the cajoling and threatening fiends who endeavour to tempt and frighten him out of it. As long as our hero remains within that circle, he can converse with his friends in the most amiable manner and yet remain safe. Only if he steps out will he be torn to pieces . . .

And how can we ever get him out? There is but one way. It is to prove to him that his very idiom is incorrect, and that he must step outside and speak the correct language. *Then* his defences cease to protect him, his ideas become falsifiable, and no doubt, in due course, falsified.

What is this one correct language? Positivism is the best theory so far – no doubt not a complete or final one – of what that language must look like. Positivism is normally, and most naturally, specified not in terms of the thought-style which it engenders or preaches, but in terms of the shadow of that thought-style on the world, its metaphysic. This is the famous granular metaphysic of positivism, with the world consisting of discrete grains, separated laterally from each other – and this lateral atomisation is complemented by the further so to speak qualitative atomisation which separates all features of the grains which can be thought of distinctly. One well-known and much lamented aspect of this atomisation is of course the separation of value from fact, which is amongst other things simply the corollary of the separation of anything separable from anything else.

But this atomised granular world is also the world, and as far as I can see the only world, in which the *modus tollens* can perform the crucial role ascribed to it by YP. The non-transcendence of this world is of course also a consequence of its thorough atomisation: everything being atomised, laterally and qualitatively, there is nothing outside the atoms and their summation *is* the world. 'The world is the totality of facts not of things' (Wittgenstein). Nothing else. In fact, the granular world of Hume and others is the shadow or reification of a cognitive style which insulates separable questions and facts, and which is rewarded with cognitive growth in consequence.

How does a granular world differ from a Hegelian or holistic (e.g., a

---

[25] The hope that this point could constitute the solution of the problem under discussion was urged to me, many years ago, by Professor J. Agassi.

Quinian) world?[26] In a holistic world, theories are indeed related to facts; but when those fact-supporting theories are examined, they in turn are found to be theory-dependent. In old-fashioned language, this is known as the Principle of Internal Relations, and in the contemporary idiom, the correct phrase is something like the theory-saturation of facts or concepts. It amounts to much the same. The practical consequence is the same. The facts which might kill a theory (thus satisfying what is alleged to have been Herbert Spencer's conception of tragedy) do not really, in such a world, ever really acquire this deadly power. They are only granted such lethal power as they may seem to possess *by courtesy of those further theories* which are built into them, and this power can be withdrawn if those theories in turn are questioned, as eventually they may be; and when that happens, the eliminated theories are once again resurrected. In a granular world, facts are, like James Bond, agent 007, licensed to kill; but in a holistic world, Bond's homicidal potency is disastrously emasculated by being deprived of its finality. An Eternal Return periodically brings back all those who were slain.

In a holistic world, the process of falsification or elimination is never-ending, and the process of seeking the grounds for elimination oscillates interminably and somewhat absurdly between the abstract and the concrete/specific: we go down to the facts to test a theory, but move up again to other theories to be sure that we got our facts right. Not so in the granular world: it contains the facts/grains which at long last terminate the quest. That is what a granular world is.

It is this consideration which persuades me that, irrespective of how he himself characterises his own position, Popper ought to be classed as a positivist. The granular metaphysic is of the essence of positivism (and it also pervades, I think the spirit of the work of YP). Without that granular metaphysic, the eliminationist view of science, which in turn is of the essence of Popper's vision, does not work. Hence Popper's vision, if it is to be coherently defended and developed, must maintain and return to the granular metaphysic and so, in that sense, to positivism. It is his clear commitment to definitive eliminations, his stress on the *modus tollens* as the heart of science, his pin-pointing of *elimination* as the clue to the nature of cognitive progress, which also commit him to the positivist position.

An objection can be raised against my contention that the granularist metaphysic is presupposed by falsificationism and the stress on the *modus tollens* as *the* method of inquiry. Even if it is tentatively conceded that this method presupposes the existence of granular facts/falsifiers,

<hr />

[26] Cf., for instance, Quine, *From a Logical Point of View*, p. 42.

why should it follow that these exhaust the world? Why indeed? Obviously, the existence of one set of things does not entail the non-existence of others. But it remains the case that these facts/falsifiers are the only points at which theories can impinge on the world, or vice versa. There may indeed be other things in heaven and on earth not dreamt of in the atomistic philosophies; but our theories, our intellectual activity, will never meet them. Our theories can touch the world only at those points at which they risk falsification through non-congruence with facts. All this is, of course, merely a way of making explicit the argument which has always tended to lead empiricism to epistemological atomism. Empirical investigation is piecemeal, so the world comes to appear as being made up of little pieces. Whether one then goes on to conclude that it is exhaustively made up of those little pieces, and that putative more diffuse parts of it, which cannot make such clear and firm contact with our inquiries, do not matter, or more brutally, simply do not exist, is perhaps a matter of metaphysical taste.

Science as conceived by Popper presupposes the possibility of fairly definitive eliminations. But that, in turn, presupposes a reasonably granular world, a world containing something tolerably close to self-contained, unambiguous *facts*, capable of delivering an irreversible *coup de grâce* to theories. Just this is the essence of a 'granular world', and is what in effect is intended by this metaphorical phrase.

The argument contains numerous strands, and these intertwine at a number of levels and make a complex pattern. Hence it is useful at this stage to offer an overall summary, intended to highlight that overall pattern:

Two styles of thought confront each other. Each of them reflects, or attempts to explain, prominent (though not wholly unambiguous) traits of, in the one case, the tradition of astonishingly cumulative and consensual investigation of nature which has developed since the seventeenth century, and in the other, of the rich, complex, but essentially inconclusive, 'essentially contested' (to use Bryce Gallie's apposite term) flow of social ideas.[27]

[27] If Thomas Kuhn is to be believed, then this package-deal and discontinuous quality is something found not merely in social ideas, but equally, and perhaps especially, in natural science. But one may well wonder whether he doesn't exaggerate both the 'bulk purchase' and the 'leap between incommensurate worlds' aspects of the revolutions *within* science, and correspondingly underrates the far more radical discontinuity between paradigms in non-science and in science. In fact, he can hardly formulate the problem in these terms, inasmuch as he had defined science in terms of the presence of paradigms (though he has

The commonest label attached to the viewpoint which admires the former, and holds it up as a model of all human intellectual, or at least cognitive, endeavour, is *positivism*. The arranged battle between the two camps failed to come off because the most important contemporary champion of the first tendency, bewilderingly, but firmly and passionately, dissociated himself from 'positivism'. This totally confuses the issue. Is he justified?

To answer this question properly, one must consider the terms of reference of modern epistemology. It is, essentially, a *differential* inquiry: it must explain why it is that some *do* know, and others do *not*. It must explain the great *Wissenschaftswunder* of modern times. The cognitive wealth of most societies is more or less stable, or grows at most imperceptibly slowly. How has one Faustian society managed to purchase the secret of eternal cognitive growth?

Whether or not it is valid, positivism has an acceptably clear and precise answer to this. The answer is in fact presupposed by Popper's central doctrine. It is a precondition of the implementation of the great Imperative which he prescribes for our cognitive endeavours – the obligation to render our cognitive claims *falsifiable*. The requirement of falsifiability is a vacuous demand, which passes the buck to some anonymous, unspecified further authority, unless it specifies the source or nature of those falsifiers who are to carry out the necessary eliminations, *independently of our will*. Positivism had specified what those falsifiers are, and the whole tenor of Popper's early work suggests that he accepts or presupposes that specification. Falsifiability without that

---

somewhat modified this view later), and non-science in terms of their absence. The great leap would be then over a river where one bank was missing!

Yet on occasion he comes close to realising something which could be summed up as the recognition of the difference between the meta-paradigm of science (distinct from the specific paradigms within it) and non-science. Consider for instance pages 291 and 292 of his *The Essential Tension* (Chicago, 1977), where quite obviously he is discussing, in his comments on Karl Popper's views, the social inculcation not of *a* specific paradigm, but of the scientific spirit in general, which transcends individual paradigms and must constitute a kind of meta-paradigm.

The correct way forward from this seems to me to distinguish between science and non-science not in terms of the presence and absence of paradigms, but in terms of the presence of different *kinds* of paradigms. When this is done, the meta-paradigm of science may turn out not to be so very different from the account of the world presupposed by the theory of knowledge in the empiricist tradition. (In fact, that tradition is best seen as a codification of the meta-paradigm which makes science possible.) The difference, however, will be that it will then be seen as *a* paradigm or *a* world, and one which happens to be cognitively fertile, rather than, as used to be naively supposed in philosophy, as *the* world, or *the* way of knowledge in any world. For instance, R. Carnap should perhaps on this view have called his book *A Logical Construction of the World.*.

specification degenerates into mere instability. So, in that sense, Popper is indeed a positivist.

The tenor of his later work changes: less stress on circumscribed falsifiability, more on the uncircumscribed, *carte blanche* critical spirit. Moreover, a number of themes appear which seem intended to perform that differential, sheep-and-goat-selecting job, previously performed so much more effectively by the more or less tacitly presupposed positivist-style falsifiers. We have seen what these devices were – clarity (wrongly assumed to be manifest), non-violence, and the pragmatist-type suggestion that all in all our cognitive practices have been sound ever since the amoeba, barring a short-lived Age of Ignorance. They are most unsatisfactory. So Popper cannot evade the positivist classification by invoking the use of some other devices for the required task of explaining why some attempts at knowledge work so well and why others fail: because these devices will not do the job in question. So, once again, one must conclude that he is a positivist *malgré soi*. And, as we shall see in the final stage of the argument, the supposition that he can rebut his idealist opponents by appealing to his own views on the nature of the social sciences will not do either.

So we can return to our initial issue, and that of the volume under discussion: the issue of positivists v. Hegelians. But the situation has been clarified and made neater. Positivism takes its rightful place in it, instead of being roundly abused – to the justified puzzlement of spectators – by *both* the teams brought to the match; and the positivist team is now strengthened by the (admittedly reluctant) recruitment of that most formidable of Viennese strikers, Karl Popper.

There is a further issue which hinges on the 'positivist' label. There is another problem, just as septic philosophically and politically. That issue is the unity of the world, the unity of the natural and the social sciences, the ultimate amenability of both the human and social world on the one hand, and of the natural world on the other, to the same methods of investigation. This is a very central issue for all those who, like the Frankfurt school, have of late striven so hard to make 'positivism' a dirty word. The reintroduction of idealism in the guise of hermeneutics, by Frankfurters, Wittgensteinians and others, had as its principal aim to free man from the indignity of a purely factual, external, impersonal, inhuman inquiry. It is hard not to note that an incidental, or perhaps not quite so incidental, pay-off of this attitude was to free favoured theories, e.g., Marxism, from the danger of being falsified by mere facts. Once hermeneutic and holistic interpretation is king, favoured theories are safe.

But in the light of this issue, it is very difficult to see why Popper should be so eager not to be tarred by the positivist brush. He has himself eagerly advocated the unity of method in the natural and in the human/social spheres, which is of course the 'positivist' thesis. Admittedly, he combines this insistence by turning on his idealist opponents and accusing them of misunderstanding the methods of natural science – by which he seems to mean that they fail to appreciate the role of daring speculation and empathy in natural science, which are both commendable provided that in the end, factual checking remains sovereign. They seem to think, on his account of their views, that the natural sciences are somehow narrowly fact-bound, without room for imagination, *feel*, and radical transcendence of the available 'data base' in theory construction.

The situation here is very complex, involving as it does layer on layer of cross-referring mutual misinterpretations. The idealists call him a positivist because, they allege, he insists that basic method is identical in the natural and in the social sciences. The allegation is entirely correct, and he himself insists on this identity of method.[28] Nonetheless he retorts, the imputation is not valid when it comes from *them*, because they are quite misguided about the veritable nature of method in the natural sciences. But is it the identity of method which matters (in which case, by this criterion, he is a positivist); or is it the *specific nature* of method in the social sciences (in which case they are mistaken in the views they attribute to him, because they infer them from misguided accounts of his opinions about the social sciences, inferred in turn from an incorrect assessment of his thoughts on natural science, via the correct assumption that he has the *same* view on both)? I believe the former alternative to be the correct one. Popper does not exclude imagination and empathy, let alone theoretical daring, from the social sciences, any more than he excludes them from the natural sciences. He merely does not allow hermeneutics to overrule facts. Our neo-idealists do exactly that. Hermeneutics as a heuristic device is not excluded by Popper; only, at most, behaviourists do that. What defines our modern neo-idealists is the use of hermeneutics as a method of validation, or of exclusion, putative falsification, of theories they do not like.

Those who are so eager to distinguish between natural and social inquiry are not really committed to a narrow, fact-constrained, unimaginative and cautious view of inquiry in the natural sciences. They are not *merely* saying that the social sciences, or the humanities or the *Geisteswissenschaften*, must be more daring and imaginative. (They are

---

[28] For instance, in *The Positivist Dispute in German Sociology*, p. 89.

not committed to denying these qualities to natural science, and hence identity of method in the two fields would not deprive 'human' inquiries of those qualities either.) What they are arguing is something more radical – they are arguing against the sovereignty of fact in the human sphere. Facts are not sovereign because they are interpretation-bound, in a sphere where the interpretations of *participants* as well as those of investigators are relevant (investigators *only* are relevant in natural science, where the objects of inquiry contribute no interpretations of their own) – if indeed investigators and objects of investigation are distinct and separate, which is precisely what the hermeneuticist idealists deny.

So, once again, it seems to me that Popper is rightly classed with the positivists. He does insist on the ultimate unity of method, and the issue is not affected by whether or not his opponents are in error about the nature of natural science. (I rather doubt whether, on this point, they commit the error with which he credits them.) The supposition that positivists oppose theoretical daring is in any case an odd one. Auguste Comte himself certainly does not fit this stereotype: 'the true positivist spirit is basically as far removed from empiricism as it is from mysticism . . . True science consists of the *laws* of phenomena, to which facts in the proper sense of the word . . . only supply the indispensable materials' (*Discours sur l'Esprit Positif*, Paris, 1898).

On the whole, the argument so far has endeavoured to bring out what is at issue between the Hegelian/holistic and the positivistic/granular visions, rather than to adjudicate between them. But can one rationally choose between them? Each of these worlds tends to vindicate itself, but such self-validation is obviously suspect. W. W. Bartley III attempted to show that the Popperian version of the empiricist version is at least not incoherent and inconsistent;[29] but that hardly constitutes a positive validation. Is it in fact possible to find some natural vantage point, acceptable and legitimate for each of these rival visions, from which one could judge both? It seems unlikely.

Empiricism and positivism contain an ethic of cognition which, *on the assumption of the validity of the granular metaphysic*, can work. But why should we assume the truth of that axiom? The greatest of the empiricists, David Hume (and others within his intellectual lineage) tried to smuggle in this metaphysic as a piece of descriptive psychology. When treated as such, however, it simply isn't true, and it now seems that it is actually more plausible if candidly presented as a cognitive

---

[29] *Retreat to Commitment*, New York, 1962; London, 1964.

ethic[30] rather than as a corollary of an untenable psychology . . .

Still, the granular metaphysic has some measure of inherent plausibility. We experience the world not as a whole but as a succession of bits. The jigsaw model of the nature of things does have some appeal. But not enough to persuade us. So what is it that does persuade us, to the extent to which we do indeed seem persuaded?

The granular or atomistic picture and all that goes with it is *a* vision amongst others. It has its associated ethics, politics, aesthetics, based generally on the twin doctrines of atomism and non-transcendence. Consent in politics, hedonism in ethics and aesthetics, summation of parts rather than *Gestalt* package deals – these tend to be the themes within it. Atomism denies the authority of global or synoptic visions; but, ironically, it does itself constitute one of them. And why should we choose *it* rather than one of its rivals, given that the inherent plausibility of epistemic atomism is not sufficient to convert us, and that it has no automatic, self-guaranteeing authority?

The vision has been linked to science and the authority of its atomic experiments, and it has been linked to a science-using society. Considered globally, such societies have certain important features: they display greater cognitive, technological and economic growth than any other society in human history. They appear capable of maintaining social order with less violence and oppression, with less deprivation and inequality, than any other large and complex society in human history.

In fact, in choosing such a vision, we choose a kind of society which sustains it and which is sustained by it. This cannot be done from the outside, for there is no external vantage point, no inter-social empty space from which it and its rival could be judged. How then is it done? Well, the Hegelians had told us a parable about how it can: global, inter-penetrating, historically successive, incommensurate yet overlapping worlds do constitute our predicament, and yet also provide the only solution to which they are susceptible. Global package-deal choices are made because we cannot but make them: the rival worlds are not merely incommensurate, they are also interconnected and have overlapping criteria and idioms. One of them seems richer, more fulfilling than the others, and also historically dominant. It seems to be winning and to be better, though we should be embarrassed to say either that it was better simply because it was winning, or that it was winning simply because it was better.

The essence of Hegelianism was Pirandellism: a systematic jumping in and out of our socio-historical skins. This had to be seen in contrast to

---

[30] I have attempted to show this in *Legitimation of Belief*, Cambridge, 1975.

the other major solution of the problem of choosing and justifying one vision in a period of change and disorganisation: that other solution was classical empiricism (of which positivism is an offshoot). Empiricism was very much like a conventional, classical theatre, pre-Pirandellian: it consisted of stepping *out* of the world and looking at it from outside, like a well-insulated, impartial spectator. *Die Welt als Idee* . . . The observer, the Pure Visitor, looked at the data presented to him, and came to his conclusions. Of course he had to refrain from any special connection with the actors or characters, which would have biassed him. Descartes had sketched out this programme, and the great British empiricists had carried it out.

The weaknesses of this solution are well known. On the one hand, the data presented to the Spectator are never adequate; he ends up with the Spectator's Egocentric Predicament, possessing only himself at most as his data. At the same time, his jury-like insulation is never genuine, for he always does have backstage connections with the play. In epistemology as in ethics, the world is not a spectacle but a predicament . . .

The Hegelian counter-solution contained a number of themes. The solitary individualist spectator was replaced by a kind of collective *Geist*. This was justified – *nur mit ein bisschen anderen Worten* – by an appeal to the fact that it is collectivities or cultures, not individuals, who carry the conceptual equipment through which we construct a world. But the collectivities which had passed in history seemed to form a progressive series, with the later ones somehow encompassing, incorporating, the merits of their earlier ancestors . . .[31] This was the evolutionist use of diversity as a solution to the problem of relativism: diversity was not random. Although it had originally inspired the problem of relativism, seen in this light it also constituted its solution!

This could be combined with the Pirandellian answer to the question as to whether philosophical thought was Inside or Outside the world. (The old dilemma was: if inside, then prejudiced; if outside, hopelessly cut off. In any case, the outside stance was illusory.) The answer was to be that the *Geist* was both In *and* Out. It was more Out at the beginning, and more In later on, and Its gradual, though occasionally dramatic and jumpy, self-revelation is the secret of progress. It came to know Itself, reveal Itself to Itself, as the historical series progressed. Thus It could

---

[31] H. Marcuse, *Reason and Revolution*, London, 1954, p. 10: 'History is organised into different periods, each marking a separate level of development and representing a definite stage in the realisation of reason.'

Hegelians were wrong in attributing so important a status to all the many post-historical transitions. Many of them were but minor crossroads. The one important transition to our intelligible world and cumulative science, codified by post-Cartesian philosophy, *is* the one really important transition.

perform the dance of the seven veils to Itself and for Its own edification. Knowledge was after all ultimately self-knowledge, which solved the problem of how Subject and Object could ever meet; but it was self-knowledge with an inbuilt delay-mechanism, endowing the story with a certain tension and drama. The separation of *Is* and *Ought* was overcome at the same time and by the same process, which also helped divinise this world and make the divine accessible to us. The Frankfurter position is only the umpteenth avatar of Hegelianism, spiced up with various sociological and philosophical themes that had come out of both Left and Right in the ferment of Weimar, and adjusted to the requirements of the Protest period of the post-war world.[32]

The Hegelians got some of the details of this story wrong. The choice is *not* in fact made over and over again in a whole series of cumulatively reinforcing changes, but basically once only. Thus the collective leap loses the reinforcement of repetition. But with this important proviso, they had a point. The empiricist vision, with its atomism, its fact – value separation, its growth-addiction and comfort-deprivation, seems to win, and seems to validate itself somehow more cogently than its rivals. But the whole great transition, in which a choice precisely is made between *it* and its rival, between two incommensurate historical packages, happens once only; it does not happen with that comforting Hegelian historical repetitiveness.

But we choose that empiricist vision, or some variant of it, in a manner which cannot be characterised in the terms which itself prescribes for the justification of intellectual choices. Ironically, we choose it as a total package deal, involving a whole social order, and our own identity with it. We know that the excluded alternative is also by its own lights justified, or self-justified. We make our choice after indulging in a Pirandellian hopping in and out of our conceptual skins, looking at the one we ultimately endorse both from the inside – by its own plausible lights, systematically elaborated by western epistemology, it is most sound – *and* from the outside: an entire civilisation, of which that vision is an integral part, seems both preferable and inevitable, given our general situation.

This double validation is inelegant but inescapable. The endorsement of a vision by those already indoctrinated by it is also a bit suspect. This can't be helped. But we did give the alternative a good run for its money. We did not altogether prejudge the results of the inquiry. Though indoctrinated, we are not all that sold on our own social order and its vision. A penumbra of doubt continues to shadow our commit-

[32] See John Orr, 'German Social Theory and the Hidden Face of Technology', *Archives Européennes de Sociologie*, 15, no. 2, 1974.

ment. But we *have* made our commitment, and we have made it in that squinting, double-thinking, in-and-out, self-involving, Pascalian-bookmaker manner on which, in their more ponderous language, the Frankfurters insist so much.

Popper's philosophy is the most sophisticated formulation of the empiricist/positivist tradition which firmly opts for one cognitive style against its rival. W. W. Bartley III endeavoured, in *Retreat to Commitment*, to vindicate Popper's vision. He was hampered by the consideration that he must not justify it: for to do so would be to commit a kind of contradiction. He took it as an essential part of Popper's vision that it repudiated the pursuit of justifications, replacing that by the requirement that all positions should be open to criticism. Within these terms of reference, all that Bartley could do for Popper's Critical Rationalism, so as to make it Comprehensive, was to show that it itself made itself open to criticism and survived it. (This was to contradict its existentialist-style critics, who insisted that it too, like any other position, was in the end based on a brute, blind Commitment.) This made it coherent or 'comprehensive', though still hanging in thin air, and not invalidated. If Bartley was successful, he left Popperism untainted by contradiction, coherent, but (inevitably and inherently) devoid of validation.

What I have done is the mirror-image of what Bartley tried to do. I have tried to show that this position, and more broadly the empiricist/positivist tradition of which it is part, *can* and *should* be positively justified. But the manner of this justification is *not* congruent with what the position itself preaches, with the style of validation which it commends *inside* the world of which it is the Charter. On the contrary: it involves making a choice between total, identity-involving, social and conceptual package deals, in a shamelessly, brazenly Pirandellian manner. It requires us to be Inside and Out of the play all at once. The Hegelian or Frankfurter account of our intellectual life can claim at least one positive instance: and this is it.

So in the end, the positivists are right. For Hegelian reasons.

2 | The gaffe-avoiding animal or A Bundle of Hypotheses

There are a number of notions of rational behaviour. The most important, and also most readily intelligible, is *Zweckrationalität*. Conduct is rational if it is optimally effective in attaining a given specified aim. (Alternative reading: if, in the light of the evidence available to an agent, there is good reason to believe it to be so.) Instrumental rationality contains, as an important part or corollary, the requirement for the efficient use of relevant information. He who wills the end must will the means; information relevant to the choice of most effective means is itself a means, perhaps the most important one. Thus *Zweckrationalität* required not merely that one should choose the optimal means, but also that one's beliefs, in the light of which the means are chosen, should themselves be in some sense optimal, given the data at one's disposal. The second most important sense of rationality is rule-observance, consistency, like treatment of like cases. Unless an authority, an organisation, or for that matter a segment of nature, is rational in this sense, we feel rather helpless in the face of its unpredictability, its caprice. This sense can be extended to a third one, namely the rationality of a coherent system of rules. *Wertrationalität* does not strictly seem to me a form of rationality at all: the idea behind it seems to be the implementation of a value, as contrasted with the attainment of an end. But this only differs from, say, the fulfilment of any whim whatever in so far as a 'value' is solemnly adhered to, consistently respected in its diverse manifestations, and 'deep', i.e., coherently related to other aspects of one's identity. In other words, when we look at what it is that makes a *Wert* into a *Wert* we find *Wertrationalität* dissolving into one or more of the other types of rationality.

The Consistency and Instrumentality senses of rationality overlap: inasmuch as optimal effectiveness is uniquely determined, in any given situation or assessment thereof, efficient instrumental behaviour will also be consistent. The same aim in similar circumstances will call for the same action. There is another and more debatable overlap: consistent, rule-abiding behaviour on the part of an organisation or individual may be held to be the most efficient from the viewpoint of a wide range of possible ends.

The easy intelligibility of the notion of instrumental rationality is liable to give the impression that the thing itself is fairly unproblematical; or that the problems which it engenders are mainly technical rather than fundamental. (The most important instrumentalist theory of ethics, Utilitarianism, generates a host of technical-seeming issues in connection with its own implementation, such as the problems of interpersonal comparisons and discounts for risk or future.)

The notion of instrumental rationality, or efficiency for short, seems to me problematical in a way far more profound than that; and the reasons and factors that make it so appear to me to have become particularly prominent of late. This is not an artificial, academic problem: in real life, the sheer identification of what is to count as rational conduct has become much harder.

There are two elements which enter into the definition of *zweckrational*, instrumentally rational, conduct: means and end. The notion presupposes that we can isolate, identify ends, aims, criteria of that which will satisfy us, which will warrant our treating the endeavour as having been crowned with success. It also assumes an objective world of causally interconnected things, some of which are under our direct control. A 'means' is in the first instance something that is under our control and also in turn has an effect on our ends, and by an extension which can be repeated, anything which is under our control indirectly and/or indirectly affects our end.

These assumptions underlying the idea of efficiency seem relatively uncontentious, or alternatively, problematical only in such a very general philosophical way that the problems raised ought not to create any specific difficulties for efficiency as such. There may be problems about the existence or accessibility of an objective world, or about causality, but need we worry about them specifically in connection with efficiency? Those problems would seem to touch virtually everything in the world; like the rain which falls on the just and unjust alike, they do not discriminate, so why should they bother us?

This is an illusion.

The notion of efficiency presupposes not merely an external world, it presupposes a *single* world. I think that most theoreticians of knowledge, philosophers of science and so on have indeed assumed something of the kind in their very formulation of the problem. The model with which they more or less tacitly operated was something like this: the individual, using the tools and materials supplied to him (the mix of external material and self-supplied tools varying with the epistemological theory in question), constructed *one world*. Of course, on occasion his world was fractured, but that constituted an anomaly, a problem, and it was up to him to set it right by reordering his ideas.

David Hume considered man to be *a* bundle of sensations, but note that the famous phrase was in the singular. It was assumed that the sensations would coagulate into one single bundle, as a lot of small snowballs may congeal into one large one in the process of making a snowman. It is not at all clear why this should be so, nor why the bundles should be as relatively neat and discrete as in fact they mostly are. For Immanuel Kant, the process of gluing the bits together so as to make a single bundle plays an important part in the construction of the world-picture, and is given a name – the synthetic unity of apperception. In fact, for Kant, the central job for the epistemic ego is precisely this, to be a kind of link man or anchor man, as they say in television: when the ego is attached to each single one of the sensations, it causes them to become indirectly fused to each other and make up a World. For Hume, the bundle arose mysteriously by some kind of spontaneous generation or accretion. So Kant at any rate has the merit of seeing the problem, or half-seeing it: for he used the unity of the perceived and conceived world as a step in solving the problem of causation, rather than being imbued with the problematical and dubious status of that unity itself. (His left-handed 'proof' of causality amounted to the following: if we have or assume a single world, with each thing assigned a definite place within it, then causality is *already* presupposed, for without it, things could not be given unambiguous locations in the world; so causality must be taken or left in a single package deal with an unambiguous single world; none would forego that single world (so Kant assumed), and hence causality is established.)

One bundle, one world. During the period when the epistemological question was reformulated in terms of language, this assumption was nevertheless retained. The question about the relationship of language to the world was formulated on the basis of the tacit assumption that one language faced one world.

I think I can say, without fear of immediate and virulent contestation, that I am not widely known as an uncritical and enthusiastic admirer of Ludwig Wittgenstein's later work. Nevertheless, if I were asked to single out some idea in his work which seems to me both valid and important, I should pick out the denial of the Single Bundle thesis which, *nur mit ein bisschen anderen Worten*, thoroughly pervades his approach to language. One does not need to sympathise with the philosophical uses to which he put the idea of the plurality, disparateness and incommensurateness of diverse 'language games' to recognise that this plurality and disparity have profound implications. The matter is really simple: Wittgenstein supposed that this plurality and disparity, or rather its recognition, somehow solved something, and absolved us from the unnecessary and self-imposed burden of seeking general validations. In fact it does nothing of the kind. Used in that way, his discovery seems to me to have little merit. But if treated as a *problem*, not as a solution, the idea becomes significant.

Language games, i.e., presumably, clusters of tokens and the rules governing their use, do *not* add up to one single overarching language with one set of rules and casting a single categorical shadow on the world, as Kant supposed. I take this to be the central philosophical point associated with the notion of 'language games'. Games are many and not one. Moreover, they do not all interact with extra-linguistic reality, whatever it is, in the same kind of way, and some of them perhaps do not interact with it at all. In so far as they do interact with it, they do so in diverse ways for diverse purposes in diverse contexts; thus the 'bits' of reality which they capture, record or report are not all of the same kind. The diversity of the games is reflected in the diversity of the material they dredge up. The incommensurateness of the various games is reflected in the incommensurateness of the material which they pull into their respective nets. And just as you cannot meaningfully reply to a move in chess by a move from dominoes, replying then with a move from Scrabble, so equally you cannot expect the diverse 'worlds' to add up to one perspective, one vision, one system. A plurality of interrelated but incommensurate worlds replaces that unitarian world tacitly assumed by classical epistemology, a world rather like one of those reconstructed panoramas of battles one sometimes finds in museums which offer a *single* picture as it may have appeared from one definite viewpoint, with all objects obeying the requirements of perspective from that viewpoint. Traditional epistemology saw the cognising individual as located within his single prospective cocoon, assembling one mosaic from the items supplied to him.

Within such a world, he could then, if he chose, be instrumentally rational. To be rational in this way might have required exceptional clarity of mind, firmness of purpose and character, and great ability or luck in extrapolation towards the as yet uncompleted parts of the mosaic. But allowing for these practical difficulties, which were not unsurmountable for someone with character and ability, *Zweckration-alität* was an available option.

Is it, in fact? A man can be a good, *zweckrational* chess player, bridge player, poker player, and so on. The criteria of success and the connections between available means and desirable ends are adequately defined within each of these universes of discourse, and efficiency is consequently identifiable within them without undue difficulty – and is indeed on occasion contrasted with other considerations which influence players, such as elegance, truculence, or sociability. But what conceivable *Zweckrationalität* can be credited to a life as a whole, where that life encompasses a multiplicity of diverse games?

The question is not rhetorical and is not intended, or not yet, to provoke an immediate reply – *any* reply. It may be that the multiple games add up to one world after all, and it may be that some more abstract aim can be identified in terms of which scores from disparate games can be added and subtracted. Possibly: but it is obviously no easy matter, and there is no immediately evident answer.

It is interesting and relevant, though perhaps not conclusive, that I instinctively find the model of plural and incommensurate overlapping games much closer to life as I know it than the single-bundle observer, assembling one homogeneous world with one perspectival structure based on a single vantage point. Each mood, each milieu, each relationship, has its own idiom. Communication between them does exist, but it is partial, incomplete, awkward, sometimes merely embarrassing. They commit treason against each other. That which is sacred in one context may be trite and easy to treat ironically in another. You have to know your way about if you are not to make a fool of yourself. What is known as *savoir-faire* is largely the ability to switch from one key to another and to recognise the clues which make such switches appropriate. But too much *savoir-faire* is morally suspect. It suggests pliable, adjustable principles. Yet moral consistency, the unwillingness to switch from the conventions of one game to another, the insistence on staying within the bounds of one of them, is a kind of madness – admirable madness, perhaps.

A great part of our life is spent not so much (as those social sciences which are inspired by the ends–means model would suggest) in the pursuit of aims, but in the avoidance of gaffes. We try to learn our part as we go along and to get by without too much unfavourable comment. Of course you could say that 'avoiding gaffes' either is, or constitutes part of, an overall aim, but that is twisting the facts a bit into the mould of the ends–means model. It is of course notoriously a feature of the ends–means model of human conduct that it *can*, if necessary, be imposed on all human behaviour. When this is done, we are then rational whether we like it or not. By inventing appropriate ends, any conduct becomes *zweckrational*. Whether it is useful so to impose that vision is another matter.

But if we are, as seems to me to be the case, gaffe-avoiding rather than rational animals, treading our way gingerly through a variety of games to which we are only in part habituated, then our condition is very different from what the theory of instrumental rationality suggests. Thus far, at any rate, I agree with those romantic thinkers who, in opposition to the means–ends rationalists, see social life as the mastering of a language, the use of a code, the participation in a conversation. They are right to this extent – for much of their life, men are not maximising anything or striving for some concretely isolable end, but are simply eager to be included in, or to remain within, a continuing play. The role is its own reward, not a means towards some further end-state. The point at which these romantics go wrong is this: the role can indeed be understood only through the concepts internal to the play. The role is a fulfilment and not an instrument, they say. So far so good. But from this there is only a small, but disastrously wrong, step to an idealist view which ignores material, non-conceptual, non-conventional constraints. Man may indeed be a convention-seeking, gaffe-avoiding animal; but even the perfect mastery of an idiom will not save you from violence or starvation if objective conditions impose them on you, and conversely, if you are powerful enough, you may commit any gaffe you choose, you may violate the local code or idiom, you may write your own ticket, impose your own code with impunity.

But these (quite fashionable and pervasive) errors of sociological idealism, current under various names, are a side issue to the present argument, which is concerned with the plurality of idioms in life, the plurality of 'worlds' which are their shadows or correlates, and the consequent plurality of overlapping worlds, within which, according to my argument, a general, pervasive *Zweckrationalität* simply makes no sense. Such rationality is possible within delimited areas; if the argument sketched out is correct, it simply makes no sense as an overall life-style. If this argument is correct, what is at issue is not whether a life-style of this kind is attractive – romantics find it repellent – but whether it is logically possible. On this view, when John Stuart Mill was plunged into a depression and concluded that it was not possible to live life in the direct pursuit of a single aim, namely happiness, as Utilitarianism commended, what he was facing was not a psychological, but a logical impossibility.

The point is this: not only is it questionable whether there is, in the required sense, a single world; it is equally questionable whether there can be a single *aim*. On this point, let me first of all specify my conclusion before indicating the argument which supports it. There is a kind of Inverse Law: the Specificity and the Plausibility of aims vary inversely.

By Specificity of an aim I mean its usability as a criterion for efficiency, for the success or failure of an enterprise – in other words, the testability of assertions concerning its attainment. For the purpose of measuring efficiency, an aim can be of a simple yes/no variety, or can allow of measurable degrees. For instance, if my aim is to ascend a certain mountain, I either succeed or fail, and it is normally easy to tell which. A miss is as good as a mile. If my aim is to amass wealth as measured in a given currency, the precise amount of it can also normally be measured. Climbing mountain peaks or making money are *specific* aims, and in consequence the *Zweckrationalität* of strategies for attaining these ends is open to fairly reliable assessment.

By contrast, each of these aims has very low *plausibility* as an overall end of the life of a human individual or community. If we perform the *Gedankenexperiment* once recommended by G. E. Moore for the evaluation of the *intrinsic* goodness or desirability of things, and think of the states of affairs satisfying these ends *in complete isolation*, as if there were nothing else in the world, we end up with something which is absurd in itself, let alone as an object of desire. Standing on a peak in a universe containing naught else, or possessing gold ingots in an otherwise empty world: each has a somewhat surrealist quality. (G. E. Moore, if I remember rightly, also used this method to discredit pleasure as an end, with the further aid of the somewhat odd argument that pleasure alone meant pleasure without the consciousness that you had it, and there you were . . .)

But something rather serious and important does underlie Moore's rather Dali-esque method. It is this: the kind of aim which can *plausibly* be ascribed to a human life or a human community is a highly complex, holistic state of affairs, which contains the specific objects of isolated endeavours only as components or internal options; these insulated sub-aims, however, are worthless or meaningless in isolation. The moral philosophy which tried to articulate itself in the idiom of Means and Ends, Utilitarianism, only attained plausibility through the use of an ambiguous, stretch-and-contract notion, namely *happiness*, the meaning of which fluctuated between being the attribute of an approved total way of life, and (when defined as 'pleasure and absence of pain'), being the alleged name of a more or less measurable and isolable specific experience.

Social sciences which operate with means–ends models require, so as to be able to reach testable consequences from the premises of their models, that men should maximise or aim at *something*, never mind what. The trouble is that they are caught in a fork: either they choose realistic aims, which, however, are complex and diffuse and thereby frustrate all calculations or instrumental efficiency, or they choose aims which allow of such calculations, but whose resemblance to actual human aims is generally minimal.

Thus it is doubtful whether *Zweckrationalität* often has, in important contexts, any plausible aims on which to work. It does of course have application in limited fields. If Weber is to be believed, the paradigmatically *zweckrational* conduct of capitalist enterprises came as the consequence of the compulsive enactment of a *role*. The role was compulsively enacted in an illogical, double-think-permeated effort to demonstrate to the agent himself something which was at the same time outside the power of the person attempting to provide the demonstration through his own conduct, and something which was already decided and thus not the possible object of *zweckrational* behaviour. (By a further irony, if Weber is right, the instrumentally rational world, in which human activities and roles become volatile under the impact of the requirements of efficiency, was brought about by a rigid attachment to the notion of a *calling*, an attachment which, through that rigidity, was itself impervious to instrumental considerations of efficiency.)

This unavailability of plausible aims is important for the ideal of instrumental rationality, but the unavailability of a single world, within which efficiency could be judged by a single measure, so to speak – if the aim were there – is even more important. I believe that this plurality of worlds has always been part of the human condition, and thus constitutes nothing new – but that we have recently become more aware of it.

There are interesting reasons for this development. It is precisely because recent times have witnessed a more persistent and determined effort to unify our world that we have become sensitive to the failure of these unification-attempts. In the past, precisely because the world as a whole was seen as some kind of coherent cosmos, qualitatively distinct incommensurate sub-realms within it, each with its own style of being and evidence, were perfectly tolerable. But something quite different has happened to the modern, post-Cartesian vision. (Note, incidentally, that the latest exegesis of Descartes, that of Bernard Williams, sees him primarily – though this is not the terminology used – as a kind of hero, clown or martyr of *Zweckrationalität*; as a man who adopts the method of doubt in consequence of abandoning temporarily the normal plurality of human aims, and serving instead one end exclusively and ruthlessly, that end being the augmentation of truth in his possession, with a manic disregard – whilst in this temporary condition – of other considerations; a truly paradigmatic case of *zweckrational* lunacy.)

What is it that has happened?

The basic plot of post-Cartesian philosophy is the perfectly sensible attempt to find a general criterion, or legitimator, of our ideas about the world, as a reaction to the erosion, fragmentation and destabilisation of previous world-visions.[1] This endeavour leads in due course to the empiricist theory of one-kind-of-evidence-only, namely sensory grains. The homogenisation of evidence leads automatically to the unification of the world (which, as I insisted early in the chapter, this tradition anyway assumed to hold, and on the whole uncritically). Man, as Hume put it, becomes a bundle of sensations; and of course other subjects in the world are likewise bundles, and made up of similar raw materials. On this account, the world really does become a remarkably homogeneous place.

There is, however, a sense in which (within this picture) the world at large is a bit different from things within it, including people. 'The world' is not just an accumulation of things (or facts, according to Wittgenstein's *Tractatus*, in many ways a fine specimen of that tradition), it is also the system of connections between them, of 'laws' and so on. The vision of approach which turns man into a bundle of sensations turns the world itself into a *Bundle of Hypotheses*. The question now is – and this leads us straight back to our general problem of Rationality – can one, and if so how, live in or with a Bundle of Hypotheses? *Ein Zollverein ist keine Heimat*: and is a Bundle of Hypotheses a livable world?

Note the route along which the world was made into a Bundle of Hypotheses. It was a consequence of the attempt to rationalise evidence and conviction, which in turn is a precondition or part of the *Zweckrationalität* ideal. *Zweckrationalität* called for standardisation of evidence, so as to evaluate it systematically and by a common yardstick. Unless you assess evidence rationally, you cannot assess efficiency, for efficiency is conduciveness to some aim. Choice of means on the basis of sloppily selected evidence is worthless. But if various beliefs are to be compared, they must be in a similar idiom. Thus world-levelling, unificatory epistemologies were elaborated in the service of instrumental rationality. If you are to choose the most efficient Means, you must *know* (and not take on trust, uncritically) the world within which means are links in those causal chains which you manipulate in getting, in the most economical way possible, to your desired Ends. This means suspending faith in objects, realities, unbased on evidence. The end-point of this story is that the world becomes a Bundle of Hypotheses, selected either for optimal corroboration, or for maximum daring and anticipated future fertility (to take two relatively recent rival philosophies of science).

[1] I have argued this in detail in *Legitimation of Belief*, Cambridge, 1975.

At this point I wish to become dogmatic and make some unsubstanti-ated assertions (not because I wish to avoid discussion of them, which on the contrary I'd find interesting, but because there is no space for it, and intelligibility of exposition requires that the point be asserted long before it is defended): mankind has never in the past tried to live within a Bundle of Hypotheses. It is extremely difficult and probably impossible to do this. Instead, mankind has generally lived by means of the joint employment of Fixed and Variable Cognitive Capital, to borrow phrases from another context and to give them a new sense.

Anthropologists and philosophers of anthropology sometimes raise the question of whether or to what extent peoples who held or hold very strange, and to us eccentric, views were also capable of recognising and using ordinary sound empirical evidence in the way which is so highly prized amongst us and which has made us the men we are. Field observation suggests that they are perfectly capable of it. That then raises the puzzled question – if so, how can they *also* believe that other nonsense? For instance, how can those fishermen be so intelligently sensitive to all the sound empirical preconditions (as we would say) of a successful fishing expedition, and yet also say and evidently believe that their success is conditional on various ritual performances and omens which, to our minds, have not the slightest connection with it . . .?

I suspect that part of the answer is to be sought in the distinction between what I have called Fixed and Variable Cognitive Capital. At any given time and in any given society, a large, probably an overwhelmingly large, part of the view of the world is frozen into the Fixed Cognitive Capital. To treat this part of the society's beliefs as a set of *hypotheses* is misleading and somewhat offensive. It is not just that they are held with a rigidity which makes them quite insensitive to contrary evidence, should it turn up. There is more to it than that. The identities, roles, personal relationships, power and hierarchy structure, allocation of resources of the society, are all articulated and legitimated in terms of the concepts and ideas of this Fixed Cognitive Capital. This means that, on the one hand, a tangled and weighty network of vested interests and habits helps ensure that the Fixed Capital cannot be changed: anyone inclined to tamper with any single part of it soon finds that he is trying to dislodge a vast and intertwined mass of other things, and he rapidly desists from so enormous, and perhaps dangerous and bewildering, an effort. It also means, on the other hand, of course, that if for some reason that interconnected mass were dislodged, the movement of the resulting avalanche would be hard to arrest, and unpredictable and destructive in its course. This happens rarely, but plainly it did and does happen when the fundamental changes associated with slogans such as 'industrialis-

ation' or 'modernisation' dislodge either social/institutional or intellectual elements in the mass.

But in the relatively stable traditional situation there is no avalanche,
and the big bulk is in a stable, frozen condition. Variability of opinion,
sensitivity to evidence, permitting the rapid inversion of the truth-value
attributed to individual and isolable bits in the world-picture mosaic
('propositions'), are restricted to a fairly small and reasonably well-
insulated area. The superstitious fishermen do not revise either their
cosmology or their social organisation, and would not understand what
was being suggested if someone were to propose it to them; but within
the limited field of connections between various weather signs and
tomorrow's state of the sea, they make perfectly rational inferences from
the former to the latter, and are quite capable of *Zweckrationalität* and of
the construction of an evidence-sensitive sub-world, within which
instrumental efficiency can be practised and assessed.

And it is this which brings us to the greatest problem for the notion of
Zweckrationalität: rational, evidence-sensitive cognitive behaviour is
perfectly feasible within such delimited spheres. If the framework is
fixed, then a sub-set of details, of specific ideas, can be variable, and can
be tied to 'evidence' (or, no doubt, to other things, for not all flexible
ideas are also rational, in the sense of meeting the recommendations of
scientific method). But it is by no means obvious that any sense can be
attached to evidence-sensitivity, to cognitive rationality, to a system as a
whole. Alternatively, even if some sense can be attached to it, it is doubtful whether the practice of such rationality is psychologically tolerable.

When I say that it is doubtful whether any sense can be attached to
evidence-sensitive, rational assessment of total visions, I do not have in
mind the familiar point about the infinite regress of justification, which
leads people to say that 'in the end' there is a blind leap of faith in *any*
vision whatever (and therefore, to the delight of believers, all faiths are in
the end equal in the eyes of Reason, and so never have any need to feel
inferior *vis-à-vis* agnostics and rationalists). The point is rather that
there is not much sense in attaching probability weightings to *sui generis*
hypotheses, which are not parts of any kind of series or wider class, and
whose probability consequently cannot be derived from a background
hypothesis, either because there is no such hypothesis, or, if there is, it is
simply the idea-to-be-assessed restated. Pascal attempted to assess the
rationality of belief in God in precisely this manner, in a remarkable
essay in cost–benefit analysis of *Zweckrationalität*. But his famous Wager
is a bit of a joke, it doesn't feel serious, it is not to be taken seriously;
more than half its point is, precisely, to bring out the uniqueness of the
question posed, through the ineptness of a procedure which in other

and more limited spheres would be perfectly rational and sensitive. Fixed Cognitive Capital simply cannot be dealt with in the same way as Variable Capital.

In ordinary life, we bang our heads against the wall of the Fixed Cognitive Capital not merely, like Pascal, when we encounter theological issues, but also in much more mundane matters. To hazard a sociological generalisation: the presence of *ritual* is a good sign of the limits of the variable world, of impinging on the fixed. The essence of ritual is, precisely, its rigidity, its evidence-*in*sensitivity, which makes it the very antithesis of *Zweckrationalität*. (No wonder the puritans, who were the instruments by which the Cunning of Reason introduced instrumental rationality into the world, also minimised ritual in their religious life.) Now what is the point of that rigidity?

A man can be instrumentally rational in choosing, let us say, a business partner, a tennis partner, or a holiday companion. There are moderately precise and formulable criteria for the successful occupancy of such a role. But does it make sense to speak of a rational choice of a spouse? No doubt the mystique of romantic love, the requirement of a *coup de foudre*, arises in part in a society which has abandoned prescriptive or preferential marriage, and where the requirement of this allegedly quite unpredictable, free-floating element of 'love' provides an ever-ready excuse for those who do not propose to otherwise suitable and eligible partners; without the presence of such an in-built excuse, the matter could often be embarrassing. But the other reason is that for such a weighty and many-stranded relationship, rational calculation breaks down, and is bound to do so. Calculation is of course present, but it is overruled by some kind of global consideration or summation, in which so many imponderables, incommensurables and unpredictables are weighted in a mysterious half-conscious and private algorithm that to pretend to fit it into *Zweckrationalität* is a bit of a fraud. The change of status and identity which is involved in a *rite de passage* such as marriage involves far too much to be eligible for rational calculation. Yet the participants have to go through with it. The ritual and its rigidity are a kind of hand-rail which guides them through a passage in which reason is no longer available, and where they might otherwise waver.[2]

---

[2] In complicated modern conditions, it can also work in reverse, by a kind of double-take. I knew a young woman who came from a country in which, traditionally, the preferred form of marriage was with the parallel patrilateral cousin. In fact, she was educated in Britain, and lived the life of an emancipated western woman. She did, however, *marry* in her own background; a young man who was in fact her parallel patrilateral cousin, and whom she knew only for a brief period before their wedding.

No doubt she was embarrassed at the thought that she might seem to her

Likewise, and notoriously, no rational attitude is possible in the face of death, whether one's own or that of others. The enormity of the thing makes it impossible to weigh it against other things, and it is offensive and repugnant to try. Judges and insurance companies are of course often obliged to assess death in calculable, monetary terms, but that is viewed apologetically and with embarrassment, and the judges themselves are protected by a certain ritualisation of their own procedure. Armies are perhaps the most ritualised institutions in society, more so even than Churches (whose special business is the Global and incalculable), and the reason for this is not only that ritualisation helps enforce discipline by creating so many secondary transgressions which can be invoked against the defiant. It is said that during the last war, the German army had a set drill for the capture of machine-gun nests, doing it by numbers, and that it worked. One would think that a highly specific concrete task, like the capture of a fortified point, would be eminently suitable for pliable, evidence-sensitive *Zweckrationalität*; but when the actions involved also imply, for the participants, the facing of an incalculably weighty risk – their own death – then ritualisation, by freeing the mind from the need to ponder, is probably effective.

Unique and weighty political decisions are similarly incalculable and thus evade *Zweckrationalität*. For a Jew in the 1930s or early 1940s, in a country occupied or about to be occupied by Hitler, was it rational to flee, whatever the dangers involved? With hindsight, we know of course that it was. But genocide and coldly organised mass murder were so discontinuous with, at least, European history for some centuries, that assigning some precise probability to it in advance of the event would have been absurd. The *sui generis* nature of the possibility made it virtually impossible to evaluate evidence about the contingency.

Or take the much-debated and emotive issue of nuclear disarmament. It is said that as part of an intelligence exercise, military experts advising the US government have on occasion ascribed a definite figure to the probability of nuclear war breaking out within a defined period. These figures have an air of silliness about them similar to that which attaches to Pascal's calculation of the rationality of the belief in God. It

---

'western' friends to be a slave of tradition and of social constraints. So she made a point of telling people that she and her cousin did in fact experience a *coup de foudre*, and that had they met in the West, they would of course simply have lived with each other as is right and proper, but that they promptly married simply as a concession, on a superficial matter, to the feelings of their archaic relatives. I am not suggesting that her story was untrue. But it is interesting to see an upside-down situation, in which the idea of an irresistible, sudden and spontaneous passion is invoked not as an excuse for avoiding, but as an explanation of conforming to, traditional requirements.

is, of course, easy to construct an argument which shows that nuclear war is, in the long run, overwhelmingly probable. But once again, we have reached the limit of our Variable Cognitive Capital, we are tinkering with something like the total stock, we are trying to deal with the Fixed Capital as if it were variable, and calculations acquire an air of unreality.

Or to take something not so ultimate, consider the dilemma which recently faced West European liberal socialists – whether to take liberal Eurocommunism at face value and cooperate with Communist parties. There is no record of a Communist regime in power remaining liberal, which of course does not entail that the thing is impossible. The issue is exactly like that of Immortality and the existence of God, in that by the time we *know* the answer, it will be too late to revise the wager if we have made the wrong one.

A competent stockbroker, whose job and essence is to practise *Zweckrationalität* on behalf of his clients, can more or less advise them about the instrumental rationality of alternative forms of investment, within the assumption of an overall economic/political stability. His views on the probability of the maintenance of that framework are about as worthless as those of anyone else. The boundary between areas where instrumental efficiency can be a guide (owing to the easy insulation of Variable Cognitive Capital, and the availability of fairly clear aims and criteria) is, I suspect, also closely linked to the delimitation of economics and politics. (This, amongst other reasons, makes the recent revival of social-contract theories in politics, in a form which tries to incorporate them within instrumental rationality, so weird.)

To sum up my contentions (and I have no illusion that they are adequately substantiated):

Instrumental rationality is feasible only within limited sub-spheres of our world, where rational evidence-sensitivity, which it presupposes, is also possible, and where fairly precise aims are too. In other words, it is possible within sub-realms within which hypotheses can be evaluated within a wider given framework.

The modern industrial/scientific world is simultaneously impelling us in two incompatible directions. By eroding the old frameworks and requiring neutral, homogeneous legitimations of beliefs, it pushes the world into becoming a Bundle of Hypotheses, and thus a home fit for instrumental rationality, if not perhaps for much else. It has diminished Fixed Capital, it has extended Variable Capital. This after all was the essence of the Scientific Revolution. It has led to rapidly cumulative knowledge and an unprecedented control over the environment. At the same time, this extension of the Bundle of Hypotheses and the corresponding reduction of the rigid framework also eventually make rational calculation harder in many areas where it is now expected and which were previously exempt from it. The more general or fundamental features of the world, though now demoted to the status of mere hypotheses, often elude rational assessment because they are unique or *sui generis* or very fundamental. They have become relativised, optional, and deprived of their privileged, entrenched status – but without becoming, for all that, eligible for rational, instrumental evaluation.

By secularisation and 'disenchantment', our world reduces or eliminates the ritually protected, entrenched areas, thereby propelling us towards an ever more general 'rationality'. By increasing human power over nature and society, it also greatly increases the number of occasions on which fundamental, unique imponderable choices need be made. But by including, by these two processes, a far bigger dose of issues not easily amenable to *Zweckrationalität* within our collective agenda, so to speak, it also makes it that much harder for us to live by the principles of instrumental efficiency. (In the days in which the area in which those principles were to be applied was restricted, it would at least have been possible, within that restricted area, to implement it.)

Thus we need *Zweckrationalität* most when we can least use it.

I'm not clear where this leaves us.

3 | Relativism and universals

A spectre haunts human thought: relativism. If truth has many faces, then not one of them deserves trust or respect. Happily, there is a remedy: human universals. They are the holy water with which the spectre can be exorcised. But, of course, before we can use human universals to dispel the threat of cognitive anarchy which would otherwise engulf us, we must first *find* them. And so, the new hunt for the Holy Grail is on.

The underlying and interconnected issues, as I see them are these: just what is the problem of relativism, or rather, what *are* the problems of relativism? How are they related to the issues of human uniqueness or the existence of human universals? What are the general features of explanation of human conduct which are pertinent to this? What are the influential themes in recent thought which provide the terms and assumptions in which they are likely to formulate both questions and answers?

There are (at least) two problems, but those two problems are absolutely fundamental: is there but one kind of man, or are there many? Is there but one world, or are there many? These two questions are *not* identical; but they are not unconnected either. However, it is quite wrong to identify or confuse the two questions, as is sometimes done. The second problem – one world or many – can also be formulated as: are there many truths or one?

The two issues are of course intimately connected, as indeed is visible from the occasions at which the discussion strays from one to the other: if man is not one but many, then will not each kind of man also make his own kind of world, and if so, how can we choose amongst them? What happens then to the uniqueness and objectivity of truth? Our moral intuitions tend to impel us in different directions at this point. Liberalism, tolerance, pluralism, incline many to find pleasure in the idea of a multiplicity of men and visions; but the equally reputable and enlightened desire for objectivity and universality leads to a desire that at least the world and truth be but one, and not many. (The tolerant endorsement of human diversity becomes very tangled if one realises that very many past and alien visions have themselves in turn been internally exclusive, intolerant and ethnocentric; so that if we, in our tolerant way, endorse *them*, we thereby also endorse or encourage intolerance at second hand. This might be called the dilemma of the liberal intellectual.) By contrast, extreme Leftists are sometimes addicted to the thesis of the plasticity or malleability of man. This tends, especially in the case of Marxists, to form part of a polemic against the alleged habit of their opponents of turning the conceptual artefacts of one particular social order into a human universal, so as to discourage any questioning of that social order.

The pursuit of universals, of the unity of man, is also on occasion inspired by the desire to underwrite the brotherhood and equality of man. Whether indeed our values are or should be so directly at the mercy of scholarly findings may well be doubted. I do not anticipate that on the day of the publication of a generative grammar of colloquial Bongo-Bongo, definitely establishing the absolute uniqueness of Bongo-Bongo syntax, I shall promptly conclude that the discriminatory measures imposed on the Bongo-Bongo by hostile authorities are henceforth justified.

But it is, I believe, profoundly significant that by and large, whilst the ultimate motive of the inquiry may be the establishment of a unitary world, the method employed is the pursuit of the unity of *man*. Yet the unity of the world seems at the same time tacitly *assumed* within the inquiry, as providing the framework within which it is carried on (even though one also senses the tacit hope that it will also in turn be demonstrated, *through* the unity of man).

I believe this to be significant twice over. It tells us something about the current intellectual climate: we are fairly sure about which world we inhabit, and that there is but one, though we are much less sure about the foundations of this conviction, or its precise definition. We flirt with relativism, which we then try to refute by showing mankind to be one, by means of an inquiry nevertheless carried on within a unitary, unrelative world . . . We are less sure about the unity of man, or precisely what it would mean. This also constitutes a clue, to my mind, concerning the only solution to which the problem of relativism is really susceptible.

Relativism is basically a doctrine in the theory of knowledge: it asserts that there is no unique truth, no unique objective reality. What we naively suppose to be such is but the product – exclusively, or in some proportion, which varies with the particular form the relativism takes – of the cognitive apparatus of the individual, community, age or whatever. (Relativisms differ in many respects, including the identification of the units to which the relativity is meant to apply.) If this is inherently and necessarily so, then perhaps no sense attaches to speaking about a unique, absolute or objective truth, but only of a truth or reality relative to the unit or cognitive apparatus in question. Notoriously, there is no room for the assertion of relativism itself in a world in which relativism is true. The previous sentences have sketched out a world; but if they did succeed in painting a relativist world, do they not at the same time, willy-nilly, say something absolute about it? This difficulty should not be overstressed. It does not inhibit our intuitive capacity for visualising a relativist world; and to use this difficulty as a reason for treating the fear of relativism as groundless, seems to me facile and superficial. Despite all the problems which attach to articulating the idea of a plurality of worlds and truths, intuitively the notion does make sense, and I believe this intuition to be justified.

Note, however, that such relativism is perfectly compatible with the existence of any number of, so to speak, *de facto* or contingent human 'universals'. In a world unbounded by any unique truth, it might still be the case, by accident, that all human languages had a certain grammatical structure, that chromatic perception was identical in all cultures, that all societies proscribed certain relations as incestuous, etc., etc. A priori one would perhaps have less reason in such a world to expect that these universals or constants should obtain. That is so because *one* reason, but one reason only, for this expectation would be absent in a 'relative' world: the reason being the direct constraint by objective truth. 'Objective truth' being absent, it could no longer constrain anyone. But *other* constraints could still operate.

If, on the other hand, in objective and unique truth, or in independent reality, colours 'really' are such and such, and if certain types of relationships 'really' are wrong and incestuous, and so on, then, *in so far as* the human mind also apprehends the unique and rational truth, it will be canalised into a unique, universal and constant channel. Diversity of perception or opinion could then spring only from the presence of *error*. But truth is only one of many factors influencing the mind, and incidentally not always a powerful one: so despite the uniqueness of truth, some societies might still be under the sway of chromatic, moral or other error. In fact, societies have often believed this about each other, and sometimes about their own past.

On the other hand, whilst not necessarily led to a unique position by Reason – which notoriously holds but a feeble sway over the human spirit – men might *still* be led to a unique position which was *not* the 'right' one by *other* and possibly less praiseworthy factors. There might be non-rational constraints of a neurological, social or other kind, compelling mankind to remain within some moral, linguistic or other universal, even though objectively this single path was not unique – or possibly not even correct at all.

So it is conceivable that relativism may be true, and yet human universals obtain; and equally, it is possible that relativism may be false, and yet no universals obtain (or only trivial ones) . . . There seems nothing at least intuitively or prima facie absurd about a uniquely determined universe, available in principle for cognition in one correct form only; but one such that, within it, inside such a metaphysically well-favoured and attractive universe, it should so happen that grammatical, conceptual, kinship, moral, etc. systems were so highly variegated that comparative grammarians, anthropologists and the rest had to despair of ever finding any universal traits. A God outside this universe would know how its variegated sub-systems all successfully operated within one total system, without any one of them embracing the totality and without any being mutually translatable. In so far as this diversity extended to all aspects of life, things might indeed become very difficult. First of all, if the cognitive equipment of cultures varies so much in such a unique-truth universe, it follows that all their cultures (with at most one exception) must be cognitively in error, at least in some measure; and their inability to grasp the *others* must make them, at best, incomplete. There is nothing absurd, or at least nothing unusual, in such a supposition. More difficult still, if the cognitive equipment of societies differs radically, there may be some difficulty in the practice of intercultural anthropology *at all*, for obvious reasons.

It is an interesting fact about the world we actually live in that no anthropologist, to my knowledge, has come back from a field trip with the following report; *their* concepts are *so* alien that it is impossible to describe their land tenure, their kinship system, their ritual . . . As far as I know, there is no record of such a total admission of failure. Perhaps sanctions applied by anthropology departments are too severe? Perhaps such anthropological failures do not present their theses, or even report back from field work at all. This doesn't prove, of course, that it has never occurred; and if it had occurred, it would not prove that it was due to the inherent inaccessibility of the material, as opposed to the deficiencies of the particular investigator. What one does quite often hear are admissions of partial failure of comprehension: 'I simply cannot imagine what the so-and-so, a West African tribe, mean when they speak of washing their souls'; 'I thought I knew the Himalayan hill folk well, having lived amongst them for a considerable time, but when a death occurred in the family, I saw from their reactions that I did not understand anything.' Such partial incomprehensions are common, but they have not, to my knowledge, prevented the drawing-up of an account of at least large parts of the social life, language and so on of the community in question. I have heard an anthropologist who had come back from a but recently discovered group in New Guinea say that they really were 'very very distant' in their way of thinking, implying that the strenuousness of his effort had had to be much greater than on his other field experiences with 'closer' cultural communities; but he did not report *failure*.

I think all this is significant, and indicates something (at worst, it could indicate complacency and a misguided supposition that we understand when in fact we do not); but, on the often rather a priori reasoning of relativist philosophers, who start out from doctrines such as the ultimacy and self-sufficiency of 'forms of life', we might have expected such failure to be much more common. It is *success* in explaining culture A in the language of culture B which is, in the light of such a philosophy, really puzzling. Yet shelves groan with the weight of such books.

So, the truth of the matter seems to me this: the issues of relativism, and that of the existence of human universals, are *not* one and the same issue. The problem of relativism is whether there is one and only one world, in the end; whether all the divergent visions of reality can in the end be shown (leaving out cases when they are simply mistaken) to be diverse aspects of one and the same objective world, whose diversity can itself be explained in terms of the properties or laws of that world. There are some reasonably persuasive, if not formally compelling, reasons for holding a belief in such unique reality.

But this is not the same question as that concerning whether or not man is one and unique, whether in basic features, humanity is internally alike, and perhaps also externally unique (whether all men are alike, and unlike everything non-human). Not only are the two questions about whether there is one world and whether all men are alike not identical, but the widely diffused assumption that a positive answer to the first depends on a positive answer to the second seems to me quite mistaken. In my view, the reasons for which will be given, the reverse relationship obtains: the positive answer to the first hinges on a negative answer to the second. The uniqueness of the world hinges on the diversity, the non-universality of man. There is one world only, there are many men; and just because there are many kinds of men, there is one world. For the unique world is the achievement of *some* men only; and had men and cultures not been diversified, the single world might never have emerged, for social forms would not have differed enough to hit on this special one; and all this is of the essence of the thing. But this paradoxical claim requires clarification and defence.

It is, as stated, a striking feature of the explorations of – one is tempted to say, flirtations with – the idea of the diversity of man, of radical differentiation in the human conceptual or other equipment, that it is carried out in the context of *one unitary world*. The assumption, if it becomes conscious and explicit as a result of challenge, can, I suppose, be defended as follows: but what else do you wish us to do? Where else, other than in the shared and assumed common world of the scientific and scholarly tradition in which we were trained, do you want us to carry out our investigation into the Diversity of Men? This doesn't mean that we necessarily grant that shared world more than a kind of interim status. If our researches lead us to conclude that man is irreducibly diverse, and that each kind of man has his own kind of world, then we shall accept and endorse that kind of plurality of men, visions, worlds, and refuse to endow the unique world, within which our inquiries were initially conducted, with any kind of special status. It was the door through which we entered the many-chambered mansion, but once safely within it, we see that it is not a unique or privileged door. This ladder we may throw away when we have ascended. . .

Perhaps such an attitude is possible. But I doubt it. I believe that our attachment to the unique world, within which alone the inquiries into the diversity of man and hence the diversity of his visions is carried out, is far deeper and more significant than that. It is not *a* world; it is *the* world.

Before discussing why this should be so, it may be essential to consider, as briefly and schematically as possible, what this world – *the* world – is like: what are its general traits?

This one privileged world is a public and symmetrical world: symmetrical in that it contains within itself no privileged places, times, individuals or groups, which would be allowed to exempt cognitive claims from testing or scrutiny. On the contrary, all claims and all evidence are deemed to be ultimately equal: some, of course, are treated with respect due to past distinction, and some with derision; in intellectual matters as in social, equality is far from complete. But an idea is an idea for a' that: and their status differentiation is not absolute, total and eternal. Reality is not ranked and stratified in dignity and availability for scrutiny, as it is in other and more traditional kinds of vision. Amongst civilised members of the republic of the mind, it is recognised that in principle no idea is so silly as not to deserve any hearing at all, and none so elevated as to be exempt from discussion. All must submit to the same base-line of evidence. Quite literally, this means that nothing is sacred. Decent cognitive comportment, the observance of proper epistemological rules, cast a secularised world as their own inescapable shadow. Evidence in turn is broken up into small packages, and is not allowed exemption from scrutiny. Practice may not fully live up to this idea, but it does not altogether violate it either.

Equality of ultimate civic rights of all ideas and evidence, so to speak, is not the only feature of this shared and unique world of ours. It also has traits which seem to attach more directly to the stuff of the world rather than to the ideas about it (though this distinction may itself be questioned). What are these substantive traits? A kind of orderliness of behaviour: it is assumed that like causes will have like effects, thereby making generalisation and theory-building possible. This feature used to be given names such as the Regularity of Nature or the Principle of Sufficient Reason.

The orderliness of the world is also assumed to be systematic: not only are there regularities to be discovered, but these form a system, such that, if we are successful in our inquiries, the more specific regularities turn out in the end to be corollaries of more general ones. Ideally, the system might even one day turn out to possess an apex, an all-embracing theory. In the mean time, the fragments of it which we do possess seem to point towards such an apex and to urge us on in the pursuit of it.

What reasons have we to believe in such a world – and in its unique validity – over and above the contingent and in itself plainly inconclusive and, indeed, suspect fact that it happens to be the vision within which, at least in office hours, most of us think and work? This is the one world *within which* we inquire whether mankind is unitary. Yet it is itself the world of *some* men only (including *us*). Is it more than just our vision, is it the account of how things actually are? And if so, why?

There is, of course, no non-circular way of establishing this Single World or Unique Truth. (Other visions validate themselves by their own rules, and will not play according to ours. Hence any move which eliminates them also breaks their rules, and is consequently question-begging.) But there are at least partially non-question-begging ways of supporting this position, and these are probably all we can ever have. *If* it were the case that there existed a number of centres of consciousness or knowledge, each as it were plugged into a different cosmic programme, and in turn remaining unrelated to each other, then that would be that, and there would be nothing we could do about it. (I leave aside the intriguing question whether in such a universe the above sentence would not nevertheless contain a unique *and* all-embracing truth, relating the centres and their experiences to each other precisely by the assertion that they are not congruent.) But that does not seem to be our world. What reasons can we adduce in support of such a conviction?

There are two converging arguments, the epistemological and the sociological. They need to be sketched out briefly.

(a) The epistemological

Here we start out with the minimum of assumptions, so as to beg no questions. Initially *anything* may be true. We ask: how can we pick out the correct option of belief, seeing that we have no prior indication of what it may be? The answer is contained in the epistemological tradition which has accompanied the rise of modern science, at first to help it along, and later so as to explain its miraculous success.

The answer is, in rough outline: eliminate all self-maintaining circular belief systems. As the main device of self-maintaining systems is the package-deal principle, which brings about the self-maintaining circle of ideas, break up information into as many parts as possible, and scrutinise each item separately. This breaks up the circles and destroys the self-maintenance. At the same time, nevertheless assume the regularity of nature, the systematic nature of the world, not because it is demonstrable, but because anything which eludes such a principle also eludes real knowledge; *if* cumulative and communicable knowledge is to be possible at all, then the principle of orderliness must also apply to it . . . The inherently idiosyncratic has no place in a corpus of knowledge. Unsymmetrical, idiosyncratic explanations are worthless – they are not explanations. Inconvertible currencies are not suitable for trade, and ungeneralisable explanations are useless for a practical and cumulative body of knowledge. If like conditions did *not* produce like effects, then the experimental accumulation of knowledge would have no point and would not be feasible. Only theories built on the assumption of symmetry and orderliness can be negotiated and applied. Material not amenable to treatment within this assumption is worthless, and must either be reinterpreted or discarded.

In brief: the atomisation of information and the orderly systematisation of explanation are imperative. Neither of them is established except as a *precondition* of having real knowledge at all. But, *ex hypothesi*, they do generate a unique world, one subject to a unique set of laws only. Information is atomised and thus obliged to shed excessive and covert theoretical loading; and theories are systematised, and thus incoherences and putative idiosyncrasy are eventually eliminated.

(b) The sociological

In our actual and shared world, diverse cultures, though not sharing their beliefs, nevertheless seem to have little trouble in communicating with each other. The world contains many communities, but they are seen to inhabit the same world and compete within it. Some are cognitively stagnant, and a few are even regressive; some, on the other hand, possess enormous and, indeed, growing cognitive wealth, which is, so to speak, validated by works as well as faith: its implementation leads to very powerful technology. There is a near-universal consensus about this, in deeds rather than in words: those who do not possess such knowledge and technology endeavour to emulate and acquire it.

As it happens, the cognitively cumulative and powerful communities apply; in their serious intellectual life, an epistemology roughly of the kind singled out previously in the specification of the epistemological argument. Powerful technology is based on a science which in turn seems to observe the rules of an information-atomising inquiry, and of symmetrical and orderly theory-construction.

The epistemological argument is abstract and, on its own, shares all the weaknesses of abstract arguments. The history of thought must contain countless specimens of abstract arguments which sound plausible enough but which either failed to carry conviction or were eventually shown to be false, or both. The sociological argument, on the other hand, is crude and pragmatic to the point of meretricious opportunism.

Moreover, the conjunction of the two is extremely inelegant. The epistemological one deliberately starts from scratch with the absolute minimum of assumptions, whilst the sociological one makes itself a present of the world which we think we live in, of our shared and often unexamined views of what is going on in it, and incidentally of some rather crass earthy values prevailing in it. Thus, a totally impractical abstraction, an argument beyond all contexts, excogitated in a putative Cosmic Exile, is fused with a meretriciously crude and all-too-worldly consideration based on greed for wealth and scramble for power. What strange bedfellows! – but they do point one and the same way, and jointly constitute the grounds we have for choosing and accepting the unique world we think and live in.

Thus, for all the inelegance of their juxtaposition, the incongruity of this bizarre marriage of convenience, and for all their great faults taken singly, this conjunction and its two elements are the best we have, the most we shall probably ever have, and they do, in fact, jointly carry conviction and – I am myself tempted to add – rightly so. But perhaps that adds nothing (other than complacency) to the preceding statement.

But if it is accepted that it is by this kind of reasoning that we have attained a Single World and Unique Truth, then the somewhat para-doxical conclusion follows that a Single World, and Single Man, do *not* go together at all. On the contrary: for the particular thought-style which alone generated this unique, converging, cumulative world, as the object of human cognition, was *not* universally dispersed amongst men. On the contrary, it was but one tradition amongst many, and a very untypical one. It prevailed, *and* we hold it to be valid. Within it, and on its terms, we carry out investigations into the other visions which were once its rivals. *It* provides the single context within which we investigate and interpret all other visions. We do not hold it to be valid only because it has prevailed, but the fact that it generates a kind of technology which helps its adherents to prevail also indisputably constitutes *a* consideration.

This position differs from pragmatism in a number of important ways. For one thing, practical success is but one consideration, as indicated. This view asserts that a given vision is valid *and* therefore is practically effective, but it does not identify validity and effectiveness. There is in fact no reason to suppose that effective science does increase the survival prospects of the species which carries it. The self-destruction of humanity, through nuclear or other war or ecological disaster, is perfectly possible and perhaps probable in the post-scientific age, whereas previously mankind did not possess the power to destroy itself, and, owing to its dispersal, was virtually certain not to face destruction by any outside force. So if truth were equated with that which increases the probability of survival, then science would certainly be untrue.

But perhaps the most significant and profound difference philosophi-cally hinges on the fact that pragmatism, like various related strands in the evolutionist and Hegelian thought-styles, believed the true cognitive vision, or rather practices, to be something ever-present in history (including, for pragmatism, *biological* history), only becoming ever more effective and manifest with the progress of time. In one famous formulation of this kind of view, the amoeba and Einstein use the same method, which is the key to all real knowledge (namely, trial and error). On the view which is here advocated, and presented as the (only) way in which we have overcome relativism, or can ever do so, this is not so at all: the correct vision or cognitive style appears at *a* definite point in time, and thus introduces a radical *dis*continuity in history. Just as it is not universal in space – it characterises *some* men, not *all* men – so it is also not universal in time. Pragmatists and Hegelians believed in a kind of Permanent Revolution; the valid thought-style or its underlying ultimate principle was confirmed by eternal repetition, and its authority reinforced by such reiteration. On the present view, no such reiteration occurs to underwrite the One True Vision. This difference is the crucial one between the nineteenth- and twentieth-century philosophical uses of history. The twentieth-century version has not yet been properly formulated philosophically.

So the Singleness of Man is *not* required for the Uniqueness of the World or of Truth. These were initially carried only by an eccentric minority, and they are not underwritten either by human universality or by permanence in time. This vision is underwritten – if valid at all, as I hold it to be – in quite a different manner, which I have sketched briefly.

So the universality of a single model of man, so to speak, is not required for the philosophical purpose (the overcoming of relativism) for which it is, I suspect, often introduced. But, whether or not required for this end, it also has an inherent intrinsic interest, and deserves consideration for its own sake. So, what is the state of play with respect to the Universality of a Single Human Model?

There are (at least) two ways of approaching this: firstly by asking whether there are manifest and, if you like, surface similarities in men; and secondly, whether there are underlying identities or similarities in explanatory principle or mechanism. Furthermore, of course, each of these questions can be asked separately for various aspects of human activity and experience, and the answers may vary from field to field.[1]

A proper survey of the phenomena in each field could only be carried out by competent specialists in that field. Nonetheless, it may be useful for a non-specialist to give a general impressionistic overview of what the findings suggest, when such surveys are completed.

In fields such as sensory sensibility and motor performance, differences do exist, but they are not very striking or extensive. It appears harder to locate them than it is to locate inter-cultural or inter-ethnic similarities in these fields. Moreover, when they do occur, it seems quite reasonable to expect them to be explained by the impact of, for example, climatic or social environment on basically similar underlying physiological equipment. So, differences are not striking, and furthermore, they tend to become eliminated at the next explanatory level. To put this in another way: men seem to move and act in pretty much the same world and with much the same physical equipment.

Truly enormous inter-cultural differences, on the other hand, occur in certain other areas, where societies, as one is tempted to say, are free

---

[1] Cf. for example an excellent survey of this problem in connection with the perception and conceptualisation of colour: *Voir et nommer les couleurs*, Laboratoire d'Ethnologie et de Sociologie Comparative, Nanterre, 1978.

to indulge their fantasy: mythology, cosmology, metaphysics, and in some measure, in social, political, and ritual organisation. The profound and radical differences in world-vision between sophisticated cultures are reasonably evident: when they translate their doctrines into each other's language, the results sometimes sound very odd indeed. Yet the translations are widely recognised as reasonably accurate by bilingual or bicultural persons. In this area, the view that the oddity enters only through mistranslation is implausible and difficult to sustain.

The situation is somewhat different and complex when it comes to identifying and interpreting the 'world-view' of 'primitive' peoples, i.e., those which have no script and no clerical class to codify that view. Here, the interpretation and systematisation is carried out by outsiders (or those who were trained by outsiders), and the view that the oddity lies in the translation, and not in the view translated, acquires some plausibility. In what sense, for instance, can a tribesman who is no theologian, and whose society does not have theologians, be credited with a theology which seems implicit to the outsider in his ritual or myths? This question is highly pertinent to the once fashionable attribution of a distinctive 'primitive mentality' to populations living in simple societies; but it is equally pertinent to the more recent revival of the attribution to them of the scientific and experimental spirit. The issue is open and methodologically difficult. Just how different one finds the savage, seems to hinge largely on whether one goes by what he *does* (which is not strange – he acts in the same world as we do, and in a similar way), or by what he says (very odd by most translations), or by functionalist interpretations of what he says (not odd after all), or whether in the end one is swayed by the thought that though odd the statement is context-bound in ritual (hence also not odd). And yet, its impact on him in the ritual hinges on its sounding odd *to him as well*, if interpreted in parallel with daily ordinary statements – and so it is odd after all. As far as I can see, you can pick and choose as to which of these levels of sophistication you select as your resting-place, and hence which conclusion you reach.

So to sum up: minor and, so to speak, explicable differences at sensory and motor level; very great differences at the level of self-conscious, codified civilisation with codified criteria of valid belief – though interestingly, a very good measure of translatability exists at the same time, which facilitates the highlighting of this divergence. (Translatability does not seem to mean agreement.) There are all kinds of 'translatability' (e.g., 'they say such-and-such, combining what seem to be equivalents of such-and-such notions in our language, in a way which makes no sense to us but does appear to make sense to them'). In between these extremes, dealing with societies which do not themselves codify their own views, one is not clear what one should say: the answer appears to hinge on just how *we* codify *their* views for them.

But the really significant difference is between what may be called validation systems: the procedures and principles employed for extending and deciding the acceptance of new items. Primitive societies do not codify these, and they can only be extracted from their practice, which need not be consistent. Literacy, by creating a norm outside custom, or rather, providing the means for stabilising such a norm, is supremely important. In the end, however, it is the establishment and institutional underpinning of the *one* outstanding cumulative cognitive style, atomistic and symmetrical, which produces the really decisive parting of the ways. It is then that the practice of *some* men finally generates *one* world.

Such, roughly, are the inter-social differences at the phenomenological or descriptive level. What about the explanatory or structural level?

The Chomskian theory of language may serve as a useful baseline, precisely because it is so very clear on the issue both of the universality and uniqueness of man. If that theory is correct, then human linguistic competence is explained by an innate equipment which is identical in all men, but which is not shared by any other organism. The argument for the identity of this equipment is simple and important: the evidence available to language-learning children is so very fragmentary and feeble that the transition from it to internalising the complex grammatical rules involved in the generation of an indefinite class of utterances, as employed by mature language-users, constitutes a truly tremendous leap. But infants of any genetic background appear able to make this transition to whatever language they are exposed to: hence not only *is* there a tremendous leap, inexplicable without hidden (innate) aid, but it also appears to be the *same* leap which is made by all mankind. If a hidden key (which is not seen, but which is inferred from our amazing linguistic competence), opens a multitude of doors, we may conclude that the locks are identical.

The theory claims the leap is towards one and the same underlying linguistic structure. Hence the acquisition of familiarity with the *idiosyncratic* traits of individual languages must somehow be explicable as a consequence of the reiterated use of the same shared innate principles, as identical bricks can be used to erect different structures, or alternatively, as something requiring only very small and hence perhaps less mysterious 'leaps', which might consequently be explicable without any recourse to the assumption of special innate linguistic equipment. To a non-specialist, this seems a difficult programme: the idiosyncratic aspects of languages *also* seem most complex, over and above the complexities which they share, and the prospects of explaining them all in the manner indicated, dubious. I doubt whether the argument for innate equipment loses its force even with the *tiniest* 'leaps'. But we can leave that problem with structural linguists. Our present use of this theory is a kind of yardstick, and does not actually require that theory to be true or demonstrated.

Whilst postulating a pan-human shared mechanism as the explanation of human linguistic competence, the theory at the same time insists on the radical discontinuity between human language and animal systems of communication. Thus, on this theory, in the field of linguistic phenomena, *one* mechanism explains all men, and *nothing* but men. The situation can be represented diagrammatically (Fig. 1.1), where horizontal shading covers humanity, and vertical shading is that which is covered by the theory. If B indicates the apex or genus, so to speak, covering all living or biological phenomena, and H and L cover human and linguistic phenomena respectively, then the areas covered by H and L are congruent, and jointly constitute a single segment of the biological. More simply: the class of men and that of proper language-users are the same class.

The thesis of the uniqueness of man, or of the existence of 'human universals', presumably means that such a congruence does hold, in the

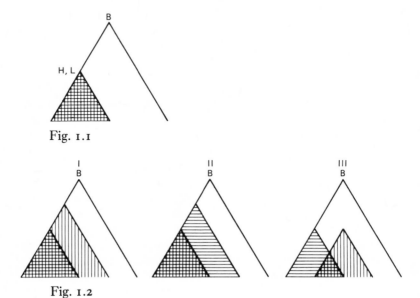

Fig. 1.1

Fig. 1.2

fields of linguistic and other behaviour. Schematically, it means that if, once again, horizontal shading covers humanity, and vertical shading covers the field of application of some explanatory theory, then one might require that situations should not arise which can be schematised as in Fig. 1.2.

But it seems obvious that non-congruence of type I *does* occur: mankind obviously shares physiological mechanisms with other organisms. One's inclination is to say that these mechanisms explain aspects of behaviour which are not characteristically or distinctively human. But if only behaviour which is 'distinctively human' needs to be explained by distinctively human explanatory mechanisms, then the uniqueness-hypothesis clearly risks becoming tautological.

Non-congruence of type II raises more complex issues, as does that of type III. In a sense, it is obvious that explanatory mechanisms or structures of type II also occur. Suppose a political anthropologist or a political scientist develops a theory of all possible forms of political organisation, by isolating the elements which go into state-formation, and then deducing all the possible forms generated by their various combinations. This theory – if the elements had been correctly isolated and the manner of their possible combinations correctly described – would constitute an explanation of possible political forms, but clearly would not cover societies too small or too decentralised to have a state at all. Would such a theory contradict the 'human universals' thesis?

Similar considerations apply to non-congruence III. It is quite possible that some explanatory mechanisms or principles are applicable both in *some* human societies and *some* non-human ones (say those of primates or insects). Does this contradict the 'human universals' thesis?

Once again, the thesis risks becoming tautological or trivial if it is reduced to the mere assertion that there are *some* (unspecified) human explanatory universals in some fields, covering all mankind, but without excluding the possibility of important *specific* explanations for *some* men only in other fields. What presumably those who uphold the idea of 'universals' mean is that in important fields (politics, kinship, economy, mythology, ritual – either in all, or perhaps more modestly, just in some of them) – identical principles do operate for all human societies; and if the uniqueness of man is added to universality, that they operate only in human societies. What would be the evidence for or against such a view?

Partly, this will turn out once again to be a matter of definition, in a number of ways. If some organisational principles only apply to, say, societies endowed with agriculture, or to societies above a certain size, pre-agrarian or small societies can still be incorporated into the scheme if the absence of a certain factor or variable (e.g., agriculture, size) is itself included as one possible variant in the range of situations 'generated' by the elements in the theory.

In brief, in so far as theories endeavour to unify, the question about the unity of mankind, at the explanatory level, risks having a trivial answer, an affirmation which simply reflects our theoretical aspiration towards unitary explanation.

Nevertheless, I suspect that those who assert the unity-of-mankind thesis have a non-trivial point in mind, and one which hinges on the distinction between genetic and social explanation; what is asserted is that social forms are as it were indifferent to the individual human material which is fed into it. Just as any man could have been brought up in any language, so also no social formation depends on the *genetic* specificity of the men composing it. There is a good deal of evidence to support such a supposition: the diversity of human performance appears to depend on socio-cultural factors to an incomparably greater degree than it does on individual genetic equipment. The regions of the world which produced most of the innovations which lie at the base of modern industrial civilisation, for instance, were themselves cultural backwaters a fairly small number of generations earlier, and yet it is unlikely that their 'gene pool' changed radically. (If anything, one might suspect that mediaeval clerical and monastic celibacy may have caused it to degenerate.)

At the same time, the argument requires refinement. Genetic equipment imposes a ceiling on performance, even if socio-cultural factors are crucial beneath that ceiling; and a community with a higher average ceiling would presumably have a different range of possible performances from one with a lower ceiling. A community artificially recruited, say, from physics professors, would presumably, in the next generation, have a different range of possible performance from a randomly selected one, even if the two new populations were given similar training.

In other words, if some potentialities are genetically limited (or rather, if the limitations are not distributed with absolute evenness), as indeed is plausible, and if communities were recruited so as to accentuate such uneven distribution, we could *then* possibly have a so to speak non-universalistic sociology. This doesn't, however, appear to be the world in which we actually live. Whilst there is no reason to suppose that the genetic ceiling is absolutely even and flat all over humanity, any more than anything else is distributed with total evenness (such an assumption is terribly unplausible), the differences in performance by the same and genetically continuous community at different times are *so* much greater than are the differences between individuals which may be attributed to differences in inherent equipment, that for most problems it would seem bad strategy to seek genetic explanations. It seems to me extremely unlikely, moreover, that such genetic unevenness as may exist, correlates at all with the historical performance of communities. The two things are probably often related *inversely*. For instance: some gene pools must be richer than others in potentially great footballers. But is there the slightest likelihood that the point of high concentration of such talent is *also* the area where football historically emerged? The same argument applies to other cultural achievements. Yet it would be wrong to treat any interest in genetic preconditions as logically absurd.

Those who exclude it, moreover, assume what could be called the Continuity thesis, which has at least two aspects: that, although the genetic ceiling can be assumed to vary, and that its distribution need not be even, any more than the land surface of the earth is totally flat, nevertheless, it only varies statistically and the unevennesses are not very extreme. If, for instance, a given social performance requires the presence of some individuals with special talents, i.e., with a high ceiling with respect to some specific kind of performance, then the *numbers* required to ensure that some such individuals are found will not vary very much in different human populations. If a given social performance requires the presence of, say five people of unusual mathematical potential, the population size required so that it should contain five such persons *may* vary in different parts of the world, but probably does not vary very much.

The second aspect of the Continuity thesis is this: that although human performance or individual ceilings vary, they do so in degree rather than in kind. The difference between the ability to speak at all and to use language like Shakespeare is great and important, but it is in some sense much less radical than the difference between having and not having the potential of speech at all. Not all men are Shakespeares, but all sane healthy men have the power of speech. The genetic precondition of social forms consists of the former kind of potential rather than the latter.

Neither aspect of the Continuity thesis has been formulated with any precision; and perhaps it would be in principle impossible to do so. What precisely is, in general, the difference between a difference in degree and a difference in kind? Nevertheless, despite this imprecision there *is* something like a natural interpretation of the Continuity thesis; and it is also reasonable to suppose that it holds true. In other words, the existence of explanatory schemata which apply to some human societies only, if such schemata exist at all, need not be attributed to the non-universality of some human *element*, but only to the specificity of some forms of social *organisation*, which, however, remain open to all human populations in similar circumstances.

These, as far as I can see, are the ideas or issues which underline the question about 'human universals'. The issue can be advanced, but it can hardly be settled. But to recapitulate:

The problems of relativism and that of the existence of human universals are *not* identical.

The doctrine of 'human universals' is often tacitly conjoined with that of the uniqueness of man: the claim is not only that the essentially human *is* present in all of us, but also that it is *not* present in anything else.

Universality at the phenomenological level is highly questionable or trivial. At the explanatory level, the notion is complex and obscure.

The solution of the problem of relativism does not hinge on the establishment of human universals. If it has a solution, it lies elsewhere.

Relativism is about the existence of One World: and the conceptual unification of the world is, precisely, the work of one particular style of thought, which is not universal amongst men, but is culturally specific.

But this in turn does not actually subvert the Universality thesis: for although the conceptual unification of the world does have specific socio-historic roots, it is evidently accessible to all men, and is in fact now being diffused generally.

Science needs one world. It does not need one kind of man within it. But one *kind* of man did make the single world. His historical situation may have been unique, his basic constitution was *not*. The single world seems to be gradually adopted by all of them, and appears manifestly accessible to all men.

4 | The scientific status of the social sciences *(und leider auch Sociologie)*

Habe nun ach! Philosophie,
Juristerei and Medizin,
Und leider auch Theologie
Durchaus studiert, mit heissem Bemühn.
. . .
Und ziehe schon an die zehen Jahr'
Herauf, herab und quer und krumm
Meine Schüler an der Nase herum –
Und sehe, dass wir nichts wissen können!

Goethe, Faust, opening speech

No intelligent and honest teacher of the social sciences can fail on occasion to have had similar feelings. *Und leider auch Sociologie.* Of course, there are some about who lack either intelligence or candour. They strut about, shaking their paradigm like a coxcomb, instructing the students, advising authorities. They are a dreadful sight. I was always amused by the virulence of Noam Chomsky's denunciation of the American social scientists who had helped the American administration wage the war in Vietnam: he damns their political morality, but he cannot refrain, at the same time, from scorning their scientific pretensions. Not only had they prostituted themselves morally, but as scholars they were frauds, their verbiage and techniques had no cutting edge. . . Possibly so; but does not the one charge cancel out the other? Would it have been better or worse, if their understanding of the situation had been genuine and their advice sound, and if that had made it possible to wage the war effectively?

But let us leave out the confident and strutting social scientists and look at the issue from the viewpoint of the more becomingly doubt-ridden, Faustian social scientist. No Mephistopheles seems eager to buy his soul. How willingly many of us would sell!

The problem – are the social sciences genuinely scientific? – immediately raises two questions: what are the social sciences? and what is it to be scientific?

The first gives rise to no deep problem and can be answered by ostension or by enumeration. The social sciences simply are what social scientists professionally practise. Social scientists are the people listed as such in the calendars of reputable universities, plus fellow-members (whether employed by universities or not) of professional guilds manned by reputable practitioners of the said disciplines. The definition thus contains a covert (but hardly very covert) reference to the consensual or majority or uncontested judgements prevalent in contemporary societies and which identify, by their tacit or express ranking, which universities, professional associations and individuals are as it were norm-setting or paradigmatic, and in effect define, by their own attribution of labels, the nature and range of the social sciences.

This covert reference to public opinion or consensus does not vitiate the definition or make it circular. Majorities, consensus, the general cultural 'sense of the meeting' – all these are of course not infallible, stable or unambiguous. There is no contradiction in the suggestion that public opinion at a given date is in error. If such sources can be mistaken, could they mislead us in this case by falsely identifying the object or cluster of objects with which we are to be concerned, namely, the social sciences? No. The central object of our inquiry is precisely the social sciences, *as actually practised and identified in contemporary societies*. Public opinion, however loosely defined, cannot here mislead us, because the object which concerns us is, precisely, one defined by reference to current cultural norms. We may of course *also* be interested in some trans-social, culturally neutral, ideal social science, if there is such a thing; but our primary concern is with the concrete practices recognised currently as 'social sciences'. So there is no problem here. We can simply enumerate or point to the objects/activities which concern us.

But the situation is quite different when we come to the second term which needs to be defined – 'scientific'. Here, ostension or enumeration are of no help whatever. We are not specially interested in the question of what our society happens to *call* 'scientific', or at any rate, the actual use of this label by our contemporaries is *not* conclusive. As a matter of fact, our society is disunited on this issue, and there is a lot of very significant pushing and pulling going on about just how far the blanket of the 'scientific' is to be stretched. But we are not interested in holding a referendum about this, or in seeing which of the many warring groups manages to impose its view at any given time. Instead, we are deeply concerned with some normative, genuinely authoritative sense of 'scientific'. We are interested in finding out whether the social sciences are *really* scientific. We want to know whether they are genuinely worthy of this accolade, and not merely whether others have been willing from one motive or another to bestow it.

Here we have an interesting and significant fact in itself. In formulating our question, are the social sciences scientific? we seem to employ for our subject a term which is defined conventionally or by denotation – anything currently in fact *called* by that name, *ipso facto* falls under it – whilst our predicate is Platonistic or normative, and intended not to be at the mercy of human whim or convention. The rules of its application are meant to be based on some higher, independent authority.

Our sentence thus seems logically a hybrid – the subject is nominalistic or conventional, the predicate is Platonistic, essentialist and prescriptive. Is such double-talk permissible? I do not think that the situation is actually all that anomalous or unusual. But it *is* significant.

If both terms were defined conventionally, by reference to the actual or majority or agreed use of each, the question would be easy to answer and lack any profundity or importance. All we should need to do would be to commission a survey, set up to find out whether and to what extent people use one label ('social sciences') in a manner such that it falls within the range of use of another and broader label ('scientific'). But no such survey would in fact be felt to be relevant or at any rate conclusive to the question which we are in effect asking.

This 'Platonism of the predicate', which obliges us to treat the term in question as though it referred to something constituted quite independently of our choice and custom, and endowed with authority over us, is interesting and significant.

Note that it is an old and pervasive feature of discussions concerning the delimitations of 'science' or 'meaning'. One would have thought that people like, for instance, the logical positivists, who were deeply imbued with nominalism and a 'concepts maketh *man*' spirit, would have had an attitude something like the following: it is for us, for humanity, to fix the convention which delimits the scientific or the meaningful, in the light of our convenience and our consensus, and of nothing else, for there are no norms/Ideas that would dictate to us. Not so. On the contrary, those famous demarcation disputes had all the passion and intensity of circumscribing the Saved and the Damned, of defining the licit and the illicit, of *discovering* an important and *given* truth, aside from just allocating labels. And that is, of course, precisely what those disputes were.

Conventionalism with respect to the delimitation of concepts was only invoked, with some embarrassment and visible lack of conviction, when the theorist found himself cornered, by, for instance the insistent question concerning the status of the Verification Principle itself. Was it itself an experiential report, or a convention determining the limits of a term? Well, said people like A. J. Ayer, with perceptible lack of ease, we suppose it had better be a convention, an 'analysis' of what is contained in the notion of understanding something. What else could it be? It *could* hardly be an experiential report, and there is nothing else it could be, so . . .

But this view was only affirmed with a bit of head-scratching and a puzzled expression. It didn't feel like a mere convention, that's for sure. It had better be one, though. There was nothing else it could be, within the positivist scheme. So the pretence was maintained that the Verifiability demarcation of meaning or of science was merely a convention of ours. But the real spirit in which this delimitation was proposed was obviously quite different. It was propounded as an objective, authoritative, Platonic *norm*. It circumscribed cognitive Salvation.

There is no shadow of doubt but that in fact, discussions concerning what is and is not 'scientific' are carried on in this utterly Platonistic, normative and non-conventionalist spirit. These are debates about whether something is really, really scientific. The debates seem based on the assumption that what is at issue is an important conceptual boundary, in the very nature of things, and altogether beyond the reach of what we *choose* to call what. Is it that all of us, including the officially nominalist empiricists of our age, are secretly, for some strange reason, crypto-Platonists? Is the lure of Plato and of essentialism greater even than Popper suspected? I think not.

Another explanation is available. It isn't really the case that we are conceptually rigid because we are Platonists; we become Platonists because we are conceptually rigid. It is *when* concepts constrain us that we turn Platonist *malgré nous*. We cannot always choose our concepts, and our concepts do often have authority over us. Man can do as he will, but he cannot will as he will; and he cannot always choose his concepts at will. Sometimes they have an authority over us which we cannot resist. And why are we in some cases so conceptually rigid, and why do we allow ourselves to be bondsmen to the values and imperatives incapsulated in some ideas?

Generically, one may say that this happens because some cluster or syndrome of features, locked in with each other in this or that concept of a given language or style of thought, have good reasons, so to speak, for being locked in with each other in just that manner, with that particular set of ingredients, and for having some kind of compulsive hold over our thought. Moreover, the moral charge, positive or negative, with which such concepts are loaded, cannot be prised away from it. It seems an integral part of the package, and cannot be separated from it. That is why the emotive theory of ethics (and its variants) sounds so paradoxical: it seems to be saying that the moral (emotive) charge is only contingently associated with the other ('descriptive') features of the package, and that we could rearrange these clusters at will.

The reasons which lead to the crystallisation of such a concept binding a cluster of traits may be general or specific; they may be inherent in the human condition, or they may be tied to some definite social or historical situation. But the overall formula for this occurrence must be something like the following: situations arise (and sometimes persist) which impel a given speech and conceptual community to think in terms of a concept T, defined in terms of attributes, a, b, c, etc.; moreover, great importance for the community as to whether a given object, practice or whatever does or does not fall under T is part and parcel of the very life, use and hence operational definition of that concept. So is its moral charge. Some conceptual boundaries have an importance for given societies which arises from the very nature of their situation, and which cannot be abrogated by fiat.

There is no shadow of doubt in my mind but that, *in our society*, the concept of the 'scientific' is precisely of this kind. We need it, and it cannot but be an important and authoritative notion. As so often, we may or may not be able to specify precisely what it is that we mean by it; what may be called Socrates' paradox, namely that it is possible to use a notion without being able to define it, does apply here, as it does so often. But whatever it is that goes into the cluster of traits which defines the idea, the idea is indisputably important, and is, so to speak, non-optional. We do not know what precisely it is, but we do know that it is important and that we cannot tinker with it at will. We cannot freely and arbitrarily decide what does and does not go into the cluster, into the definition. Nor can we refrain from using it. Of course, we can define a given word in any way we choose, and we can also invent as many neologisms as we like; but it is not for us to decide what is important to us, and which concepts we are compelled to use, whether we like it or not, by the objective circumstances of our condition. If we redefine the old words, the notion will simply come back in some other verbal clothing.

The idea of the 'scientific' is such a notion. But it has not always been so. No doubt it has some mild affinity with the old desire to define true knowledge as against mere opinion, and with the even more acute concern with the identification of the true Faith. In the later case, we knew only too well why the notion was so important: personal salvation and damnation depended on it. But the demarcation of the scientific, though it may overlap, certainly is not coextensive (let alone co-intensive) with either true knowledge or with the true Faith. . .

If this be granted, then what is it?

The 'scientific' was not a crucial and authoritative notion in all ages and all societies. In societies in which the institution of the 'sage' was well established, it was natural that a preoccupation with the distinction between real and spurious *knowledge*, genuine and fraudulent access to recipes for good life-styles and excellence, should become widespread. It was a kind of consumer protection service for those who entered the market place for wisdom and counsellor services about the Good Life; and it seemed to provide the first powerful stimulus for the development of the theory of knowledge. In the days of competing putative Messiahs, the criteria for identifying the true one seemed to be demonstratively spectacular rather than epistemological. By the time revelation came to be monopolised and codified in scripture, the central preoccupation became, naturally, the identification of the unique or nearly unique point of revelation, and of the authenticity of the putatively unique message, messenger, or of the permanent institution, or series of personal links, between the authentic point of communication and the present. Against the background of these various institutional and doctrinal assumptions, each of these questions, and no doubt variants of them, made sense. Though they do have some overlap and affinity with the question which concerns us here, they are obviously not identical with it.

The main point of overlap is that in all of these questions, men were concerned with the validation or legitimation of more specific claims, in terms of some more general criterion. When one determines whether or not something is 'scientific', one is *ipso facto* deciding whether or not it has a certain legitimate claim on our attention, and perhaps even on our credence. In other words, the question is not purely theoretical: according to whether the answer is yes or no, authority is conferred on or withdrawn from the more specific claim in question. The status of being 'scientific' is not necessarily the only or the dominant way of conferring such authority on specific claims; but it is most certainly at least one amongst such widely heeded and respected ways of validation. Time was, when it wasn't even one amongst many; when it was, in fact, unknown, absent from the repertoire of claim-enforcing authorities available to men who wished to persuade themselves, or others, of the validity, or at least of the respect-worthiness, of this or that proposition.

Here, to my mind, is a crucial clue. We need first of all to identify those background social conditions which have engendered this particular manner of validation, which bring forth this new and potent notion of 'scientific', and endow it with authority.

If this is granted, it automatically pushes our inquiry in a sociological direction – by obliging it to be sensitive to and concerned with general differences in *kinds* of society. At the very least, we shall need to be concerned with the difference between the kind of society which does, and that which does not, engender the concept in question.

There are at least two ways of approaching the problem of defining 'science': the philosophical and the sociological. The philosophical can be characterised as follows: the practitioner of this approach works in terms of some kind of model of discovery or of the acquisition of knowledge, where the elements in that model are items drawn from individual activities, such as having ideas, experiences, setting up experiments, relating the lessons of experience or the results of experiments to generalisations based on the initial ideas, and so forth. An extreme individualistic theory of science would be one which offered a theory and a demarcation of science without ever going beyond the bounds of a model constructed in this way. Such a theory might concede or even stress that, in fact, scientists are very numerous and that they habitually cooperate and communicate with each other. But it would treat this as somehow contingent and inessential. A solitary Robinson Crusoe could, according to such a theory, practise science. Given resources, longevity, ingenuity and ability, no achievement of science as we know it would, 'in principle', be beyond his powers. He could criticise his own past theories furiously, devise ingenious experiments for confounding them, refer to them ironically in footnotes, denounce the weaknesses of his past interpretations in incisive and covertly vitriolic letters to *Nature* (which, admittedly, he would also have to edit, print, and deliver to himself). An arduous life, but a rich one; and for an individualistic philosopher of science, there would at any rate be no contradiction in imagining it. People who hold theories of this kind are not debarred from admitting that in fact, criticism, testing and corroboration are, generally speaking, social activities, and that they depend for their effectiveness on a mathematical, technological and institutional infrastructure, which is far beyond the power of any individual to establish; but they are, I suppose, committed to holding that whether or not a social environment makes these preconditions available or not is, as it were, an external condition of science and not in any essential way part of it.[1]

[1] Sir Karl Popper has propounded the much-discussed doctrine of methodological individualism, which requires all explanations in the social sciences to be, ultimately, in terms of the aims and beliefs of individuals, and which precludes the invocation of holistic social entities, other than as a kind of shorthand. (See, for instance, Karl Popper, *The Open Society and its Enemies*, 1966, Princeton, NJ.) At the same time, Popper has more recently argued in favour of a World Three (*Objective Knowledge*, Oxford, 1972), a realm of objects of thought, in addition to the

There are various ways and degrees of injecting a sociological element into such an individualist vision. Minimally, one might insist that society constituted an essential precondition – but only society as such, and not necessarily this or that *kind* of society. Durkheim would be an example of one who held such a position: he maintained that thought was impossible without conceptual compulsion, which in turn depended on the existence of society and above all on communal ritual. This, if true, turns society into an essential precondition of science and indeed of all thought; a genuinely pre-social individual, however able, long-lived and well-equipped, could never rise to the formulation of a general idea.[2] Crusoe would only be a scientist because he had brought his entire society along with him, internalised in his own thought – which was indeed the case.

A second degree of the sociologising of the theory of science involves insisting not merely on the presence of a society, but of a special kind of society. Popper's theory of science seems to be of this kind: society is not enough, for the womb of science requires the 'critical spirit'. Closed Societies cannot engender science, but an Open Society can. An Open Society is one in which men subject each other's views to criticism, and which either possesses institutional underpinning for such a practice, or at least lacks the institutional means for inhibiting it. Popper's views on this matter have a number of aspects which may not be altogether in harmony.

---

relatively well-established Cartesian worlds of External objects and Internal experiences. It is interesting that *some* of the arguments invoked in support of this doctrine – the incorporation in a social tradition and its equipment of a wealth of ideas never accessible to any one man – are *precisely* those which led some others to be tempted by social holism. Is there much gained by opting for an essentialist rather than holist terminology for indicating the same facts? I suppose it depends on whether all such cultural worlds are simply parts of one and the same Third World, or whether they are allowed, each of them, to make its own world, which need not be commensurate or compatible with others. In the former case, a Platonic language for describing this would seem more appropriate; in the latter, a sociological–holistic one. It should be added that his individualism does not oblige him to see science as only contingently social; on the contrary, in the appropriate sense, he sees it as essentially social. This is discussed later in the chapter.

2 Emile Durkheim, *Elementary Forms of the Religious Life*, tr. Joseph W. Swain, New York, 1954. The main contrast between the two great sociologists Durkheim and Weber is precisely in their attitude to rational thought: Durkheim sees it as a characteristic of any society and correlative with social life as such, whereas Max Weber is preoccupied with it as a differential trait, present in one tradition far more prominently than in all others. So one sees rationality as ever-present, and its explanation is *ipso facto* the explanation of society: there was indeed a social contract, but it had the form of ritual, not of a compact. Durkheim sees it as present in an uneven manner, and its explanation as coextensive not with society as such, but with the emergence and distinctive nature of one kind of society, namely that which concerns us most, our own.

When stressing the continuity of trial and error as the basis of all cognitive advance throughout the history of all life, it would seem that the core secret of scientific method is something we share with all organic life and never needed to learn. (We have only learnt somehow to do it a bit faster and to show mercy to carriers of unsuccessful ideas.) No special institutions seem to be required. In the context of turning the tables on relativists who invoke the human inability to overcome prejudice and interest, however, he seems willing to concede that many (perhaps most?) men are unwilling to correct their own views in the light of contrary considerations, and perhaps even need prejudice to make discoveries at all; but he insists that science is the kind of institution which is not at the mercy of the virtues or vices of the persons who man it. Public testing by a diversified and uncontrollable community of scientists ensures the eventual elimination of faulty ideas, however dogmatic and irrational their individual adherents may be. According to this version, science and its advancement clearly do depend on the institutional underpinning of this public and plural testing. On the other hand again, in the context of the discussion of the origin of the scientific spirit, he is inclined to invoke the figures of heroic, Promethean Ionian founders–liberators, who somehow overcame their own human proclivity to dogmatism, and encouraged their disciples to criticise, thereby inventing science. The Ionian proto-Popper plays a role in this system, similar to that of the philosopher in *The Republic*: he and he alone, by his somewhat mysterious emergence, can break through the vicious circle, to which mankind is otherwise in thrall.

Popper's overall philosophy is curious in that science had to be invented in human history, when seen as the great act of liberation from the Closed Society, though it had *not* originally needed inventing in the general history of life, for the amoeba had it as its birthright. Within nature, red in tooth and claw, organisms eliminated faulty hypotheses by eliminating each other. Savage, pre-scientific men, however, gleefully eliminated each other, but not hypotheses; for some reason they allowed ideas to survive, or rather, they uncritically preserved them instead of eliminating them. Harsh with each other, they showed tender solicitude for ideas. Modern scientific men eliminate hypotheses, but not each other, at any rate when on their best behaviour. The curious consequence of this philosophy of history is that there is a kind of Dark Age or Fall, an unfortunate Detour, an expulsion from the cognitive Garden of Eden, which took place between the first emergence of humanity and the beginnings of science and the Open Society. The amoeba's birthright was lost somewhere during the early tribal, over-collectivistic period of human history, and was miraculously, heroically, recovered in

Ionia. It is interesting that the Regrettable Detour theory is something shared by Christianity, Marxism and Popper, though in different form.

The current second most influential philosopher of science, Thomas Kuhn, would also seem to sociologise the subject to the second degree. Society appears in his view to be essential for the existence and advancement of science, and not any old society will do: it has to be one endowed with a paradigm. There appear to be societies not so endowed – for instance, the community of social scientists.[3]

As far as one can make out, the crucial differentia between science-capable and science-incapable societies in his view is just this: the presence and absence of a paradigm. Kuhn does not seem to have any views concerning the difference between scientific and *un*scientific paradigms; a crucial weakness in his position, to my mind. Paradigms seem not merely to be incommensurate, but also to constitute a curiously undifferentiated class. The prophet of their incommensurability seems to have little sense of how very different in *kind* they are – that some of them are more incommensurate than others. But in so far as the importance of paradigms, and the fact that they are socially carried, perpetuated and enforced, leads him openly and avowedly to turn to sociology, he does make himself open to Popper's taunt: *which sociology* is the philosopher of science to use? Which sociological paradigm may he trust, when using sociology to grapple with the general problem of the nature of science, so as to illuminate the standing of all sciences, including sociology itself? By making all scientific activity relative to paradigms, and the philosophy of science dependent on sociology (which is presumably no more exempt from paradigm-dependence than any other science or inquiry), his position would seem to have an element of circularity in it. Was it some Cretan who had once observed that anything a Cretan said was paradigm-bound, and that all paradigms were mutually incommensurate?[4]

But what does concern us here is this: both Popper and Kuhn sociologise the philosophy of science to the second degree by my count, i.e., they make science dependent not merely on the sheer existence of society, but on the availability of a special kind of society.

The ways in which they do so, however, are contrasted and indeed diametrically opposed. For Popper, the only science-capable (I suppose *wissenschaftsfähig* would be the right word) society is one so loosened up in its social control as to permit criticism even of its most respected sages (or better still, perhaps, one endowed with institutional guarantees of

---

3 Thomas Kuhn, *The Structure of Scientific Revolutions*, 2nd edn, Chicago, 1970.
4 Thomas Kuhn, *The Structure of Scientific Revolutions*, 2nd edn, Chicago, 1970, pp. vii–viii.

the possibility or even the encouragement of such criticism); for Kuhn, science is made possible only by the presence of social–conceptual control sufficiently tight to impose a paradigm on its members at most (though not quite all) times, notwithstanding the fact that paradigms are not logically, so to speak objectively, binding. They are made binding by social pressure, which thus makes science possible. Unless the deep questions are arbitrarily prejudged, science cannot proceed, it appears. But just as Thomas Hobbes insisted that any paradigm is preferable to anarchy, so Thomas Kuhn insists that any paradigm is preferable to the dreadful freedom of contemporary social scientists, ever questioning and debating fundamentals and for that very reason, through their great 'openness', inhibiting the emergence of genuine science in their own midst.

It is not necessary here to choose between the near-anarchism of Popper (anyone is to criticise anyone, though within the limits of some presumably self-imposed but not too clearly identified rule of rationality, which sometimes seems to wither away to a very exiguous minimum – abstention from physical violence), and the authoritarianism of Kuhn, recommending loyalty to paradigms at most times though evidently retaining the right of occasional rebellion (during similarly ill-defined, and I think in principle indefinable, conditions of 'scientific revolution'). What is relevant for our purpose *is* to single out an error which they both share. To define science, one needs to sociologise the philosophy of science to the *third*, and not merely the second, degree. It is not sufficient to allow the relevance of society and to distinguish between science-capable and science-incapable societies; it is also necessary to make this distinction in terms of features of society which do not pertain to their cognitive activities alone, and to consider those societies when involved in activities other than cognition. We shall need to look at the impact of cognition on its other activities. This, in my terminology, is to sociologise the subject to the third degree; and it needs to be done. How is it to be done?

If we are to understand why the notion of being scientific is so potent, why this accolade is so very significant, we must look at *what* it is that 'science' does *to* society, and forget for a moment the usual and fascinating question of *how* it manages to do it. Philosophical theories of science, such as those which are incorporated in various philosophical attempts to demarcate science, basically endeavour to answer the question concerning *how* it is that science works, how it is that the great miracle of scientific progress and consensus is achieved. But from the viewpoint of identifying what it is that confers such magic and charm on to science, we must look not so much at how it is done, but *what* it is that is done which is so enchanting. Why is it that science makes so much difference to society, that a special prestige attaches to any activity which may be included within its charmed circle, and can be withheld from anything that fails to qualify as 'scientific'?

This contrast, as I formulate it, somewhat simplifies a more complex reality: philosophers of science are of course also concerned with the features of the *output* of science, with the kind of theory it produces. Nevertheless, that tends to be a datum for them: their problem is – how was it achieved? It is the sociologist who is concerned primarily with the effects and implications of the kinds of knowledge that science provides. In the interest of simplicity of exposition, I shall pretend that this division of labour is neater than in fact it is. The complexities and nuances can be reintroduced if required without undermining the argument, I think.

The question as posed can best be answered by offering a highly schematic but nevertheless relevant sketch-history of mankind – one which divides this history into three stages. Trinitarian philosophies of history are common: there is, for instance, Auguste Comte's theory of the religious, metaphysical and positive stages, or Sir James Frazer's doctrine of the successive dominance of magic, religion and science, or Karl Polanyi's less intellectualist account of the succession of the communal, redistributive and market societies. The new pattern of world history which is now crystallising in our time and which con- stitutes, I believe, the unofficial, unformulated and sometimes unavowed, but tacitly pervasive view of history of our age, is somewhat different. It shares some of the intellectualism and the high valuation of science of the Comtian and Frazerian schemes, though it is more preoccupied than Frazer, at least, with the impact of science on the ordering of society.

The crucial stages of human history are the following: first, that of hunting and food-gathering; then, that of food production (agriculture and pastoralism); and finally, that based on production which is linked to growing scientific knowledge. Theories of historical stages in terms of social organisation do not work: it is the cognitive productive base which seems to provide the Big Divide; and on either side of the Big Divide we find a diversity of social forms. In the present context, the world of hunters and gatherers does not greatly concern us. But the difference between the agrarian and the scientific/industrial world does concern us a very great deal.

The notion of a fully developed agrarian society includes not merely that of reliance on food *production*, but also two other important features:

literacy and political centralisation. Developed agrarian societies are marked by a fairly complex but relatively stable division of labour. But it is a mistake to treat the division of labour as a so to speak homogeneous commodity: its implications for society vary according to just what it is that is being turned into a specialism. Literacy and political centralisation, the emergence of a clerisy and of a polity, have quite distinctive consequences, which cannot simply be assimilated to the minor economic specialisations which occur within the process of production taken on its own.

Agro-literate polities are not all alike. In fact, they differ a great deal amongst themselves. The diversity of agrarian political regimes is well known. The clerical classes of agrarian polities also vary a great deal in their organisation, recruitment and ethos. In one place, they may be part of a single, centralised, and jealously monopolistic organisation; in another, they may be a loose and open guild open to all men of pious learning. Elsewhere again, they may be a closed but uncentralised caste, or constitute a bureaucracy selected by competitive examination, with an administrative but not a religious monopoly.

But notwithstanding this variety, certain important common or generic traits can be observed. Recorded knowledge in such societies is used for administrative records, notably those connected with taxation; for communication along a political and religious hierarchy; as parts of ritual and for the codification of religious *doctrine*, which has a kind of shadow in the form of word-magic, the compliment paid by manipulative magic to scriptural religion. Conservation of the written truth, and possibly its implementation, are central concerns, rather than its expansion in the form of acquisition of more truth. (Cognitive growth is not yet a plausible ideal.) Despite inner complexity, sometimes very considerable, both the status system and the cognitive systems within such a society tend to be fairly stable, and the same tends to be true of its productive system. The normative and conservative stress on the written word, in the keeping of the clerisy, tends to produce a cultural dualism or pluralism in such a society, a differentiation between the Great (literate) Traditions and Little Traditions. Parts of the written Great Tradition may contain general ideas of great penetration and potential, or acute and accurate observations of reality, or deductive systems of great rigour; nonetheless, generically speaking, one may say that a corpus of this kind somehow or other had no firm grip on, and cumulative penetration of, nature. Its main significance and role lies rather in social legitimation, edification, record-keeping and communication, and not in a genuine cognitive exploration of nature. When it comes to the manipulation and understanding of things, the cognitive content of the corpus tends to be inferior to the skills, such as they are, of the craftsman or artisan or working practitioner. The cognitive despair expressed with such vigour in the opening speech of Goethe's *Faust* is clearly a commentary on this situation.

With less anguish and perhaps more indignation, and with a missionary zeal on behalf of a putative alternative, a similar sentiment can be found in, for instance, what might be called the pan-human or *carte blanche* populism of Professor Michael Oakeshott.[5] Oakeshott's work enjoyed a considerable vogue in post-war Britain, and he probably continues to be Britain's foremost conservative political philosopher. His work is highly relevant for the present purpose because, at its base, there is a premiss which is half-epistemological, half-sociological, and which runs as follows: genuine knowledge is 'practical', which means that it is maintained and transmitted by the practice of a skill, and can only be perpetuated by a living tradition; and its content can never be adequately seized in written documents, and certainly cannot be transmitted from one man to another by writing alone. The illusion that this can be done, which endows abstract and written assertions with independent authority, he names 'Rationalism', in a highly pejorative sense, and he clearly holds it to be the bane of modern life. His reaction to Faust's opening speech could only be: the more fool you for ever having sought knowledge in the way in which you did. You were looking in the wrong place. Oakeshott's doctrine vacillates somewhat between on the one hand, a global pan-populism, endorsing all traditions, and damning all their scholasticisms, which they develop when they adopt writing and printing and take it too seriously; and on the other hand, the endorsement of one specific and blessed tradition, which, thanks presumably to an unwritten constitution, common law, and the pragmatic wisdom of Whig politicians, has resisted 'Rationalism' somewhat better than others – though around 1945, it did so less well than it should and aroused his wrath. If it is the achievement of one distinctive tradition, can it also be a valid recipe for all of them – without implicitly contradicting its own central principle, namely the absence of any abstract and universally valid principles?

This issue concerns the propounder of the theory – he does not seem to have published any solution to the problem and does not seem too troubled, though by rights it should worry him acutely – but it does not concern us. The reason why this Oakeshottian position *is* highly relevant for our argument is this: whether or not it provides a good diagnosis of

---

[5] *Rationalism in Politics and Other Essays*, London, 1962.

the political predicament of modern man, it does unwittingly provide a very accurate schematic account of the role of abstract knowledge in the agro-literate polity. It is a rather good account of the relation between codified knowledge and practical skills in the agro-literate polity – but *only* in the agro-literate polity. The scriptures, law codes, epics, manuals and so forth in the keeping of its scribes, jealously preserved and fairly stable over time, are not superior to the inarticulate practical wisdom of the life-long member of the clan or guild. They echo, formalise, distort and travesty that wisdom; and though, contrary to the anti-'Rationalist' diatribe, reverence for the codified version of the wisdom may on occasion be beneficial – because, for instance, reverence for the codified rule makes it less amenable to opportunist manipulation – nevertheless it is true that the absolute authority claimed for the writ in the scribe's keeping is not justified. The written theory is parasitical on the lived *praxis*. So be it; or at any rate, so it *was*, once, in the agro-literate polity. It is so no longer.

But it is manifestly untrue of modern science and the society based on it. As a social phenomenon, modern natural science has a number of conspicuous features:

(1) Though not completely consensual, it is consensual to an astonishing degree.

(2) It is inter-cultural. Though it flourishes more in some countries than in others, it appears capable of persisting in a wide variety of cultural and political climes, and to be largely independent of them.

(3) It is cumulative. Its growth rate is astonishing. This is also, amongst cognitive systems in general, unique.

(4) Though it can evidently be taught to men originating in any cultural background, it requires arduous and prolonged training, in thought-styles and techniques which are in no way continuous with those of daily life, and are often highly counter-intuitive.

(5) The continuously growing technology which it engenders is immeasurably superior to, and qualitatively distinct from, the practical skills of the craftsmen of agrarian society.

It is these features, or others closely related to them, which have engendered the persistent and haunting question – what is science? The question is no longer: what is truth, wisdom or genuine knowledge? Men possessed by the haunting question concerning the nature of science do not necessarily deny (though some of them do) that knowledge or truth also exist outside science; they do not all say, as an antiscientistic book once ironically put it, 'Extra scientiam nulla salus'.[6] But they are generally imbued with the sense of the distinctiveness of this kind of knowing, and wish to locate its source. They do not want to kill the goose which lays the golden eggs, they only wish to identify it, so as to use it to the full, and perhaps to guide it to new fields. (Some do wish to equate knowledge with scientific knowledge, not because they despise and abjure pre-scientific cognitive styles, but because they consider them to be basically similar to science, being just earlier and feebler, and to deserve the same label. I believe this kind of 'Continuity thesis' to be mistaken.)

This as it were external, sociological account of science, described from the viewpoint of what it does to the cognitive map and productive processes of society (leaving aside the question of its inner mechanics, the secret of its success), may of course be challenged. It may be denied that science constitutes the victory of trans-social, explicit, formalised and abstract knowledge over privately, ineffably communicated insights or skills or sensitivities. It may be asserted that the golden-egg-laying goose is not, after all, radically distinct from the old practical skills. The perception and understanding of a scientific problem, the capacity to propound and test a solution, requires — it can be argued – some flair or spirit or 'personal knowledge' which is beyond the reach of words or script, and which cannot be formalised. The *Fingerspitzgefühl* is alive and well, and, more important, remains indispensable. The late Professor Michael Polanyi was only one adherent, though possibly the best known, of such a view.[7]

It is difficult to say how one could evaluate this claim. It is sometimes supported by arguments such as the infinite regress of formalisation, which can never catch up with itself:[8] whatever is asserted is only a case of *knowing that*, and presupposes one further practical *knowing how* to apply it – and if that in turn is articulated and made explicit, the initial argument applies once again, and so on for ever. Or it can be supported by the widely held and plausible view that whilst there can be a logic of testing, there is no logic of discovery – only free-floating, uncontrollable inspiration, which comes or does not come as it wills, but appears to be more willing to descend upon well-sustained, but elusive and indefinable, research traditions.

But even if all this is admitted, what matters from the social viewpoint

[6] Paul Feyerabend, *Against Method*, London, 1975.
[7] *Personal Knowledge: Toward a Post Critical Philosophy*, Chicago, 1974.
[8] Gilbert Ryle, 'Knowing How and Knowing That', Presidential Address, *Proceedings of the Aristotelian Society*, 1945–6, 1–16, and Lewis Carroll, 'Achilles and the Tortoise', in *The Complete Works of Lewis Carroll*, New York, 1939.

is that the ratio, the entire balance, between ineffable practical skill or flair on the one hand, and explicit formal knowledge on the other, is transformed out of all recognition in a science-using, industrial society. Even if an element of flair or tradition which is beyond words *is* crucial for the occasional outstanding great new discovery, or, in small regular doses, for the sustaining of a vigorous research tradition, yet the enormous mass of ordinary research and technological activity works quite differently: it rather resembles the old explicit scholasticisms of agro-literate society, except in one crucial way – it *works*. Scholasticism, for all its ineffectiveness, seems to have been a good preparation of genuinely productive vigour. Talmudic societies take to science with alacrity.

Its general implications for the society which uses science are also fairly obvious. A society endowed with a powerful and continuously growing technology lives by innovation, and its occupational role structure is perpetually in flux. This leads to a fair amount of occupational mobility and hence to a measure of equality which, though not sufficient to satisfy out-and-out egalitarians, is nevertheless far greater than that of most agrarian societies. It is egalitarian because it is mobile, not mobile because it is egalitarian. Mobility, frequent abstract transmission of ideas, and the need for universal literacy, i.e., fairly context-free communication, also lead to a completely new role for culture in society: culture is linked to school rather than home and needs to be fairly homogeneous over the entire catchment area of an educational system. At long last, Great Traditions really dominate, and to a large extent supplant, Little Traditions. So the state, which once may have been the Defender of the Faith, now becomes in effect the Protector of a Culture. In other words, the modern national state (based on the principle One State, One Culture) becomes the norm, the Irredentist nationalisms emerge where this norm fails to be satisfied. The unprecedented potential for growth leads to Cornucopianism, the attempt to buy off discontent and to smooth over social conflict by incremental Danegeld all round – and this in turn, as we now know only too well, becomes a dreadful trap when, the incremental Danegeld having become an engrained, as-of-right expectation, the cornucopia temporarily dries up or even just slows down, as from time to time in the nature of things it must.

These seem to be the generic traits of science-using society. They differentiate it profoundly from most or all agrarian societies, which are Malthusian rather than growth-orientated, cognitively and productively stable rather than growing (innovations when they occur involve changes of degree rather than kind, and in any case come as single spies, not in battalions). Theories of historical stages or epochs in terms of social organisation (capitalism–socialism is the most popular) seem to have failed, in so far as science-using (i.e., industrial) society appears to be compatible with diverse forms of organisation, within the limits of their shared generic traits; but those traits in turn distinguish it from all its predecessors. The question about the nature of science is in effect the issue of the nature of this distinctive style of cognition, which in turn defines an entire stage in the history of mankind.

Philosophical theories of science, as here defined, do not define science, as was done above, in the sociological manner, in terms of what it does *to* society. They tend to ignore that. Instead, they try to identify the secret which enables it to do it.

It is impossible to list here all the contending theories in the field, and even if we listed them, we should have no way of deciding between them. There is no consensus in this area. Science may be consensual; the theory of science is not.

But it is worthwhile, for our purpose, to list some of the main contenders:

(1) Ultra-empiricism: stick to observable facts. Accumulate them, and only go beyond them when the accumulated data strongly point in some one direction. Above all, do not trespass into the transcendent! (This cautious version of empiricism, associated with Bacon or Hume, and surviving in modern behaviourism, has been much decried of late. Its detractors do not always fully appreciate that the interdict on cognitive trespass once had a great value. The belief-systems of agrarian societies were often so constructed as to be cunningly self-maintaining in a circular way, and the Interdict on Trespass was the best way of eliminating these.)

(2) The Kantian diagnosis, which is a mixture of the Interdict on Trespass with recommended daring within proper bounds, and within the conceptual limits allegedly imposed by the structure of the human mind.

(3) Collective self-propulsion by the resolution of internal con-tradictions, with deference to privileged *praxis* – the *praxis* of the privileged class is a privileged *praxis* – and to the direction of a prescribed social development. This is the nearest I can get to formulating one of the theories of knowledge commonly associated with Marxism.

(4) Maximum daring of hypothesis within the limits of testability – the Popperian theory.

(5) Obedience to a given background picture (thus eliminating the chaos characteristic of unscientific subjects, and ensuring comparable work and thus cumulation) except at rare, 'revolutionary' occasions, which cannot be generically characterised or presumably predicted, and which then lead to a progressive replacement of one background picture by another. (Within the limits of this theory, which declares these successive background pictures to be incommensurate, there *cannot*, however, be any rational way of showing that the post-revolutionary picture is superior to the one it replaced. Though the idea of scientific progress is presupposed, and indeed sets the problem, it cannot coherently be asserted, for it would require the comparison of successive 'paradigms', which are said to be incommensurate, by comparing them to some meta-paradigm, which *ex hypothesi* we do not and cannot possess.) This is the much-discussed theory propounded by Thomas Kuhn.[9]

(6) The successive improvement of collectives of propositions with a view to enhancing both external predictions and manipulation and internal coherence and elegance, by methods asserted to be continuous with those which governed biological evolution. This is pragmatism, ably represented in our time by Quine.[10] In his version, it asserted the Continuity thesis more coherently than in the work of Popper (where it clashes with the discontinuity between Open and Closed thought). If a major break in the cognitive history of life occurred at all, in this logical-pragmatist version, it arose at the point where abstract entities came to be used and in a way acquired reality, thus permitting the dramatic growth of mathematics:

The unrefined and sluggish mind
of Homo Javanensis
could only treat of things concrete
and present to the senses.

(Quine, *From a Logical Point of View: Nine Logico-Philosophical Essays*, Cambridge (Mass.), 1953, p. 77)

This is not the place to debate the merits of these theories. No doubt there are others. But we shall need to refer to the themes which occur in them – accurate observation, testing, mathematicisation, shared con-

9 In *The Structure of Scientific Revolutions*.
10 Willard van Orman Quine, *From a Logical Point of View: Nine Logico-Philosophical Essays*, 2nd revised edn, Cambridge (Mass.), 1961.

ceptual currency, the abstention from transcendence or circularity, and perhaps others.

My argument has been that by 'science' is meant a type of cognition which has radically, qualitatively transformed man's relation to things: nature has ceased to be a datum and become eligible for genuine comprehension and manipulation. Science is a distinctive cognitive system with some mysterious in-built mechanism ensuring sustained and perpetual growth – which has been profoundly beneficial for human productive systems, and corrosive of our systems of social legitimation. We do not really know *how* this sustained and consensual growth is achieved, but we do know *that* it is achieved, and 'science' is the name for the manner in which it is done, whatever it may be. Hence the question whether social studies are or are not properly to be included within the limits of science is by no means merely terminological. We are asking whether the same kind of thing is happening in our understand-ing and manipulation of society.   ·

   But this way of presenting the issue contains one important simplifi-cation. It suggests that the evaluative charge contained in the appellation 'science' is, because of its implied promise of understanding and control, entirely, wholly and unambiguously *positive*. This is by no means so. Though there exists one major academic industry producing books telling the social scientists what science really is and how they can turn themselves into genuine scientists, there exists another, with at least as flourishing an output, putatively establishing that the study of man and society cannot be scientific, or alternatively, if the positively loaded term 'scientific' is to be retained, that they are scientific, but in a sense radically different from that which applies in natural science. The idea that the methods of natural and social science are basically identical is nowadays almost a definition of 'positivism', and 'positivism' is a term which in recent years has more often than not been used pejoratively. This is significant: originally, the central theme of positivism was the interdict on transcendence. Modern anti-positivists seek to escape from the weaknesses that flesh and fact are heir to (notably contingency and corrigibility) no longer to some transcendent realm of pure and certain truths such as were fashionable in agrarian days, but to the social and human realm; and to do so, they must insist that the human or cultural is radically distinct from nature. One also sometimes has the impression that a 'positivist' is anyone who subjects a favoured theory to the indignity of testing by mere fact.

   The arguments purporting to prove that the study of man and society cannot be scientific (variant reading: can only be scientific in a sense radically different from that applicable to the study of nature) can also be catalogued. Authors upholding this view of course often combine or conflate these various points. Nonetheless, it is useful to list them separately.

(1) The argument from idiography. Human, social or historical phenomena either *are* inherently individual; or our *concern* is with their individual and idiosyncratic aspects; or, of course, both.

(2) The argument from holism. Society is a unity; the Principle of Internal Relations, which insists that everything is what it is in virtue of its relationships to everything else within the same system, applies to it. If the main device of old metaphysics was the reality of abstract objects, then this idea, in various terminologies, is the central device of modern socio-metaphysics. Empirical inquiry, however, can *ex hypothesi* deal merely with isolated facts and cannot seize any totality. Hence it essentially distorts and misrepresents social reality. This doctrine can be combined with the view that it is the actual function, conscious or latent, of empirical factual inquiry to hide social reality and distort our perception of it in the service of the established order, which has cause to fear clear-sighted perception of social reality on the part of the less privileged members of society. The latter view can also naturally be fused with a special dispensation for the propounder himself and those like-minded, who possess some means of privileged cognitive access to the real nature of society – insights which are beyond the reach of mere atomic empirical facts garnered by the ideological *chiens de garde* of the established order.[11]

(3) The argument from the complexity of social phenomena can be used to reinforce the preceding two arguments.

(4) The argument from Meaning. Human actions and institutions are identified not by some shared physical traits, but in terms of what they mean to the participants. This fact (if such it is) can be held, wholly or partly, to entail the exemption of human or social phenomena either from causation or from external and comparative empirical investigation, or of course from both.

The argument can be put thus: the nexus which exist between natural phenomena or classes of events are independent of

---

[11] 'Sociology and Empirical Research' in *The Positivist Dispute in German Sociology*, by T. W. Adorno, Hans Albert, Ralf Dahrendorf, Jürgen Habermas, Harald Pilot and Karl Popper, London, 1976, pp. 68–86.

any one society, common to them all, and blind to the meanings prevailing in any one of them. But actions are identified by what they *mean* to the participants, and the meanings which identify them are drawn from the as it were semantic pool of a given culture, which need not be, and perhaps never is, identified with the reservoir of meanings used by another culture. Hence there cannot be a valid causal generalisation in which one of the links is a class of actions, i.e., events only bound together by the so to speak collectively private meanings which happen to be in use in a given culture, for these do not overlap with any so to speak natural kind or category. Nature could not recognise and identify them and thus cannot apply any causal lever to them. As for the links obtaining between two or more such socially meaningful categories, they are themselves established in virtue of the semantics of the culture in question, and can only be apprehended by penetrating, learning that system, and *not* by external investigation. Comparative inter-social research and generalisations are absurd and impossible, inasmuch as the systems of meanings of diverse cultures are not comparable or overlapping, or only contingently and partially so.[12]

A historical comment which one may allow oneself on this position is that idealism is alive and well, and operates under the name of hermeneutics. The views which had once been articulated with the help of terms such as *Geist* or 'Spirit' now see the light of day in terms of 'meaning' or 'culture'.

(5) 'The Social Construction of Reality'.[13] This argument clearly overlaps with the preceding one; perhaps it is identical with it, differing only in the style of presentation and in its philosophical ancestry. The preceding formulation is rooted above all in the work of Wittgenstein, whereas this one springs from the ideas of E. Husserl and A. Schutz.

[12] An argument of this kind is found in Peter Winch's *The Idea of a Social Science and its Relation to Philosophy*, Atlantic Highlands, NJ, 1970. An even more extreme formulation of this position, combined with an ideographism *à outrance*, is found in A. R. Louch's *Explanation and Human Action*, Oxford, 1966. This position has been frequently criticised – see, for instance, Robin Horton's 'Professor Winch on Safari' in *Archives Européenes de Sociologie*, 27, no. 1, 1976; or Percy Cohen's 'The Very Idea of a Social Science' in I. Lakatos and A. Musgrave, eds., *Problems in the Philosophy of Science*, Amsterdam, 1968; or my own 'The New Idealism' in Ernest Gellner, ed. I. C. Jarvie and J. Agassi, *Cause and Meaning in the Social Sciences*, London, 1973.

[13] Peter L. Berger and Thomas Luckman, *The Social Construction of Reality: A Treatise on the Sociology of Knowledge*, New York, 1980.

(6) The Individual Construction of Reality (as you might say). This slogan, though not as far as I know actually used by the movement in question, could be used to characterise the approach of a recently fashionable school known as Ethnomethodology and associated with the name of Garfinkel.[14] The central doctrine appears to be that our ability to describe (make 'accountable') events is something we individually achieve, and that consequently the only scientific understanding available is the description (?) or highlighting (?) or exemplification of the very acts of individual accountability-creation. The movement is not marked either by lucidity of expression or by willingness to indulge in rational discussion (a reluctance which can in turn be rationalised in terms of its central insight, which would preclude the testing of interpersonal generalisation, there not being any such; but which also conveniently places the movement out of reach of criticism). This movement stands to 'The Social Construction of Reality' as Fichte did to Hegel; the Ego rolls its own world, instead of the world rolling itself in a kind of collective effort. But the temporal order seems reversed this time, for Fichte preceded Hegel. This view combines idealism with idiographism.

(7) The Pirandello effect. The allusion is (as we saw in chapter 1) to the device most powerfully developed by Luigi Pirandello for breaking down the neat distinction between characters, actors, producers, authors and spectators of a play. His plays, in which characters discuss the further development of the plot with each other and, seemingly, the author or members of the audience, are of course meant to induce bewilderment in the audience by undermining the comfortable separation of stage and auditorium, by compelling involvement by the spectator. The play, he seems to say, is not a spectacle but a predicament. So in observation of social reality – and this, it is claimed, distinguishes it from nature.

One charge which has been made against empiricist or scientistic social research (though it has not as yet been made in these words) is that it pretends that a society can be a

---

[14] See Harold Garfinkel, *Studies in Ethnomethodology*, Englewood Cliffs, NJ, 1967. For critical comments, see a very witty article by A. R. Louch, 'Against Theorizing', *Philosophy of the Social Sciences*, 5, 1975, 481–7; or my own, 'Ethnomethodology: the Re-enchantment Industry or the Californian Way of Subjectivity' in Ernest Gellner, *Spectacles and Predicaments*, Cambridge, 1979.

spectacle, and not a predicament, for the investigator. This pretence, the critics insist, is false. It constitutes deception of others and, if sincere, constitutes self-deception into the bargain. We make a commitment in our choice of ideas, problems or interpretations, and the choice is not or cannot be impartial or guided by logical criteria alone, or perhaps at all. Thus, the inescapable involvement of the investigator in his subject-matter makes any pretence at 'scientific objectivity' spurious. In actual presentation, this argument is generally fused with several of those already listed.

(8) Special cognitive status for the inquiry into man or society can also be claimed not so much in virtue of *general* considerations, such as those listed so far, but in virtue of alleged special substantive characteristics of the specific object or style of inquiry. For instance, in the lively debate concerning the scientific status of psychoanalysis, the claim is sometimes made (in defence of the legitimacy of this technique) that the eccentric methods employed in it (by the standards prevailing in other inquiries) are justified by the very peculiar nature of the object investigated, i.e., the Unconscious. Its cunning and deviousness in the face of inquiry, which it tries to evade and deceive, justify cognitive emergency measures, which would be held illicit by the rules of evidence prevailing in the normal court-rooms of science. Faced with so ruthless an enemy, the investigating magistrate is granted special powers and dispensed from the normal restrictions on methods of inquisition. The Unconscious cannot be apprehended in any other way, and the difficulty and urgency of the task justifies extreme methods. (Whether these really serve to outwit the quarry, or merely protect the reputation of the hunter, by ensuring that he is never convicted of fundamental error, is another question.)

There is no space here to attempt any kind of thorough evaluation of all these negative arguments. Suffice it to say that none of them seems to me remotely cogent. Take for instance the one which may seem most powerful, namely, the one to the effect that the categories of actions or events in a given culture are defined in terms of the meanings current within that culture, which are so to speak private to that culture, and not coextensive with 'natural kinds'. This, though true as far as it goes, in no way precludes even a physical determinism for the events within the culture in question. It merely precludes the identification of the determined events (if such they are) in terms of the meanings current in the culture. The determining forces, so to speak, will select the events they bring out in terms of some characteristics which only accidentally and contingently overlap with the meanings which accompany and seem to guide the events. For instance, when we watch a film, we know full well that what will happen is already determined; and it is determined by the pattern found on the reels which is being transmitted from the projection room. The meaningful connections which interest us and which appear to guide and give sense to the series of events observed in the story on the screen are really quite epiphenomenal and powerless. We do not actually know that our life is like that, and most of us hope that indeed it is not; but the argument from the meaningfulness of social life alas in no way establishes that it cannot be so.

If on the one hand the arguments purporting to establish that human and social life cannot be subject to scientific explanation are invalid, then, on the other hand, any inspection of the lively and vigorous discussions in the field of the philosophy of science indisputably reveal one thing – that the issue of the nature of science, of the identification of that secret which has made possible the unprecedented, totally unique rate of cognitive growth since the seventeenth century, remains unsolved. We have some very impressive candidates for the solution, powerfully and elegantly presented. But to have an impressive short-list is one thing, and to have a firmly identified, recognised, acclaimed winner is quite another. And that we do not have. The situation simply is that science is consensual, and the philosophy of science is *not*.

The two contentions which have been affirmed – that the putative demonstrations of the impossibility of science in social spheres are invalid, and that there is no agreed account of why and how science works in the fields in which it plainly does work – will be crucial in answering the question to which this chapter is devoted, namely whether or not the social sciences are indeed scientific

The question now in effect answers itself – once we have broken it up into its constituent, normally conflated, sub-questions or variant interpretations.

We can first of all check the activities of the social sciences for the presence or absence of the various traits which figure prominently in diverse theories of science. Those traits are:

> The presence of well-articulated hypotheses and their systematic testing.
>
> Precise quantitative measurement, and the operationalisation of concepts.

Careful observation by publicly checkable methods.

Sophisticated and rigorous conceptual structures, and great insights.

Shared paradigms, at any rate over sizeable communities of scholars, and persisting over prolonged periods.

There can be no serious doubt but that all these traits, often in combination, can be found in diverse social sciences. Man for man, or community for community, it is doubtful whether social scientists are inferior, in intellectual daring and ingenuity, in formal rigour, in precision of observation, to the practitioners of disciplines whose scientific status is not normally doubted. As a distinguished philosopher of science, Hilary Putnam, ironically and compassionately observed, the poor dears try so much harder.[15] As indicated, we do not know the secret of science; we do not know just which of the many blazing beacons we are being offered really *is* the Sacred Fire. We do know that many beacons are ablaze, and given the short-list supplied to us by the philosophers of science, we rather think that one of them (or perhaps a number of them jointly) is *it*. But which one? I am reminded of the no doubt apocryphal story about the eccentric Holy Roman Emperor Rudolf II, sitting in the castle in Prague and looking at thirty-odd copies of the Mona Lisa, and musing – ah, if only we knew which one is the real one, we could then sell all the fakes.

More concretely, we do know that many of the indisputable characteristics of science are often present in social research. The aspects of social life which are inherently quantitative or observable with precision are indeed investigated (for example, in demography or social geography) with precision and sophisticated techniques. We know also that sophisticated and elaborate abstract models are developed in various areas and serve as shared paradigms to extensive communities of scholars (economists, for instance); and in spheres where the conceptual apparatus is not so very far removed from the ideas of common sense, we nevertheless know that a well-trained practitioner of the subject possesses understanding and information simply not available prior to the development of the subject. In all these senses, social studies are indeed scientific. Large areas of them do satisfy one or another of the many available, and convincing, theories of the Sacred Fire. And our collective life would be much poorer without them.

So much for the satisfaction of the hallmarks of science, as they are specified by the philosophy of science. But we obtain a different picture

[15] Bryan Magee (ed.) *Men of Ideas*, New York, 1979, p. 233.

if we look at it from the viewpoint not of methods employed, but of the impact on our cognitive world: if we ask whether there is a general, overall consensual cognitive activity, radically discontinuous from the insights and techniques of ordinary thought, and unambiguously cumulative at an astonishing and unmistakable rate. The answer is obvious. In this crucial sense, in terms of their impact on our social order, social studies are not scientific – much as they may rightly claim to be so by the previous criterion or criteria. They claim to have stolen the Sacred Fire. Does anyone pay them the compliment of wishing to steal it from them?

We can try to break up this failure into its constituent parts. The quantitatively accurate descriptive techniques are not accompanied by correspondingly convincing theory or similarly accurate prediction. The sophisticated abstract models do not firmly mesh in with empirical material. The powerful insights are not consensual. Paradigms exist and prevail, but only in sub-communities; and when they succeed each other, the situation is quite different from that which prevails in natural science. In natural science, we are generally sure that there is progress, but have great difficulty in explaining how it is possible that we can know that, given that there is no common measure for comparing successive visions. In the social sciences we are spared this worry. We need not puzzle about *how* it is that we can know that we are progressing, because we are not so very sure that we have indeed progressed. The partisans of a new paradigm may, of course be sure about their own particular leap (they usually are); but they are seldom sure about the whole series of leaps which constitutes the history of their subject. On the contrary, their own leap is very often a reverse one, a return to an earlier model. . .

If I am right about the logical inadequacy of the alleged proofs of the ineligibility of the social world for science, we need not despairingly conclude (or confidently hope, as the case may be), that this will always continue to be so. If, indeed, the Sacred Fire of science has not yet been identified, we do not know how to remedy that. The question remains open. But I suspect we shall know that the social sciences have become scientific when their practitioners no longer claim that they have at long last stolen the Fire, but when others try to steal it from them; when the philosophy of social science becomes a search for an *ex post facto* explanation of a cognitive *Wissenschaftswunder*, rather than for a recipe/ promise for bringing it about.

5 | What is structuralisme?

A spectre is haunting Europe, or at any rate Cambridge: 'structuralisme'. But what is it? Or perhaps: what the devil is it? Popular explanations of it fluctuate between the unintelligible and the obvious, with a heavy list toward the former. Communism at least had a Manifesto that articulated its central ideas with vigour, lucidity, and authority. To my knowledge, there is no corresponding 'structuraliste manifesto' that could tell us just what it is that is haunting us, or some of us. On an occasion that most impressed them, archaeologists were advised to embrace structuralisme by Sir Edmund Leach. But what exactly is it they are to embrace?

I was once involved in translating what is probably the most theoretical and synoptic work by the best-known structuraliste. This exercise on my part was not due to any ambition to set up as a translator in order to make money that way or to test or refute theories about the indeterminacy of translations. Not at all. It happened quite differently. The original translator, after submitting a couple of sample chapters to the top structuraliste and exchanging some amiable letters, or perhaps letters that began as amiable, soon came to illustrate the Indeterminacy of Translation thesis by getting involved in a flaming row with the author and ceasing to be on speaking, or indeed writing or translating, terms with him. The publishers had already paid an advance and wanted to see the translation completed, and they commissioned a conceptual go-between, a *tertius quid*, to mediate between the two warring parties. Unfortunately, far from becoming a *tertius gaudens*, he rapidly became a *tertius perdens*, if there is such an expression, as the chain reaction continued and he too ceased to be on speaking, writing, and translating terms with the original translator. There was indeed no reason whatever why the chain reaction should ever cease. At some nth stage I was sucked into the recursive process, more for reasons of personal friendship with the $(n-1)$th victim than by virtue of any competence or qualification. Instead of fumbling into the abyss to join the others, I managed to terminate the regress, by means largely of abject humility:

this series at any rate was not allowed to follow out its rule to infinity. I humbly stressed to the aggrieved original translator that I had no pretensions to authority in this matter, and I underlined, as indeed is the case, that I had actually failed my O level (School Certificate as it was called in those distant days) in the language in which the work had originally been composed – which is quite an unusual distinction in itself. I then worked on completing the translation. When the work was done, the original translator threatened to sue if his name appeared on it, but also to sue if anyone else's, notably mine and that of *n*–l, were credited with it. So the translation appeared without any name or names to which credit or blame might be attached – as if it had sprung into being unaided and spontaneously. One friendly reviewer described it as execrable, but several others, and I think the majority of those who commented on it at all, praised it.

The work in question is probably the main succint theoretical summary of his own position by the leading structuraliste, and as I say, I put in a lot of work on the translation of it. It might well be the nearest thing we have to a structuraliste manifesto. Yet I must confess that, at the end of all that work on the correct rendering of single sentences and paragraphs, I still had no idea of what its overall argument was meant to be. In this I do not appear to be alone: Noam Chomsky has commented on the work in question, saying that all it seems to amount to is the idea that men generally classify things. This, though evidently true, would not, on its own, amount to any kind of new illumination, so one supposes there must be more to it. But what is it and where is it to be found? This is the moral of my story: there is no facile rosy path to the central ideas or tenets of structuralisme.[1]

If, indeed, there is no such key text for the identification of structuraliste doctrine, some other method must be used for locating it. I shall attempt to use a kind of generative method – the construction of a model of structuralisme, consisting of a set of ideas or themes. Such a model then has some claim to be considered a correct rendering, if the observed activities and positions of people normally described as structuralistes follow from them, and activities repudiated or conspicuously avoided by them do not follow from them: and there is a reasonable amount of evidence to suggest that this set of ideas did operate in the minds of such people. Such evidence can be sought in their writing, but it can also be

---

[1] I know of one admirably lucid essay that sets out to clarify the principles of structuralisme, but it is not easy to locate. It is Jean Pouillon's contribution, 'Structure and Structuralism', to E. Gellner (ed.), *Soviet and Western Anthropology*, London and New York, 1980, pp. 278–82.

sought in the problem situations in which they are known to have been involved.

I believe that the philosophical roots of structuralisme are deep. One problem to which it is, I believe, related, is that of the general nature of explanation and of causation. There are two main conceptions of causation: what might be called 'emanation', and what is customarily called 'covering law'. The idea underlying the former conception can be best conveyed, at least initially, in a kind of pictorial or suggestive way, which may leave philosophers feeling uneasy and seem to them sloppy, but which nevertheless does, I think, capture the central intuition that inspires this view. The idea is this: things have deep natures or constitutions or structures or inner essences, or whatever you wish to call them. These are normally, or perhaps permanently, hidden from view, but the regularities we discern in the phenomena that are open to view emanate, or flow from, those hidden, permanent inner forms. Once those inner forms are perceived or understood or conceptually seized, all else follows and is clear. But without such understanding, any attempt to bind the visible phenomena under generalisations is bound to remain superficial, and will probably be abortive, even if it restricts itself to surface classification and prediction.

Very often, this conception of knowledge is also very satisfying morally: those inner forms tend to be not merely potent in their explanatory force but also gratifying aesthetically and ethically. They reveal a moral as well as an ontological order; in fact, these various orders converge. Truth, beauty, and goodness are one. From the viewpoint of someone interested only in the philosophy of science and explanation, of course, this blessed convergence of the axiological and cognitive realms is a kind of optional extra: the emanation view of causation can be held on its own, without these moral and aesthetic overtones or associations. They are not entailed in the emanation view of causation as such. Nevertheless, the elective affinity of these views is relevant to the understanding of the appeal of this vision. Similarly, the *rejection* of the fact–value convergence, or if you like, the cagey insurance against disillusion should it fail to hold, itself also constitutes a clue to the appeal of the *rival* view of causation.

In recent centuries, the 'emanationist' view has been, on the whole, in decline. The main logical reason for this has been an increasing reluctance to rely on inherently hidden, inaccessible entities for purposes of explanation. This might be called the empiricist or positivist trend. (It is a nice question to ask: have we lost faith in the fact–value convergence because we have become more empiricist, or have we become empiricists because we have lost faith in that convergence?) It may well be that one of the roots of this new vision itself is, ironically, ultimately theological – that antiquity lacked the notion of natural law (evidence to the contrary being at least in part due to mistranslations and conceptual retrojections) and was implicitly emanationist; and that the 'law' conception of natural order and explanation is a consequence of the doctrine of a hidden, austere, orderly, and voluntarist deity, which reveals neither its own designs nor the hidden essences of things, but obliges its creatures, if they are smitten by the desire to know, to content themselves with the tabulation of mere regularities in the surface phenomena, which alone are available to their inspection. Such a deity does not stoop to any brazen signalling of its meaning, or to self-display.[2] In any case, whatever its historical roots, this empiricism for-swears the reduplication of the world into hidden essence and visible emanation, which seems inherent in emanationism. Emanationism explains the visible world in terms of entities and forces of another world. But the only access to that other world, we now realize, is through its alleged manifestation in this world. Is this not a circular or vacuous procedure? Is it not better to be honest and treat the explanations merely as shorthand, as summaries of the regularities found in the phenomena, rather than endowing them with a 'realist' status and treating them also as simultaneously descriptive characterisations of another realm, underlying ordinary events? Positivists, given to epistemological Machismo, see them as mere shorthand abbreviations of descriptive accounts of events in *this* world. So a powerful epistemological tautology – what you cannot observe, you cannot observe – comes to reinforce a spirit that was perhaps initially inspired by the faith in a very hidden, mysterious, yet austere and order-loving deity.

It was of course David Hume who, starting from the premiss that the world we think is bounded by what we can sense, ended with an early form of the covering-law theory of causation. His inference was *from* radical empiricism *to* the 'law' theory. I am not clear whether the reverse inference holds formally, though it is a rather natural step to take. The affinity between the two positions – an empiricist reluctance to coun-tenance experience-transcending entities, whether for explanatory purposes or any other, and the law theory of causation – arises as follows: if there is nothing other than experiences, then the causal link between experiences cannot be anything either between or beyond them (there not being any such things), and therefore what else could it be, other than the pattern of similar experiences, the regular association – in

2 For this fascinating historical speculation, I am indebted to a brilliant paper by Dr John R. Milton of Imperial College, London: 'The Origin and Development of the Concept of "Law of Nature"', *Archives Européenes de Sociologie*, 23, no. 2, 1981.

other words, the observed law? Conversely, if the notion of law or regularity captures the essence of causation, then there is nothing to it other than that law and the elements that it connects or binds. Nothing else being required, it would seem to follow that nothing else is relevant. Hence experience-transcending entities, even if they exist (which this argument on its own cannot exclude), have nothing to do with causation.

It is a striking fact about the world we inhabit that at the phenomenal level, there are few good regularities (though there are some). The heavenly bodies are one sphere where regular behaviour is conspicuous: with a little less precision, there are the tides and the seasonal rhythms of nature. (It is interesting to note that of two great theories of religion, Hume's and Durkheim's, one links religion to the fear of the irregular, the other to the confirmation of the regular.) In all those extensive spheres where regularity is absent at the immediate level of phenomena, it can only be sought (and is frequently found) at higher levels of abstraction, i.e., in terms that relate to experiential ones only indirectly, in some complex way. The two theories of causation – the emanative and the covering-law one – then lead naturally to quite opposed assessments of the status of those more abstract terms, which figure in the causal laws. For the emanationists, they are names of real things, somehow responsible for the order specified in the law and providentially discovered through that very order. For the covering-law theories, it is natural to think of them as simple shorthand. But it is interesting to note that Popper, for instance, is simultaneously a warm adherent of the covering-law theory of explanation and a passionate realist and anti-instrumentalist. I am not suggesting that the two positions are in formal contradiction, but it would be interesting to know how the strain between them is resolved.

Although a hidden, austere, and orderly deity may be historically a crucial source of the descriptive–covering-law view of science and cognition (by simultaneously denying the prospect of the mind's penetrating to the heart of things, while at the same time holding out the promise of regularity and order, unlike earlier, more capricious and manipulable spirits), yet theism and emanationism can also be combined. Descartes did fuse them; he had the intuition, which most of us share, that all the various states of the world do not 'really' have the power to produce their successor situations, so that talking of one of them 'causing' the other is but shorthand. 'Really' what happens is that the deity directly generates both succeeding stages, and only their orderly continuity produces the illusion that one of them causes the other. Descartes was in effect an emanationist both with respect to the deity and the mechanical and extended realm, which persisted only because it was perpetually renewed by God. The only things that escaped this emanationism were the clear and distinct links of logical thought, whose validity had to antedate even the existence of God (though they were thereafter underwritten by God), because they alone established the existence of that God, and which were consequently independent of any emanationist core, so to speak. Just as in the movements on a watch dial, successive positions of the hands do not really cause each other, but are, all of them, caused by the central and hidden mechanism, so the successive states of such a natural system all flow from the hidden deity, rather than being 'really' linked to each other. Mechanical and theistic emanationisms have a certain resemblance to each other and were indeed fused by Spinoza. In a sense, the covering-law view of causation, which amounts to saying that there is no link, no 'power' connecting elements in a causal chain, that the only connection is in an extraneous law which is not intrinsically part of either of the connected events, is itself the consequence of an extreme emanationism: the perception that the links following each other are not really connected with each other but both emanate from a hidden core, when followed by the excision of that core (because we realise that, being inherently hidden, it is never accessible to us and hence irrelevant), leads to a Humean view of causation. Firstly, God absorbs all causal potency into Himself, making nature so to speak inorganic, inert. Then God is abstracted from this picture, and what is left is an inert, inorganic world in which connections can only be contingent regularities, noted *ex post facto*, but devoid of any inner necessity accessible to reason. In other words, Hume's account.

The repudiation of vacuous 'reduplication', the use of a transcendent realm that is merely a hidden way of referring to *this* realm that it purports to 'explain', is perhaps the most powerful philosophical motive for preferring the descriptive view of science and the associated law view of causation. But there is one region in which the reduplication of the world, the supposition of an independently existing substrate, somehow responsible for surface phenomena, is not absurd, presumptous, circular, and unwarranted – an area in which we really are allowed to peep behind the veil of Maia, and habitually do so: where the 'other' reality is accessible and really *is* known to exist. That area is the area of human performance.

In the human sphere, external experience of reduplication, contact with a second reality behind appearance, occurs in, at any rate, two forms: through the multiplicity of persons and through the passage of time. Let us take time as an example. A strict empiricist, nonreduplicationist, positivist attitude to the past, for instance, is to treat it simply as equivalent to the evidence about 'what we call the past' in the present, which alone is now eligible for experience. But we do not really believe that the past is merely the marks of the past in the present. (A. J. Ayer attempted at one stage to persuade himself of this and asserted such a view in print, but he admits now that he cannot sustain this heroic piece of positivist puritanism.) The past was once present, as *the present*, and it was real. The acts of historical personages that explain certain marks in the present are not merely summaries of those marks. They 'really' existed, and they explain those marks in this philosophically 'realist' way. Their being is not exhausted by their role as premises from which current data follow. They have a true reality of their own, transcending their explanatory instrumentality. And we believe the same, whether or not we can prove it, in connection with the independent existence of other selves.

Our faith in the independent existence of our own selves in the past gives us a kind of precedent for a similar kind of positivism-defying hubris with respect to other people.

And it is not merely the sheer existence of the reduplicated, transcendent, independently existing that is confidently affirmed in this sphere. Those transcendent objects do not merely exist; they are plausibly allowed to have purposive structures. So, at least in some measure, they are allowed to exhibit that fact–value, *Sein–Sollen* convergence that otherwise scandalises the empiricist conscience. Nature may not be allowed to be a language; but language at least *is* a language. Irrespective of whether it was designed by a creator or by the play of chance and natural selection, it is allowed to constitute a purpose-adjusted system. Whatever mechanism it is that generates all the sentences of a given language and excludes noise-sequences not acceptable in it does not merely 'exist' independently, but is allowed to be a purpose-serving system. As a system, it operates in a way to satisfy, in some measure, some specifiable requirements. The study of language, for instance, is the study of linguistic *competence*. In other words, it is the study of how a range of performances manages to satisfy certain criteria, which define competence within their realm. So, it is not merely legitimate, but actually inherent in the very inquiry, to assume that there is a system and that what it emits or generates satisfies a range defined by certain norms. A similar assumption in the study of nature might seem anthropomorphic; in the study of human competence, it is entirely appropriate. *Some* measure of anthropomorphism may be allowed in the study of man. But if this is so, then not merely the independent existence of the explanatory core structure but also its systematic and norm-satisfying nature may legitimately be assumed. So, in this field, we are not merely allowed to indulge in philosophical realism (the independent existence of external objects), but in, so to speak, morally saturated and heart-warming realism, which postulates that those extraneous realities form systems and satisfy norms.[3]

To sum up: in the human sphere, emanationism is alive and moderately well. At any rate; it is well enough to have some prospects of survival. The emanationist assumptions of the independent existence of systems that are more than mere shorthand summaries of the data and that are in some measure purpose-bound, or norm-satisfying, seem permissible, or perhaps mandatory, in this sphere.

This is one, but one only, factor underlying structuralisme: for structuralisme is a form of emanationism. But this is only one root among a number. We would misunderstand structuralisme if we thought this was all there was to it.

Let the scene now shift from the heady, stratospheric abstraction of explanation and causation in general (and the distinction between a nature that does *not*, and a culture that *does*, make reduplicationist purposiveness thinkable) and descend to the more concrete sphere of research into societies, and in particular into fairly small-scale societies, within the tradition of inquiry known as social anthropology. This tradition has for a long time had its own kind of humdrum structuralism – solid, earthy, blokey, and without any of that scent of the Left Bank that is forever attached to structuralisme. Within social anthropology, the old-fashioned, homely structuralism meant roughly this: a stress on groups, their organisation, and the constraints this imposed on the conduct of individuals. The idea was that a tribal society has a certain structure or organisation, each part of which imposed such pressures and sanctions on the individuals within it as to ensure that they behaved in a way that in turn sustained that structure, and so on for ever, or at any rate for quite a long time. Structure was important, a matter of serious concern for men (inside the society or among investigators). Culture, on

---

[3] J. W. N. Watkins, in 'Ideal Types and Historical Explanation', *British Journal for the Philosophy of Science*, 3, May 1952, 22–43, triggered off that record-breaking series of philosophical articles on 'methodological individualism' (philosophy's answer to *The Mousetrap* and still running strong). He argued, interestingly, for reduplication licence in human studies, invoking the authority of Lionel Robbins' views on the methodology of economics – we know man twice over, from inside and out. But he used this for a 'unity of science' conclusion, i.e., a view that does not radically distinguish methods in natural and social sciences (unless perhaps the obligation to attribute rationality, sometimes held obligatory in human studies, distinguishes them from natural ones). I am here arguing that it is the plausibility of reduplication in the human sphere, contrasted with its philosophical offensiveness in nature, which encourages structuralistes to return to an emanationist view of causation and explanation.

the other hand, was relatively ephemeral, accidental, epiphenomenal, and altogether suitable for women (inside the society or among investigators). Structure was, for instance, whom one could marry; culture was what the bride wore. Marriage restrictions or prescriptions were an important element in how the society actually worked; but the specific *tokens* or *symbols* by means of which categories of people were identified as marriageable, unmarriageable, eligible for political status, objects of aggression, etc. – that was a fairly trivial, superficial, and accidental matter. A token was required to identify this or that category of people, this or that ritual occasion. The classification or the ritual was important, but *which* token was used to mark it off was a matter of chance. *Structure* dictated where tokens were needed; accident or history (if indeed those two could even be distinguished) determined which concrete object was to serve as token. The deployment of tokens mirrored solid structure, but the specific nature of the tokens themselves mirrored nothing. No reason could be given, why, let us say, the colour *white* should be a sign of rejoicing in one society and of mourning in another. That could only be a historical accident and was barely worthy of the attention of a serious scholar, especially when it occurred in illiterate milieux in which historical accidents could not be established for lack of records.

This kind of anthropology was seriously concerned with structure, the organisation of groups for the serious ends of the maintenance of order and production, the allocation of roles and of obligations and of brides; and it was implicitly somewhat dismissive of culture – the set of symbols by which groups, roles, status, and so forth, were identified and recognized in a given society. Its implicit theory of culture was half an accident theory, half an echo theory. Cultural elements mirrored and thereby reinforced and sanctioned 'real' constellations of people on the ground. Culture was the decoration, often important for information or reminder, but without a direct structural role. The echo and the accident aspects of this theory of culture complement each other: it is an accident that this token signals this or that structural feature, but it is the structural features of the society that determine how many kinds of echo, roughly speaking, there are to be. I may be exaggerating or overstating a little this rather dismissive, somewhat Philistine attitude of the old structuralism to culture – but basically that was it.

It is significant that this kind of earthy structuralism was associated with the declared aspiration to turn anthropology into a natural science of societies. Structure was that part of society best amenable to the treatment. Hence there was order and regularity to be found, and these were not to be expected in the sphere of culture. There is a striking analogy between the use made by this kind of old structuralism of the distinction between structure and culture, and the Lockian distinction between 'primary' and 'secondary' qualities. It was primary quality that explained, and secondary that *was* explained. The primary quality was the central concern of science. Primary qualities like impenetrability resemble the economic and power relations of groups – in other words, structure. And just as secondary qualities are thought of as merely engendered by the interplay of primary ones and our senses, so cultural traits – the sartorial, gastronomic, linguistic, and other indicators of structure – are merely a kind of surface illusion produced by the contingent forms of the sensibility of the culture in question.

The ambience of *structuralisme* could hardly be more contrasted to that of *structuralism*. Its favoured areas are precisely in the realm of culture: symbolism, mythology, ritual, literature, art – the erstwhile secondary qualities of culture, and also, a little less congruently, kinship. Kinship may be the odd man out in the list; it may or may not be significant that in his study of Lévi-Strauss, Edmund Leach (*Lévi-Strauss*, London, 1970) singles out his celebrated work on kinship as the field in which he was least successful. But concentrating for the moment on the mainline concerns of structuralisme, it could be said that it has put culture into the very centre of anthropological concern, when it had previously been a kind of epiphenomenal echo. Whereas, by contrast, Lévi-Strauss, for instance, has on occasion vaunted his lack of interest in politics. Culture, it now appears, has its own structure of which the political system knows nothing.

It is not just the epiphenomenality of culture that is being denied (and that is being replaced by an implicit doctrine of the autonomy of culture or even an assertion of its centrality). It is the echo theory of culture that is firmly destroyed. Structuralisme has a theory of meaning that is, above all, a denial of the echo doctrine: the essence of a symbol is not its relationship to the thing symbolised. (In the empiricist theories of meaning, the symbol is a kind of shadow of what is meant or, in Hume's case, the concept is simply the after-taste of the experience.) Its essence is its place in a wider system of symbols. 'John' is given its meaning not by its relation to John but by its place in a system also containing 'Peter', 'Paul', and so on. The system is assumed to have its central set of rules, which generates everything that can occur within it. Any relationship to anything outside, one might add, is almost accidental. As in the case of old-fashioned structuralism, the actual token doesn't matter much; but whereas previously, what gave it life was its relation to the bit of reality that 'controlled' it or to which it referred or which it symbolised, now it has the breath of life infused into it by the core-generating mechanism that assigns a place to it. It should be said also that the new structuralistes can be found handling both meanings and the tokens that are their carriers: both equally are grist to this mill.

Empiricism was essentially an echo theory of knowledge. As Hume put it:

all our simple ideas . . . are derived from simple impressions . . . which they exactly represent.

Not surprisingly, when Radcliffe-Brown hoped to further an empirical science of society, he tended also to adopt an echo theory of culture. But Hume had to qualify his theory concerning the invariable origins of our ideas in our impression. There was the famous exception – the Blue Patch.

Suppose . . . a person to have enjoyed his sight for thirty years, and to have become perfectly well acquainted with colours of all kinds, excepting one particular shade of blue . . . which it had never been his fortune to meet with. Let all the different shades of that colour, except that single one, be placed before him, descending gradually from the deepest to the lightest: it is plain that he will perceive a blank, where that shade is wanting, and will be sensible that there is a greater distance in that place, betwixt the contiguous colours, than in any other. Now I ask, whether it is possible for him . . . to supply this deficiency, and raise up to himself the idea of that particular shade, though it had never been conveyed to him by his senses?

Hume answers his rhetorical question with an emphatic yes, but discounts this counter-example to the echo theory as 'so particular and singular, that it is scarce worth our observing'.

Evidently, because the 'missing shade of blue' is part of a spectrum we work with and comprehend, it generates a curious exception to the echo principle. The structuraliste approach, in a way, stands Hume on his head. This is no exception; on the contrary, this is the very paradigm of how we acquire ideas! It is only because our minds are sensitive to given spectra or polarities that impressions can provoke ideas in us. Our mind would be incapable of echoing anything not already found within the span of its sensibilities. So structuralisme seeks out the polarities that define our sensibilities.

So at the very centre of structuralisme, there is a preoccupation with culture – the set of concepts, symbols, etc., that men use – and a firm determination not to see it merely as a set of echoes (whether of things or of social groups and statuses), but instead, as a system that has its own rules, and to ensure that the manner in which its visible elements are generated is laid bare.

A version of structuralisme was already implicit, for instance, in

Wittgenstein's concept of a 'language game'. The point of that notion was to draw the reader's attention to the wide variety of such games, of systems of rules and elements, within which a given expression could have a role and hence a 'meaning'. What he was concerned with denying was the assumption that in language there was but one game, or only one game that mattered, namely that of matching linguistic units (sentences) with real-world units (facts). He held, rightly, that many theorists of language had assumed this; and he also held, quite wrongly, that what are known as philosophical problems are only or generally engendered by the failure to see this point. With the old view there also went a corresponding distinction between primary and secondary qualities, or a kind of logicians' and linguists' variant thereof: there was logical form – hard and solid – and its filling – ephemeral and secondary.

With the insistence on the diversity of games, or of structures as we can say in the present context, belief in such a neatly two-tier structured reality automatically vanished. There is no list of generic primary qualities, or secondary ones, holding over the entire variety of diverse language games. Diverse games draw quite different distinctions between the solid–substantial and the ephemeral, and some of them perhaps don't have such a distinction at all, or else have a multiplicity of them. There is a parallel here with structuralistes who also believe in a plurality of structures and who also do not look down on culture as secondary. There is also a striking similarity between Berkeley's assault on the primary–secondary distinction, through his attack on the notion of 'abstraction', and Wittgenstein's erosion of a neatly stratified world, through his attack on the notion of an underlying homogeneity of language. This assumption had played a part in the view he was destroying, entirely analogous to that attributed by Berkeley to 'abstraction'. If we could abstract, we could reach a generic substance-substratum; and if there was but one real kind of language use, its form gave us the general nature of reality – its primary qualities.

But there is also a difference between the structuralistes and Wittgenstein here. They do also seem to think that the various structures formally resemble each other and are rooted in some generically shared structure of the human mind. For Wittgenstein, the whole point of language games was their irreducible diversity.

The outlook known as structuralisme really emerges through the super-imposition of these two insights, or switches of vision. In two distinct spheres, an echo or reflection theory is denied: any set of human or cultural products are seen as really emanating from a persistent core system, emanating from it rather than merely consisting of linked elements in a sequence, and culture specifically is saved from being seen as a mere set of frills, pale shadows of true substance. The meanings that constitute it, again, are seen as systematically generated. On the one hand, epistemological realism takes over from the notion of 'explanation as shorthand and fiction', with its attribution of a merely instrumental, illusory status to the entities cited in an explanation; and on the other, an implicit sociological reductionism of culture, which had seen it as a mere set of reflections, in language, ritual, mythology, or whatnot, of the serious, weighty, substantial, structural relations in, as it were, masculine areas such as politics and the economy, is rejected. Henceforth, culture was to have its own structure, its own laws, emanating from its own persisting central core. It is odd that there should have been a Marxist-structuraliste *rapprochement*, given the Marxist view of the derivativeness of the superstructure. In part, the Marxist-structuralist syncretism was indeed also associated with doctrines conferring autonomy on theorising and intellectual activity, by treating it as one further form of *practice*. In part, I fear that those who operated this syncretism were not unduly fastidious logically. The Marxist-structuraliste union reminds me of the story of the celebrated head of a famous and very enlightened and liberal Cambridge college, who was heard to remark at a wedding, nodding at the happy couple: 'I have slept with both of them, and can recommend neither to the other.'

But the influence is richer still. There were other considerations and influences contributing to the sense that the correct or fruitful mode of explanation in human, social, or cultural studies is not subsumption under an extraneous law, but generation or emanation from a permanent core structure.

There are areas in which the pursuit of covering laws is fairly unpromising or outright hopeless, whereas the attainment of generative or emanative explanations, so to speak, is a perfectly reasonable prospect. As already stated, some realms of human activity tend to be like this, but not only human realms. In fact, covering-law and generative explanation can on occasion be related inversely. Take as an example a system that is more natural than human – namely, the roulette wheel.

The operation of the roulette wheel generates a sequence of numbers, usually between 0 and 32, also classifiable (but for the eccentric 0) as 'odd' and 'even', 'red' and 'black', etc. Now the sequence is not merely not subsumable under any law governing the pattern of numbers; the system is so designed as to ensure that this is not possible. And not merely is it not possible at the ground or phenomenological level, it is also not possible by means of that favoured strategy of covering-law theorists, i.e., by means of concepts at some remove from the ground-level phenomena. In other words, not merely is there no law saying that after a 3, we are to expect such and such a number, but equally, there are no subtler laws, of the form, let us say, of something like this: after *n* even numbers, expect an odd one. This is of course the main strategy of inquiry of the covering-law school: if, as is generally the case, no good laws are to be found in a given realm at the level of our initial and observational categorisations of objects or events in that field, we must reconceptualise the realms in 'deeper' terms that do lead us towards powerful generalisation. We do not talk physics in daily life, and few if any powerful generalisations can be stated in terms of the categories employed in daily life. But the language of chemistry and physics, while referring indirectly to an important proportion at least of the kind of events we deal with in daily life, does it in more abstract terms, not referring directly to the familiar objects of daily 'lived' experience, but making the formulation of laws possible.

But this strategy, which is the very essence of successful science as conceived by the law theorists, is not applicable to a well-built roulette wheel. Does, then, the sequence of a roulette wheel escape all explanation? If we were provided with such a sequence, from within a society whose manner of operation we did not yet understand, should we be obliged to give up in despair? Not in the least. Suppose an archaeologist from a society totally ignorant of roulette came across a partly decipherable document that in fact was the record kept by a croupier at a table in Monte Carlo. We'd better make our imaginary archaeologist a structuraliste, for we can then imagine him to be a very happy archaeologist indeed. As the language in which the croupier kept his record has not yet been mastered by the scholars of our structuraliste–archaeologist's culture circle, he does not know what those signs, like 'odd' and 'even' or 'red' and 'black', actually mean. But that does not worry him one little bit. In fact, it gives him pleasure. He is, after all, a structuraliste. Extraneous reference of a symbol is not a thing of great moment. It is the system of which it is a part that matters. The *structure* is the thing.

And here the *structure* is very plain. In fact it has that binary polarised quality that brings joy to his heart. Here is a system oscillating neatly between the polarities 'red' and 'black', 'odd' and 'even'. Whatever these terms refer to (and to hell with that), they clearly were the polar concepts entering into the construction of that world, indicating its limits, expressing its vital tensions. And what was more, this world had a number of such polarities and tensions, which combined and recombined with each other in all possible ways, thus neatly teaching the denizens of that world the limits and the dramas of their existence! And there was even, on occasion, an entry in the record, namely o, that apparently eluded those polarities. No doubt it was specially significant, indicating the ambiguous fusion, sublation, and temporary transcendence of the binary oppositions that made up that world. Clearly, the occurrence of o was a kind of climax in the series, an apex of the semantic triangle, an orgiastic suspension of the customary oppositions and of the law of the excluded middle, which like the famous suspensions of logic in central religious doctrines simultaneously signals the sacredness of the occasion and yet, by containing the suspended oppositions in an explosive, unstable, transient unity, reminds the believer of the bounds, oppositions, and tensions of the world over which the faith presides and on which it confers its conceptual structure. (As you can see, I too can write structuraliste prose when I set my mind to it.)

Let us leave the example of the roulette wheel. A roulette sequence is produced by natural, not social or conceptual, causation, though of course the significance of the series is social. I introduced the example because of its simplicity and because it shows how plausible, and in this case indeed fully valid, structuraliste explanations can be used in an area in which the searcher after covering laws is forever doomed to disappointment. But lest the example misleads someone, a point needs to be made. The shift from the search for covering laws to the pursuit of generative structures is not the same thing as the shift from causal to statistical explanation. In the case of the roulette-produced sequence, if our hypothetical archaeologist had a penchant for probability theory rather than for structuralisme, he would of course have spotted quickly that, though there seemed to be no causal order in the sequence, it was admirably amenable to calculations of probability. But that option, evidently open and indeed correct in this particular example, is not always available and, more important, is not always relevant. And that brings us to the other, more realistic precedents for the adoptions of the emanationist–generative approach.

Take the case of linguistics. Here, once again, as in the roulette case, the sequences of sounds as such are barely susceptible to causal covering laws, or any covering laws. As Chomsky observes, the probability of any one sentence being uttered at a given point of time is extremely small, so small as to be negligible. Probabilities of course attach to given sounds and sound patterns (if only because the number of phonemes in any language is finite, and indeed not very large). But these probabilities hardly exhaust linguistics.

On the contrary, revolution in linguistics some decades ago consisted precisely in the abandonment of the search for causal sequences, which would link linguistic sound patterns with antecedent situations in the extralinguistic world. *That* was the behaviourist programme, which simply confused the (plausible) doctrine that all assertions must be experimentally tested with the (absurd) view that all mental perform-ances, including assertions, must be uniquely tied to experiential antecedents. As Chomsky pointed out, the causes in the world that allegedly 'controlled' the utterances had to be invented *ad hoc* and *ex post facto*. In retrospect, this behaviourist search for the elements in the world of experience 'under the control of which' given linguistic utterances came to be made (a search given such effective ironic treatment by Chomsky) does indeed seem absurd. The new 'generative' strategy consists of attempts to specify the formal features of the core structure, from which the actual range of utterances recognised in a given language, as it were, emanates. It doesn't even try to show why a particular utterance occurred at a given time and given circumstance. It can only show how that utterance comes to lie within the bounds of the generative power of a given language. This powerful precedent no doubt provoked attempts at emulation in other areas of the human and social sciences. Whether indeed this strategy is as appropriate in other fields, whether their problems and circumstances are relevantly similar to linguistics, is something that needs to be examined.

Take the case of phonetics. As a matter of historical fact, certain developments in phonetics did indeed stimulate the efforts to develop a structuraliste method in anthropology. If I understand those advances in phonetics properly, they amount to the following: the sounds emitted by the human throat can be characterised by a set of binarily opposed characterisations, such that only one, but at least one, of each pair of opposites applies to any sound. Thus if the characterisations are A and $—A$, B and $—B$, C and $—C$, and so on, then every sound will be characterisable as simultaneously either A or $—A$, B or $—B$, and so on. Languages construct their 'phonemes', i.e., units of sound such that within the limits of one phoneme all sounds – despite whatever further subtle differences there might be between them – are interchangeable and make the same contribution to the meaning or role of an utterance. If the number of these opposed pairs is finite, as is the case, the number of possible phonemes is correspondingly finite. Languages do not exhaust all the possible phonemes available to them: they leave some of them unused, or they lump together classes of sounds that, in another language, are subdivided into a number of phonemes.

The influential precedent in phonetics has at least two very important features. One of them is what might be called its binarism. The generative mechanism is simple and really relies on the principle that each entity in the 'generated' realm must have one of two attributes, drawn one each from a finite set of pairs. Whether binarism can indeed be transferred from phonetics (without prejudice to the question concerning whether it works to perfection in that sphere, an issue on which I am not competent to speak), if so why so, and if not why not, are questions which deserve ample discussion. I see no reason why binarism should be transferable, though of course any finite set of distinctions can be presented as a series of nested binary ones.

Phonetic structuralisme, in this sense, achieves a kind of pleasing transcendence, or if you like, ontological penetration of reality. This is the second feature. Such penetration is seldom granted to us, and we must be grateful when we come across an example of it. As indicated at the beginning of the chapter, part of the appeal of structuralisme is that it links us with the old emanationist tradition, the hope that explanations give us not just shorthand summaries of surface patterns, but reveal for us a deep, permanent, morally saturated, and satisfying reality, qualitatively different from and superior to the ephemeral and amoral connections observed on the surface of things. Now it would be an exaggeration to say that phonetics propels us into some noumenal and moral realm. But, at a more modest level, phonetics does significantly bridge disparate regions and explains one in terms of another, and thus it does provide a very profound kind of explanation. The point is this: the binary characterisation of sounds, which provide the basic material, as it were, from which the bricks of language are made, are defined in *phonetic* terms, i.e., in terms of physically identifiable and definable properties, definable in neutral, interlinguistic, intersocial, physicalist, and operational terms. They are, so to speak, part and parcel of physics and not necessarily of any culturally specific perceptual space. But they generate phonemic elements, i.e., the bricks of individual languages, and these bricks – phonemes – notoriously are not the same in diverse languages.

Now this is very important. It shows how elements drawn from (or definable in terms of) the physicalist world generate the elements used for the inner phonetic world of distinct cultures – of specific linguistic communities. Given the shared and universal properties of sounds, the capacities of the human throat to produce varieties of them, and of the human ear to receive and discriminate between them, we can see how nature's material is turned into cultural bricks. The generative proto-type in phonetics, which has so much inspired structuralisme in anthropology, is a good if simple specimen of a genuine, illuminating explanation. It is of course noteworthy that all this has inspired an important piece of terminology in current anthropology, notably the distinction between 'etic' (from 'phonetic') and 'emic' (from 'phonemic').

By 'etic', an anthropologist means the characterisation of some social activity in terms appropriately used by an outsider, employing neutral, 'scientific' terminology; by 'emic', the characterisation of an activity in terms employed from the inside, by the natives themselves. If, in any given field of activity, we can identify the mechanisms by which etic materials are turned into emic meanings, we have achieved a great deal. There is of course no guarantee whatever that any given piece of emic significance can be explained as a transformation of etic materials at all. No doubt cultures possess 'private meanings', so to speak, which are not etically explicable at all; which, from the viewpoint of a scientistic philosophy, we could say the culture in question simply 'makes up' from its own head, as it were. Relativism could be redefined, I suppose, as the view that there aren't any etic concepts at all, really; that the soi-distant etic is merely somebody's emic (say that of members of twentieth-century western scientific communities), and that it wrongly and presumptuously claims a special, intercultural, or rather transcultural, privileged status. Whether this is so is an issue that can hardly be pursued here. Suffice it to say that while some anthropologists claim to hold such a relativist, etic-denying view in their working lives, in practice they behave like normal members of the western scientific community, speak 'etic' to each other most of the time or indeed all the time, and most or all of the theories and accounts they offer would simply make no sense unless this were so. In a world in which only 'emic' speech existed anthropology and comparative social studies simply would not make sense.[4]

---

[4] Some adherents of this modern form of relativism actually welcome this consequence, and are pleased that intersocial generalisations should be impossible. It enables them to treat all cultures as cognitively equal and exempt from rational criticism purporting to stand outside local cultural custom. If they extend this to their own culture (or whichever culture they favour), they are enabled to endorse what would otherwise seem to be archaic and logically indefensible beliefs. Holders of this view have received a curious reinforcement from Quine, who affirms the relativity of meanings under the name of the 'indeterminacy of translation'. His reasons are not, however, the usual ones (which are a kind of Herderian reverence for the privacy and dignity of each and every culture). Instead, his view follows in part from his exclusion of meaning from his own ontology, which in turn entails the impossibility of asserting identities of meaning (within as much as between languages), and hence excludes confident, or any, translations. This is all rather odd in so far as for other purposes operative within his philosophy he welcomes a rather physicalist–evolutionist account of the general role and manner of operation of those incommensurate clusters of ideas, allegedly debarred from communicating with each other owing to the absence of a shared, universal conceptual currency. Yet they are all described in terms of building

Now let us consider logic and metamathematics. This important and active field seems to have shifted in the twentieth century from a Cartesian to a generative or emanationist paradigm. When logic was revived around the turn of the century as part of an attempt to provide a firm basis for mathematics, the idea present in the minds of at least some of the practitioners was that the 'logicisation' of mathematics would lead to a science exemplifying the Cartesian ideal – a firm base, providing a kind of risk-free, or at least minimally risky, foundation, giving virtually no hostages to cognitive fortune and transmitting this security by means of rigorous reasoning to the entire edifice erected on it. Partly, but only partly, for technical reasons that undermined the faith in the feasibility of the exercise, this ideal no longer seems to haunt the subject. The picture is now quite different. The general strategy seems to be the exploration of the generative power of an artificially invented or postulated core and mapping it against the actual practices of mathematicians.

In substantive or empirical fields, the contrast is between emanative or generative explanation on the one hand and linear or law-linked causation on the other. In formal fields such as mathematics, emanation is contrasted not with any kind of causation (which is absent) but with deduction. The background picture in the field now seems to be this: the working mathematician does indeed work by a kind of natural deduction, employing principles of inference that he does not formalise. But mathematical logic is concerned with constructing formal systems within which the elements (axioms, inference rules, and so on) of the central structural core are strictly specified, and where the practitioner is concerned, precisely, with understanding the limits of what this system can or cannot generate. The logical understanding of mathematics then consists of mapping the relatively intuitive, naturally deductive work of mathematicians on to such formal generative models. If I am right in supposing that this is the pervasive spirit of the subject now, then it in turn provided a precedent and model for the endeavour to practise *structuralisme* in other areas of inquiry. I have little doubt but that this persuasive and prestigious exemplar did indeed exercise such an influence.[5]

world-pictures as extrapolations from their own sensory stimuli, with a view to predicting the pattern of further such stimuli – an account of cultures and world-views that not only leaves out a large part of what interests anthropologists and other philosophers but that also seems to presuppose that there is a single world and an optimal, if not uniquely correct, idiom for describing it, after all (see Quine, *La Philosophie analytique*, Paris, 1962, p. 139 and E. Gellner, *Spectacles and Predicaments*, Cambridge, 1979, chs. 11 and 12).

[5] See A. Musgrave, 'Logicism Revisited', *British Journal for the Philosophy of Science*, 28, no. 2, January 1977.

The 'generative' paradigm stands contrasted with *both* causation *and* deduction, when either of these is conceived as God-given or nature-given, to be accepted and simply explored for the connections that they just bring with themselves. Instead, the notion *generativeness* contains the key insight that whatever connections emerge on the surface are there as manifestations of the permanent core, and it is the core and the rules that link it to the surface that must be understood. The surface connections on their own have no explanatory power.

Structuralisme is basically a shift back to an emanative or generative model of explanation, from a linear or covering-law model. It is inspired partly by the consideration that when we handle cultural products, systems that men make even if they are not conscious of so doing, we believe that the central generative core or structure really is there, and our faith in this is not eroded by the empiricist interdict on inventing reduplicative and inaccessible 'other realms' when explaining the patterns of this, our accessible world. The shift is further reinforced by a transfer of attention to systematic cultural productions such as mythology, away from spheres that are so much cultural products as the result of an interplay of social and natural forces – notably, economic and political life. It is reinforced further still by apparently successful implementations of a similar strategy in linguistics, phonetics, mathematical logic, and possibly other areas.

This is itself, so to speak , the generative core of structuralisme – the elements present in the minds of actual structuralistes that manifest themselves in their actually visible, surface productions. Hence, this is the point at which it is appropriate to sketch out the overall syndrome of structuralisme.

Structuraliste work tends to exhibit the following traits:

(1) It operates with a theory of meaning that is systematic rather than representational. The meaning of a sign is its place in a system of signs, rather than its relationship to a special bit of the world of which it should be the *Doppelgänger* or shadow.

(2) The system is assumed to be generated by a kind of core set of elements or structure, persisting independently, and at least ideally located in a realm of being other than that of its own generated manifestations.

(3) A society or culture is assumed either to be, or at least to be very intimately linked to, such a system, comprising both core and manifestations.

(4) It is generally assumed that the core elements occur in

contrasted pairs, or if you like, that each of them splits into a pair of polar opposites. This might be called 'Binarism'.

(5) The core not merely genuinely exists – this approach involves a realist, not an instrumentalist theory of explanation – but also persists unchanged over time. Otherwise it could hardly extend its explanatory cover over manifestations occurring at diverse and successive dates.

(6) Structuralisme either actually favours cultural products (myths, rituals, literature, gastronomy), or at the very least treats them as equal in importance to the 'hard' elements of social life (order-enforcement, production). It is quite free of that anthropological equivalent of the distinction between primary and secondary qualities that is the old distinction between structure and culture, where the latter is assumed to be both accidental and largely epiphenomenal.

(7) When contemplating cultural products, be it say an epos or a menu, a structuraliste will seek out the opposed extremes on or in it and assume them to be the limits of the world in question *and* to be parts of the generative core that produced it. This might be called the method of 'beating the bounds'.

(8) For structuralistes, meaning is the very material of their inquiry, not merely something that accompanies, precedes, or possibly helps explain or characterise conduct.

All these various traits are of course not fully independent. For instance, the preferences for cultural products and for meaning are clearly connected and overlap. If I have separated these in effect intertwined strands, it is simply because one aspect or another of structuralisme may be more manifest from various angles, and it is worth while including them all. Also, it should not be assumed that all these elements are necessarily consistent. For instance, the timelessness of the explanatory core structure does not tally with the identification of such a structure within a society, given that societies notoriously have a habit of changing over time. Or again, is it really plausible to equate the polar extremes found in the manifestations of a culture with the core-generating elements, given that, in a well-constructed generative explanation, core explanans and surface explanandum may be expected to be articulated in different idioms, to be made of different materials?

These are some of the inner strains that may be expected to appear in structuralisme, if I have identified its essence correctly. But I shall concentrate on some of the main weaknesses or doubts one may have about the unqualified or uncritical application of the structuraliste approach to the study of human societies.

The structuraliste approach is not interested in surface or linear sequences; it is assumed that the full range or potential, as it were, of the generative core in question will play itself out, and that the precise order of appearance of the cards, so to speak, does not matter. The pack has a certain number of cards; all of them will sooner or later be played; and we work out the nature of the pack from the run, whatever its order. This assumption has to hold if the structuraliste approach is to make sense.

Does it? It does in certain spheres. No wonder structuralisme has been influenced by linguists, and no wonder that areas such as mythology, ritual, and symbolism are favoured by it. The point about the symbol tokens used by systems such as language is that they are *cheap*, the opportunity-cost of using them is virtually zero. Sounds, marks on the paper, symbolic gestures, all cost virtually nothing in terms of effort or any other price involved. That, no doubt, is one of the reasons why they came to be used as such.

To appreciate the significance of this, imagine a contrary situation. Imagine, for instance, that the letters of the alphabet constituted an economically scarce resource, which had to be secured by production or trade. Think of the following articles in the financial sections of the press:

The Polish economy is in dire straits owing to the continued shortage of Łs, without which it cannot function. The only unexhausted high-yield Ł-ore is now found in central Asia, and the Soviet government has shamelessly used this as a means of pressurising the Poles. The recent patented process for extracting Łs from the sea has proved uneconomical, and the Polish government now places hopes in its deep Ł-drilling in the Carpathians. If this fails, Ł-rationing will be imposed both on the Polish press and on private correspondence. The town council of Łodz has offered a large prize for the most suitable renaming of the city.

Or again:

A question is to be asked in Parliament about the alleged continued dumping of Hs in the British market by both the Russians and the French, neither of whom has any uses for Hs. This, however, is ruining what is left of the old Lancashire H-industry. Several Lancashire MPs of both parties are planning both to approach the Chancellor of the Exchequer with a view to introducing import restrictions on Hs, and the Minister of Education with a request that elementary schools be asked to redouble their efforts against the dropping of Hs, a habit that continues to have a severely adverse impact on the H-market.

Or again:

Following an initiative by the Swedish Ministry of Trade, the Scandinavian countries have agreed to set up a joint board for the supervision of the trade and production of ǿs, without which the Scandinavian economies cannot operate. The Danish parliament has approved the setting up of a commission that is to investigate the compatibility of this board with Denmark's obligations under EEC rules.

Now the whole point is this: in fact, the entities used in symbolism and communication operate under a rather special economy, without scarcity. Or, better, the other way round: symbolic systems choose as their units, their vehicles of communication, elements whose cost approaches zero. Because this is so, but *only* because it is so, or in so far as it is so, we can expect symbolic systems to play out their full inner potential, so to speak; and for this very reason, we can infer from the range of their production the nature of the core mechanism that produces them. The range of surface phenomena produced is not distorted by shortages, not affected by rising and falling prices. The zloty may not be worth much, but the Ł is free, and the Polish government can print as many Łs as it likes without fearing that the resulting inflation will make them unusable. Their use is already predicted on the assumption that they are to be had for free. A very, very tired and exhausted Pole may on occasion be too weary to utter even an Ł, but the majority of members of the Polish speech community can expand or contract their simultaneous production and consumption of Łs without batting an eyelid. In fact, as far as speech is concerned, we are *already* in that realm of plenty in which, as Marx foresaw, the distinction between work and self-expression lapses. It is a pity that no philosopher noticed this intriguing fact before. It could have been used to cheer us up.

But large segments of social life – need we be told? – do not operate under such blessed conditions. The economy is in effect defined by economists in terms of *scarcity*. Politics, again, is a realm that seems to be a zero-sum game; power for some means less power for others. The same holds true of prestige and status. (Some must lose, and somehow or other be constrained to accept their loss. In the telling of a story, neither narrator nor listeners need to be losers; and in *such* a situation, it is plausible to suppose that an *un*constrained code plays itself out to the full, freely releasing all its potential. But other aspects of life are not so free of constraint, conflict, and painful choice or inevitable loss *somewhere*.) In brief, there are extensive aspects of human life, alas including those that seem essential for our survival, where the actual sequence of events is determined not merely by the free play of some underlying core mechanism (if indeed it exists at all), but by the blind constraints, shortages, competitions and pressures of the real extraneous environment. A large part of the social sciences has been rightly concerned with an attempt at understanding how that kind of extraneous and straight–causal constraint can be fused with the emanative, unconstrained free play of a generative mechanism. Are we justified in trying to apply the structuraliste paradigm here? My invented examples treated phonemes as raw materials. Are structuralistes justified in treating raw materials as phonemes?

Frazer would wish us to believe that the priest at Nemi suffered himself to be killed, victim to nothing more than the association of ideas. I find it just as hard to believe that he should perish merely because his death was a message in the generative code of a culture. *Pace* the structuralistes, although society does use codes, society is *not* a code. What happens in a society cannot be inferred from even a successful working-out of the range-potential of its code, whether that code be conceived as (literally) a language or a 'tradition' or even a set of persisting institutions.

Closely related to this objection is another one. The generative or emanationist model of explanation makes sense in contexts in which there is reason to suppose that there is indeed a persisting, reasonably stable core structure, responsible for the emanations or surface phenomena. In the case of human language, this is indeed so. Notoriously, the best-known and most provocative thesis associated with the emergence of the idea of generative grammar is precisely the existence of an invariant, universal and innate linguistic human potential, activated into being and given its superficial phonetic and other traits by the experience of a specific language, but possessing a basic form manifested equally in any human language and not dependent on any. This ultimate core is assumed to be located in human neurophysiology in a manner that is not yet quite beyond the power of neurophysiologists to locate. Even if we think of the more specific generative core of a single language (as opposed to that ultimate core shared, according to this theory, by all languages), the existence of such a permanent and stable core structure is perfectly plausible. The corpus of phonetic, syntactical, and any other rules that define a given natural language can be assumed to be built into the customs of an ongoing community of the users of that language, rather in the way that some heavy object can be carried by a large number of bearers and remain unaffected by the perpetual dropping out of some bearers and their replacement by others. This is evidently how languages do perpetuate themselves. They do of course change, but they change rather slowly: compared with the speed with which single concrete utterances follow each other, languages change so slowly that they are stable for all practical purposes. They do flow, but so do glaciers; the flow of a glacier does not prevent a mountaineer or skier from treating the glacier as a fixed object.

But what is true of glaciers and languages is *not* generally true of societies and institutions. Above all, though a language is in a sense 'made up' of the utterances that occur in it, the utterances do not modify it (or only very seldom and trivially). There is no feedback from utterances to language – from *parole* to *langue*. Very, very occasionally, an earth-shaking political speech, a brilliant witticism by a man of letters or a comedian, may from the moment of its utterance introduce a new turn of speech into the language. But this is rare, and even when it happens, it does not modify the language in any very serious way. But does this hold of institutions and communities?

Some may indeed approach this kind of stability – but even then, it must be said, they only do so rather precariously, and the distance between *parole* and *langue* is, in their case, incomparably smaller than it is for (literal) languages. It might be said, for instance, that in a relatively long-lived and fairly stable institution such as the British parliament, the rules of parliamentary procedure, the core structure that limits the pattern of activities in parliament, change rather slowly and are not effects by individual performances within parliament. But even in this rather exceptional and privileged case, which might perhaps be paralleled in the rituals of stable and long-lived religions, the ratio of structural, dispositional change to episodic performance is far greater than is the case in language. If one multiplies the few hundred parliamentarians by an estimate of the number of parliamentary speech acts performed by them per generation and relates the resulting figure to the amount of deep change occurring as a result of new political situations in a generation, the resulting ratio must be far, far smaller than the ratio of speech acts performed by even small linguistic communities per generation, related to the amount of changes in a language per generation.

But in any case, whatever the result of such calculations (which would of course depend on how we decided to count acts and changes), the procedural rules of stable institutions such as the British parliament are not, for better or for worse, typical of human institutions and societies in general. In many political and economic activities, important events and decisions modify the core itself. To put it another way, there is no stable and independent core that is reasonably insulated from events in the sequence on the surface. Or to put it another way still, changes in the core are parts of the surface sequence itself. Or to put it yet another way, no useful distinction can be drawn between a core-generating structure and a generated surface sequence. For better or for worse, that is our condition, at least in very many of our activities. This may or may not make life more interesting; but one price paid for it is that the activities for which this observation holds are not easily amenable or are not amenable at all to the structuraliste paradigm. All this is merely another way of saying something that others have noted previously: it is puzzling how structuralisme could cope with basic change. It can really cope with diachronic phenomena only by treating them as synchronic – as accidentally successive manifestations of a stable, permanent core.

Another aspect of this point is that in some of the fields in which structuralistes try to impose it, one has some difficulty in imagining just where the central core could possibly be located. With language, we have no such difficulty: neurophysiology plus the disembodied, diffused, collectively carried rules of a natural language, spread out over the perpetually repeated language use of an entire community, are perfectly reasonable candidates for the locus or carrier of the core. In other spheres, no such candidate-loci seem to be easily available. This does not seem to bother structuralistes too much, but they seem to me wrong not to worry about it, for it deserves serious consideration. There is an irony in the structuraliste-Marxiste flirtation or *rapprochement*: Marxism is supposed to insist on a material base and on change. As far as I can see, the whole bias of the structuraliste model favours the assumption of timelessness, and its practitioners do not seem to mind too much when the base–core is allowed, in what would seem to be a somewhat idealist spirit, to float in thin air.

One could put it like this: structuralisme is a bit like reconstructing a pack of cards from the record of a run of dealt cards. This method works if there *is* a stable, permanent pack; and also if there is nothing that systematically interferes with the dealing out of the cards. But suppose some censoring mechanism inhibits the dealing of certain cards? If there is some such interfering mechanism, it too must be understood; or, perhaps we should say, it must be understood *first*. In the life of real societies, some of these mechanisms have familiar names – such as coercion or economic constraint.

This analogy also breaks down or is incomplete. The operation of dealing cards from a pack is easily understood. The mechanisms by which visible, surface elements emerge from a permanent cultural core are *far from* being self-evident or transparent. Cards are the same whether they sit in the pack or whether they are dealt. No such manifest identity can be assumed in cultural 'generation'. On the contrary, one may suspect that the materials used in the deep and surface structures are *not* identical, and a good explanation must show just *how* the one 'produces' the other.

Just this constitutes another and, once again, related objection to the practice of structuralistes. The method is valid if we are, so to speak, shown the generation of one world from materials drawn from another, above all independently identifiable, world. In the privileged case of phonetics, it was apparently shown that, drawing on the realm of physically identifiable noises, the range of socially significant noises, i.e., phonemes, could be extracted. Given the psychologically established competence of the human ear to distinguish the available combinations of those paired opposites, and given the sociolinguistically established capacity of speech communities to carry appropriate sub-sets of the available usable potential phonemes and to bring them effectively to the attention of children who are being socialised into them – given all that, it really has been shown how the phonemic world of particular cultures is constructed out of the phonetic world kindly provided by nature. The elements of the surface are explained in terms of the rather different elements of the core structure.

In the actual work of structuralistes dealing with phenomena such as mythologies or works of literature or rituals, I often fail to detect signs of any such achievement. There does not seem to be even any attempt to locate some deeper level so as to explain the surface in terms of it. Instead, elements plucked by some mysterious process from the surface text – usually the alleged polar extremities occurring in it – are attributed a kind of double status, both marking the limits of the emic world in which they occur and also being somehow mysteriously credited with being the (etic?) bricks out of which that inward world of the culture in question has been constructed. Can they really be both?

Now this particular objection could not be raised against those two great proto-structuralists – Immanuel Kant and Emile Durkheim. I am not defending either the former's *Critique of Pure Reason* or the latter's *Elementary Forms of the Religious Life* from other criticisms that can be raised against them. But they are, both of them, gloriously free of this particular blemish. In the great *Critique*, Kant endeavours to show how the emic world of all men (strictly, all beings endowed with our kind of reason), who for him formed but one single culture, was inevitably generated from the combination of certain core elements. Given that we are beings with sensibility (receiving sensations with spatial and temporal dimensions), and given that we had 'reason and understanding', by which he meant basically the capacity to group individual objects under generic concepts and the capacity to combine concepts into judgements and to erect pyramidal systems of concepts and judgements – given all that, he thought he could show how a certain world, containing substances, causal order, a single deity, and even Newton, inevitably emerged. A kind of minimal epistemological receptor is postulated with only the equipment specified in the *Critique*, and a habitable *Lebenswelt* tumbles out as a consequence – a world fit for Newtonian scientists and Pietist Protestants to live in. I am not suggesting that the execution of this programme was flawless, and I do not wish to defend Kant against the charge that the generated world bears little resemblance to *some* human worlds and at the same time a suspicious excess of resemblance to one special world – that of conscientious, orderly, unitarian, and science-orientated Protestants. But at least the programme itself satisfied an important criterion for a genuine structuraliste explanation. It led us from one level to another. The items used at the explanans level were very economically, non-arbitrarily chosen; and the elements in the generated explanandum would bear some resemblance to a world actually inhabited by some of us.

The same can be said of Durkheim. There is an irony about this, given Durkheim's expressed preference for explaining the social by the social. In a sense, the reason why *Elementary Forms* is such an interesting achievement is precisely because he did not follow this precept in it. The distinctively social and human (the possession of shared, compulsive, categorical concepts) is explained in terms of something that could be pre-social – namely, ritual. *Ritual maketh man.* This seems to me analogous to the phoneticians' achievement of explaining the phonemic in terms of the phonetic. I am not saying that Durkheim's theory is actually true, only that it satisfies the requirement that the explanans and the explanandum be at different levels (rather than at the same level and presupposing each other), and that it is plausible. Bertrand Russell ridiculed the 'social-contract' theory of the origin of language, which would have an assembly of hitherto speechless elders solemnly agreeing henceforth to call a cow a 'cow'. Durkheim's version would have a group of hitherto behaviourist, associationist, conceptless elders, persistently indulging in common rituals, which would *eventually* imprint and impose shared, compulsive concepts on them, thus rendering them human and beyond the reach of a merely stimulus–response (S–R), behaviourist model of conduct, and thus also propel them into the realm of thought proper. And this theory is not absurd – whether or not it is accurate.

For Kant, the generative core was not accessible to observation, but could be inferred by reasoning that locates the presuppositions of our world, our cognitive and moral judgements. For Chomsky, the core is only contingently unobservable; we infer it, but one fine day neurophysiologists may actually locate it. For Durkheim, the core was *already* observable by anthropologists. Ritual conduct had for him a kind of double ontological status: on the one hand, it was accessible to observation by the field researchers, and on the other it constituted at least part of the core that engendered our conceptual powers. Durkheim seemed to think (erroneously, I suspect) that a Humean-behaviourist–S–R psychology might work for animals, but failed with us because it could not account for the *compulsiveness* of categorical and moral concepts.

In the realm of sound, we can go to the *sub-* or basement-world of physics in order to explain the ground-level phonemic world of the sounds we perceive; and the same is possible in the sphere of colours, and indeed Edmund Leach in chapter 2 of his *Lévi-Strauss* chooses this realm to explain what structuralisme is about. But when it comes to our *entire* cultural–conceptual world, the world we live in, do we have any sub-world, some neutral base, the combinations of which would explain the bricks on our world? We have not. In practice, structuralistes then explain our world or the world of a given culture in terms of itself – of (arbitrarily?) selected polar elements within itself. Finally there is also in structuralisme a certain ambiguity concerning whether each culture has a single generative core from which its myths and rituals emanate or whether the hunt is on for a universal, panhuman core, manifested by the cultural products of *all* societies.

But our latter-day structuralistes seldom seem even to try to emulate Kant and Durkheim and locate a sub-basement that would explain the range of output of a culture or of mankind. They are content to stay at the same level, explaining a cultural world in terms of itself, merely underlining its alleged salient polarities. Admittedly, it would be appallingly difficult to do the other thing: the world of meanings of any one culture is no doubt infinitely more complex than its phonemic world. And we have little indication where on earth (literally) we could look for those pre-semantic elements that would explain the semantic to us. We have no other world to supply the bricks of this one.

The failure to be fastidious about the logic of their programme or the precision of its execution seems to me closely associated with another habitual failing. Not only are the polar extremes of a text simply plucked out and then treated as somehow explanatory of the world that the users of the said text live in, but no criteria are offered for how one is to identify the crucial polarities of a world from any old contrast that a willing and imaginative observer may locate in it. The structuralistes seem to be far too willing simply to trust their intuitions in this matter and to expect their readers to extend this trust to them. Polar extremities no doubt abound in many texts, but has anyone ever put it to the test by locking diverse structuralistes in insulated cubicles with the same text and seeing whether they all emerge with the same binary opposition in the end? And if they do not, as I suspect would be the case, how do we know which one of them got it right? Answer comes there none. If these suspicions are well founded, the conclusion could be that in these fields, the structuraliste method consists of a somewhat arbitrary extraction of polar patterns at the whim of the individual structuraliste virtuosos. As for binarism, I see no reason for even suspecting it to be true, any more than the Aristotelian doctrine of virtue as a 'mean' between two extremes, which it resembles. Admittedly any linear spectrum must point toward two extremes, but I see no reason for supposing that such spectra are the only ultimate constituents of our cultural worlds.

A number of cautions should be borne in mind. A descriptive account of the spectra or polarities with which a given society or language works is *not* the same as a generative account of how these spectra are produced. In other words, one should not confuse, so to speak, descriptive or phenomenological structuralisme with a genuinely explanatory kind. (The former is often presented as if it were the latter.) Moreover, a sheer highlighting of our polarities is not even a proper description of a world: it does not tell us how they mesh into each other or whether they are exhaustive. And is there necessarily only one unique way of distinguishing the polarities of a given cultural world? These questions do not seem to be faced seriously when the structuraliste fireworks are being let off.

All these doubts do not amount to an indiscriminate rejection of structuraliste ideas and methods. They merely amount to a recommendation of caution in the application of these ideas to fields other than those in which they were originally fruitful, and likewise, a recommendation of greater thoroughness, and fastidiousness in working out the implications of those ideas even in the fields in which they may indeed be applicable.

6 | No *haute cuisine* in Africa[1]

The brilliant, illuminating and intellectually cohesive tradition known as social anthropology has long been dominated in Britain by the thought and research styles established by Bronislaw Malinowski. Those who were close to him and attended his seminar at the LSE were the Companions of the Prophet. Many of them are still with us, active and productive; but they are by now, all of them, in retirement. In the senior unretired cohort which follows them, Jack Goody is an outstanding figure. In Eastern Europe, there is a joke about the current generation of Communist leaders, which says that its coming was predicted in the Bible: 'then came a generation which knew not Joseph'. Jack is prominent amongst those who knew not Bronislaw.

So, one is bound to look in his latest book for evidence about the way anthropology is going. In his previous work, Jack Goody has already done a great deal to give the subject a new direction. In his *Technology, Tradition and the State in Africa* he showed how an anthropologist's fine sense of the intimate internal texture of societies can be combined with systematic comparison and a sense of historical context and cumulation. At the same time, his sustained invocation of the means of coercion (or of destruction, in his phrase) was an invaluable corrective to the Marxist fantasy of a world dominated in the end by the means of production, with coercion as merely secondary. (Marxists actually talk of the 'idealist theory of violence', meaning the allegedly erroneous supposition that political domination, purely self-serving and not at all the instrument of any pre-existing economic class, could ever be the basis of a social system. It is ironic that an ideology which has helped to engender just such a system should also deprive itself of any language in which to describe it.) His work on the reproduction of the domestic unit has helped to relate anthropological questions to historical material. He has been toying with a schema of European history, linking it to kinship patterns. Crudely summarised, it runs as follows. First, tribal groups were perpetuated by the regulated allocation of brides. Eventually, the

---

[1] A review of Jack Goody: *Cooking, Cuisine and Class: A Study in Comparative Sociology*, Cambridge, 1982, 253 pp.

Church breaks up these kin units by extending the range of marriage prohibitions – in the interest of laying its hands on the land which ceases to be guarded by the now eroded kin groups. (Isolated individuals, scared about their own fate in the after-life, and with no ever-perpetuated group to worry about, eagerly bequeath their lands to the Church.) This situation, however, eventually helps to engender an individualist society in which the Church itself loses both power and land. This sequence, it seems to me, constitutes an improvement on the Hegelian formula, according to which mankind proceeded from a stage when only *one* was free, to a second stage when *some* were free, and a final fulfilment when *all* were free. In the less starry-eyed and more plausible Goody version, we go from a first stage when you *must* screw your cousins, to a second stage when you *may not* do so, leading to a final free-for-all when you do *everybody*.

Goody's volume, once again, makes a major contribution to an overall theoretical issue in the discipline. There is a piquancy about this subject-matter of food. An outsider, at any rate if of genteel background, might suppose that there is something a bit gross and vulgar about a keen interest in food. (I remember a colleague telling me how embarrassed he was in front of his grammar-school friends by his own working-class father's passionate and loud interest in food, until he went on to Oxbridge and found that at the top, it is once again perfectly in order to be demonstratively concerned with it.) You might well suppose that in the debate between idealists and materialists, the former would concentrate on the role of ideas and the latter, on the importance of sustenance. We must eat before we think. Grub first then morals, says Brecht. Man is what he eats, the German pun insists. So you might expect materialists to haunt the kitchen and scullery, and idealists to browse in the library.

If indeed you suppose that this is how scholarly interest in ideas and in grub is distributed, you'd be making a great mistake. Ideology is the favourite subject of Marxist writers. In fact, they can't keep off it. But if you want studies of that most earthly of our conditions of self-perpetuation, you must go to our neo-idealists. They are at it so much that they lend themselves to, and have provoked, parody. Jack Goody tells us of one such parody which appeared as early as 1968, *La Langue verte et la cuite: étude gastrophonique sur la marmythologie musiculinaire*, by Jorn and Arnaud. I'm glad Jack warned me that this is a parody, for otherwise I might have struggled with it in an attempt to make some sense of it. It wouldn't be the first time in modern thought that the parody was indistinguishable from its object.

The reader may not be aware that idealism is a strong, possibly a dominant, element in contemporary thought. Not under that name, of course. The notion, however, that our life should be understood not in terms of constraints, operating through fear or hunger, but, on the contrary, that what really guides social life are symbols and meanings and systems thereof, codes, etc., is extremely widespread, in and out of anthropology, and is associated with slogans such as 'hermeneutics' and 'structuralisme'. Under these slogans, it has constituted one of the major attempts to modify or transcend the Malinowskian tradition, to go beyond Bronislaw. Though people of this turn of mind have also applied themselves to texts, some of their most celebrated recent work was not about what comes out of our mouths, but what goes into them. Jack Goody sums up the views of the most influential amongst them:

> Language is therefore the model for the analysis of socio-cultural phenomena, which are interpreted in terms of communication, that is to say, of exchange. Women are like words in language systems and goods in economic systems, objects of circulation.

He then proceeds from summary to direct quotation of Lévi-Strauss:

> The rules of marriage serve to ensure the circulation of women between groups, just as economic rules serve to ensure the circulation of goods and services, and linguistic rules the circulation of messages.

Though there are indeed important parallels between these diverse fields, their assimilation to each other, the suggestion that language provides a model for the understanding of the others, seems to me bizarre. Verbal messages are cheap, sounds can be uttered almost effortlessly, whilst goods and women are often scarce. This totally transforms the rules of the game. There is a great difference between emitting a message, which costs me virtually nothing, and which I can sometimes do simply to fill time, and giving a daughter in marriage, which deprives her household of origin of her labour and her offspring. Communication and exchange cannot be so easily equated – as Goody's summary seems to concede and imply, in a disturbingly *en passant* manner, as if nothing contentious were being said.

A message can only convey information if it is one of a number of possible alternative messages. (The technical sense of 'information' hinges on this, and the amount of 'information' is in the end a matter of how many alternative constellations a given system can display: how *rare*, if you like, the message-conveying constellation of the system is, within the total set of possible constellations. Whether in fact the alternative states of the system are then actually linked to actual messages is left open.) But when goods or people are exchanged by social groups, it is *not* an essential part of this process that alternative goods or personnel also be available for exchange: or if they are available, if another daughter is to hand as a bride to be given away, this, significantly, does not alter the message. If any message is conveyed, it hinges more on the selection of donor and recipient than on the object or person exchanged, which may be rigidly prescribed. All this highlights the difference between communication and exchange, and the weakness in the recent tendency to assimilate them to each other.

Moreover, the significance of real semantic messages and of ordinary objects or persons exchanged, as evidence of status within the societies in which they occur, is quite different. It is perfectly possible that a culture plays out all its phonetic and/or conceptual possibilities in its utterances and in its myths. Hence, when these are recorded, one can work back from the text to the core generating mechanism which can be assumed to be responsible for them. But the range of political and economic possibilities is seldom, we can safely assume, played out to the full. The cost of the tokens in this game is too great, and there are too many constraints imposed by reality on their unlimited deployment. Many possible constellations of the system are never actualised, because they are contrary to the interests or inclinations of the participants. So we have no reason to suppose that the record as it were exhausts the social possibilities. Hence the possibilities which are actually realised are a very incomplete guide to the full powers and nature of the core generating mechanism, and moreover, we are more interested in those limiting constraints than we are in the hypothetical core mechanism.

No doubt cultural tokens do form systems of a kind which need to be explored, but the analogy has been greatly overplayed, and has been used without care. Take the celebrated 'culinary triangle' of Lévi-Strauss, discussed by Goody, which is meant to isolate the basic elements of the gastronomic language: the raw, the cooked and the rotten. Now everything I consume must be either in its original state (raw), or modified by human agency (cooked), or modified by natural process unaided by man (rotten). No other possibility exists. The classification is exhaustive as it works by residue at each stage. The triangle is not the hidden secret, the deep structure of our culinary messages: it simply conveys a tautology. This being so, no wonder that the aim of the analysis based on it is not, as we are told on the next page, to provide 'exhaustive knowledge' of specific societies, but 'to derive constants which are found at various times from an empirical richness and diversity that will always transcend our efforts at observation'. Well, yes. You can be quite sure that anything you've ever eaten will always have been drawn from within that triangle, which does indeed define the very bounds of our gastronomic world. . .

I am reminded of one of the dreariest phenomena in the Soviet Union, namely the fact that many restaurants, including specialised ethnic ones such as Georgian or Uzbek ones, tend to use the very same menu, evidently supplied by the Central Commissariat of Menus. It is a small booklet containing sections of Russian, Ukrainian, Armenian, etc., etc., foods, so that each restaurant simply crosses off the extensive parts which are inapplicable to that particular establishment. The difference between this Menu of All the Russias and the Lévi-Straussian deep-structure gastronomy is that the former does indeed describe quite interestingly the very bounds and polarities of the Soviet gastroworld, whereas the triangle is purely formal. Actual ethnic recipes can of course be attached to it or to its elaborations; but it is not clear to me what is achieved by that.

A few pages further on, Goody observes that 'other factors too suggest a modification of the linguistic model used in the seminal work of Lévi-Strauss . . . he argues that the language of cuisine, unlike the language of ordinary life, "translates" *unconsciously*; it is not used to communicate between me as much as to *express* a structure'. Once again, we get a terrifyingly casual, *en passant* and implied identification – this time between that which is unconscious, and that which expresses some total structure rather than a specific message. In fact, the two oppositions conscious/unconscious and individual messages/expression of shared structure are quite independent, and cut across each other. A collective ritual may express loyalty to a shared community and its hierarchy and indicate its boundaries, but the message can be blatantly overt and conscious; conversely, in any well-constructed play, characters will convey highly specific and individual messages to each other by the tone, posture or context, and yet not be consciously aware of them.

But there is more to it than this. All this cannot possibly be described as merely a *modification* of some early model. What we have here is the conflation of three radically distinct and probably quite incompatible programmes: the pursuit of the universal features of the human mind, as manifested in the ordering of food or speech; the interpretation of a cuisine as the 'symbolic' expression, ratification, or one specific social order as a totality; and the use of elements from a given cuisine to convey specific messages *within* a given social context. These must be clearly separated, not treated as 'modifications' of each other. 'La place a table ne ment jamais' (Mauriac). *Et le plat, lui, est-ce qu'il ne ment pas non plus?* If man speaks so as to hide his thoughts, as the Frenchman said, does he eat so as to betray them? I think not.

Jack Goody does not of course necessarily endorse this approach, but his doubts and criticisms are expressed with astonishing mildness:

While all theories obviously require a testing of some kind the nature of functional and structural hypotheses, with their assumption of fit and homology combined with the initial plausibility of suggestions that give an all embracing unity to the diversity of experience, place them in a special position. The danger can perhaps be gauged . . .

Goody illustrates what happens when testing is attempted by summaris- ing some evidently most interesting and valuable work by Adrienne Lehrer. But it would greatly help further testing if those who propound these ideas displayed more conscientiousness in formulating those ideas with precision, rather than being content with 'initial plausibility' plus rhetoric plus a shower of ethnographic illustration, whose relationship to the initially plausible but nebulous ideas remains obscure.

Only at the very end, when Goody comes to his conclusion, does he go a little further:

An understanding of a set of activities needs to take into account the hermeneutic dimension whenever it is relevant . . . But the sociological analysis of meaning must also take into account the social dimensions of the problem of their roles and relations, their position in the hierarchy, their membership of one society as against another and their position in the world system. The concern with culture must not exclude the social . . . I am aware that too little attention has been paid to the ritual, symbolic and cosmological aspects of food.

Why on earth is he so damned apologetic about his findings and about his emphasis? Symbolic meanink/shmeanink! Neither food nor society is primarily a code. (I do not eat my dinner in the way I read a telegram.) They have conditions and consequences, which are more important than their role as tokens. I never doubted this, but my unwavering faith is greatly strengthened by Goody's data and his conclusions. The only thing that puzzles me is his almost shamefaced tone at reaching them. This must, I suppose, be a sign of strength and authority of current neo- idealist trends. People ought to be helped to overcome them. Perhaps one could found a Hermeneutics Anonymous to give them strength to do so.

Society is not a language. Language isn't a language either, if it comes to that. Virtually nothing is a 'language' in the structuraliste sense, except perhaps systems such as packs of playing cards. In a real language, we say complicated and specific things: we do *not* exhibit and wave objects at each other, objects selected for their position at the limits of the spectra which define our world, in the interest of reminding and nudging each other about those limits, lest we forget. Nor is our alleged habit of polarities-waving somehow the basis of our capacity to say specific things and to conceptualise the world; on the contrary, structuralisme naively takes those capacities for granted – though they are far from self-explanatory – in its *simpliste* accounts of how our world is endowed with its structure. The idea that beating the binary conceptual bounds is the essence of communication is a structuralistic myth, even if it does provide a facile recipe for sparkling interpretations of texts.

Goody's summary, and his much too cautious evaluation of recent trends in this field, only take up the early part of the book. He then proceeds to a detailed account of the whole process of food production and consumption amongst two Northern Ghanaian societies of which he has intimate direct knowledge. One of them, the LoDagaa in the North, was stateless, uncentralised, and livestock-orientated; the Gonja, a little further south, had a state organisation and a formal social stratification, with an aristocracy, a Muslim clerical stratum, commoners, and slaves. They were more disrupted by colonialism than the relatively amorphous LoDagaa, and in any case they were less numerous.

Goody remarks that this last feature is puzzling to anyone starting from Middle Eastern data and expecting states and populousness to go together. I'm not clear whether he included North Africa in the Middle East, but it is my strong impression that the stateless, or rather state-resisting, Maghrebi populations of regions such as the Atlas, the Rif, or Kabylia, and probably the Aures, were thicker on the ground than many of the governed areas of the plain. Why should oppression lead to high population? Some of the sedentary valleys of the Atlas, if one counts only the actually cultivated and inhabited valleys themselves (and not the surrounding hills intermittently shared by the inhabitants with surrounding pastoralists), must have had extremely high population densities. I do not know whether these impressions have been confirmed by demographers.

From the viewpoint of testing theories about gastronomy as conveying social messages, the results of Goody's inquiry are entirely negative, interesting though they are otherwise; 'the actual shape of the cuisine in both societies was surprisingly similar'. It seems that there were no significant differences, either periodically or in terms of social strata, between the various levels and occasions of Gonja social life. As for the LoDagaa, it seems they had few differences to express. So if a local Rip van Winkle woke up in the middle of a meal, the dish in front of him would offer him no clue whatever as to season, occasion, or social standing. The most he could hope for, if Lévi-Strauss is right, is some insight into the nature of the human mind as such.

It is this feature – the absence of culinary stratification in sub-

Saharan Africa – which led Goody to the central question which, as he himself stresses, underlies this book: what are the conditions of the emergence of a high and low cuisine? Why is political differentiation, which was certainly present in some African societies, insufficient to engender *gastronomic* stratification?

His accumulation of data relevant to this takes up the major part of the volume. The data are extremely rich, diverse, and interesting, and it would be impossible to summarise them. This part of the book will also provide most entertainment and information for the lay reader. But if the details elude summary, the conclusions do not, and I hope I do not travesty his subtle, complex and qualified argument in presenting them briefly.

Neither food production nor political centralisation as such is sufficient for the emergence of high cultures. So there is another, complex and subtle, but immeasurably important Great Divide in the history of mankind, posterior to food production and the state, but closely linked to writing, and to social differentiation by access to literacy, and to domination by literate specialists. Intensive agriculture and literacy seem linked to that sustained elaboration of culture which marks off Asian pre-industrial civilisations from the societies of sub-Saharan Africa. No high cultural products without differentiation, specialisation and stratification. . .

Friedrich Engels thought that the subjection of women marked one of the great social revolutions of human history. Goody, by contrast, thinks it was a sign of a crucial transformation in human culture when cooking for great men and occasions was handed over to men. That showed it to be serious. It was then that it was linked to a well-codified regulated division of labour, going beyond that of the domestic unit. So gastronomy is not so much a code, whether universal or specific, as a reflection of the level of development of the forces of production and coercion. When writing engenders clerisy, it also makes possible a codified, recipe-born cuisine. Culinary codification accompanied systems of legal and moral recipes. It is only when the tools are available to chain man's spirit as well as his body that you can really get a decent meal. So to understand the new cookery, one must look to its preconditions rather than to the messages allegedly encoded in it. Back to pre-hermeneutic sociology. Societies are systems made up of concrete people and their activities, and the interdependence and preconditions of these activities require exploration; they are not codes, used by a mysterious and all-powerful central mind, whether culture-specific or universal, to emit cryptic messages, whose decoding can then keep our latter-day structuraliste clerisies in business.

Thorstein Veblen (not mentioned in Goody's book) had treated with irony and inverted the once much-favoured anti-egalitarian theory which had taught mankind to accept a Leisure Class as the price of cultural advance. The spirit of craftsmanship, Veblen thought, which could be self-generating, would suffice, and we could dispense with the parasites. But in fact that spirit has complex social preconditions. Using a greater range of ethnographic data than was available to Veblen, and without that special American bias which takes the work-ethic and political order for granted (Veblen's book doesn't even consider the state!), Jack Goody has stood Veblen on his head once again, with great force and persuasiveness, and has, in effect, rewritten *The Theory of the Leisure Class*, without, this time, the irony intended in Veblen's title.

7 | Concepts and community[1]

For better or for worse, Wittgenstein may well be the most influential single philosopher of the century. Saul Kripke's work is preceded (rather than followed) by a great reputation for precocity, technical virtuosity, and occasional eccentricity and self-sufficient indifference to convention. In other words, he seems well set to be the Bobby Fischer of American philosophy. All this being so, one cannot but turn to a book by Kripke on Wittgenstein with interest, and one is not disappointed.

The book does not wish or claim to deal with the whole of Wittgenstein's philosophy. But it does single out a theme, a problem and a solution, which are, in fact and in Kripke's estimation, absolutely central to Wittgenstein's thought. If anything, Kripke rather gives the impression that Wittgenstein's alleged discovery of the problem is a greater achievement than the proferred solution:

Wittgenstein has invented a new form of scepticism. Personally I am inclined to regard it as the most radical and original sceptical problem that philosophy has seen to date, one that only a highly unusual cast of mind could have produced.

(p. 60)

The most radical scepticism yet – that is a strong claim.

It is as well to begin with a specification of what this problem is. It is a crucial feature of intellectual life, our capacity to think and use language, that we use abstract terms such as 'man' which refer to an open-ended, indeed potentially infinite, class of objects. So, it would seem there must be *something* 'within us' which helps us to recognise and determine whether the next object to arouse our interest is, or is not, a man. What exactly is that *something*?

So far, this is simply the old problem of universals. Just what it is that binds together all the exemplars of one abstract notion, and just how do we deploy that whatever it is, so as to group things together correctly? What does seem original in Wittgenstein's formulation is that he rams it home by way of a new strategy, borrowed from the problem of the justification of scientific generalisations. This problem starts from the

[1] A review of Saul A. Kripke: Wittgenstein on Rules and Private Language, Cambridge (Mass.), 1982, 150 pp.

observation that all data in our possession are always, inevitably, finite. We can never be sure that data which come our way in the future will still fit into the generalisation set up on the basis of past data.

This argument can then be applied to each language user. A person applying an abstract term has already chosen a set of elements, and will go on to choose further ones. To use the kind of example much favoured in this discussion, if we overhear a man muttering '2,4,6,8,10,12', etc., it is very natural for us to conclude that for some reason he is going through the list of even numbers. But what he *might* well be doing could be something quite different. He might be performing a compulsive private ritual which leads him to list all even numbers up to a given very high number, and thereafter to repeat the number 7 as long as there is breath in his body. And the point is, however long a series we have of the numbers he has already uttered, we shall never be able to exclude a whole infinity of rival interpretations which differ from the one we had originally adopted. So how do we know what concept, what rule of inclusion (and of ordering, in the cases in which this applies), he is *really* using?

The answer is that we shall never know for certain, as long as all we have to go by is the series or class of objects which he recognises or mutters. The situation might seem to change if we are allowed to ask him a question, and he deigns to answer. Nature is mute, but men are not. So we can ask him. If he tells us he is going through even numbers, well, that's it: we now know what he is up to, or so we think.

Kripke, expounding Wittgenstein, is quick to undeceive us. Not so. The man *says* that he is 'going through even numbers' (and to simplify matters, we assume that he is truthful). But how do we know what that set of words actually means to *him*? It *might* mean to him what *we* would call 'going through even numbers up to a certain high number, and repeating 7 ad infinitum'. Well, of course, we interrogate him further by means of some further clarifying phrase, to see whether he really means what we call going through even numbers, or whether he is going through the (to us) somewhat weird ritual which in his language is called 'listing even numbers'. But he might interpret any new explanatory phrase in turn in an eccentric way. So the problem of interpreting correctly what he says reappears at each stage, and hence (claims Kripke) we are never really in possession of data other than the objects included in the list *so far*. In the end, it seems, there are only examples, specimens, but not explications, of concepts.

So you can never really identify, pin down a concept, fix the way in which a given abstract term will and will not be applied to future instances, *either* by explication, *or* by the list of examples available so far.

So what is this uniquely potent scepticism excogitated by Wittgenstein? It is best to sum it up in Kripke's words (p. 54):

There can be no such thing as meaning anything by any word. Each new application we make is a leap in the dark; any present intention could be interpreted so as to accord with anything we may choose to do. So there can be neither accord, nor conflict.

This could be called the Existentialist theory of meaning: every application of a word is a free unconstrained *acte gratuit*. Be it noted that neither Wittgenstein nor Kripke actually holds this theory: Wittgenstein's great achievement, according to Kripke (the Wittgenstein Paradox, as one of Kripke's chapter headings has it), is to show us that there is no way out of this paradoxical situation if we try to handle it with traditional philosophical tools. Kripke observes (p. 60):

it is important to see that his (Wittgenstein's) achievement in posing this problem stands on its own, independent of the value of his own solution of it . . .

If we have now seen, at least in outline, the alleged problem and its importance, let us go straight to a sketch of Wittgenstein's solution, as expounded by Kripke (p. 79):

Wittgenstein finds a useful role in our lives for a 'language game' that licenses, under certain conditions, assertions that someone 'means such-and-such' and that his present application of a word 'accords' with what he 'meant' in the past. It turns out that this role, and these conditions, involve reference to a community. They are inapplicable to a single person considered in isolation.

Or again, even more strikingly and provocatively, Kripke sums up the solution he attributes to Wittgenstein in an important and illuminating footnote which begins on p. 93:

'We do not all say $12+7=19$ and the like because we have grasped the concept of addition; we say we all grasp the concept of addition because we all say $12+7=19$ and the like' (Wittgenstein).

So, it is communal consensus which *makes* addition. As far as I know, the above is not an actual quotation from Wittgenstein, but a statement made up by Kripke and credited to the spirit of Wittgenstein's solution so as to bring out certain very illuminating parallels between Wittgenstein, William James and David Hume, and a whole class of theories which consist, in Kripke's excellent phrase, of 'reversing priorities'. For instance, Kripke sums up Hume's doctrine of causation as follows:

'Fire and heat are not constantly conjoined because fire causes heat; fire causes heat because they are constantly conjoined' (Hume).

(p. 93)

What Hume had done was, instead of aiming to explain constant conjunction by a mysterious nexus called 'causation', to say instead that all that causation amounts to is constant conjunction. And similarly, what Wittgenstein has done, as summed up by Kripke, and shorn of all qualifications and waverings and insurances, is to say that it isn't conceptual compulsion which makes for social consensus, *it is social consensus which makes for conceptual compulsion, and which indeed makes concepts at all.*

We used to think, naively, that the astonishing consensus of so much of mankind about the result of simple arithmetical additions, and some other matters, is due to the objective validity of the principles of addition, and the strange mysterious hold they have over our minds (sometimes dubbed 'Reason', as if that explained anything). Not so. *Concepts maketh community.*

if the individual in question no longer conforms to what the community would do in these circumstances, the community can no longer attribute the concept to him. Even though, when we . . . attribute concepts to individuals, we depict no special 'state' of their minds, we do something of importance. We take them provisionally into the community, so long as further deviant behaviour does not exclude them. In practice, such deviant behaviour rarely occurs.

It is, then, in such a description of the game of concept attribution that Wittgenstein's sceptical solution consists.

(p. 95)

This passage could hardly be clearer. The normal (and in my view correct) assumption that some societies have attained some concepts which can coerce thought, *in defiance* of mere consensus and, instead, in deference to national criteria, is simply denied. We had supposed that a society which operated with, say, the notion of even numbers, continued to live under the obligation to follow 6 by 8 even if some outburst of collective religious mania led to a reversal of consensus on this point. But this is denied.

The occasions in western history when a society reversed its previous consensus because it thought it recognised the implications of a previous idea which had hitherto not been implemented (the Reformation, the Scientific Revolution, the Enlightenment, ideological revolutions) are of the very first importance: but if Wittgenstein's 'solution' is adopted, they become totally unintelligible. This solution dissolves the overwhelmingly important, and admittedly mysterious normative power of concepts, into the descriptive fact of behavioural consensus. (Denials notwithstanding, a behaviourist reductionism is hidden within this theory of meaning.)

Kripke makes it quite plain (p. 97):

> On Wittgenstein's conception, a certain type of traditional – and overwhelmingly natural – explanation of our shared form of life is excluded. We cannot say that we all respond as we do to '68 + 57' *because* we grasp the concept of addition in the same way, that we share common responses to particular addition problems *because* we share a common concept of addition.

No, on this theory it is the other way round. It isn't that shared concepts bring us together. It is togetherness which *constitutes* shared concepts. *Gemeinschaft* alone breathes life into *Begriffe*. No need to ask, with Goethe, what happens *wo Begriffe fehlen* . . . As long as we stick together, concepts cannot be lacking. Togetherness in reactions *is* a concept. Nothing else *can* make a concept, nothing else can endow it with that continuity of meaning without which thought is impossible. Reason is the creature of shared custom. Men are not brought into a consensual community by the shared compulsion of Reason: it is a consensual community, and it alone, which endows us with shared concepts, and thus bestows on us the gift or the illusion of Reason. *Am Anfang war die Gewohnheit. (Und auch am Ende, nichts bleibt als die Gewohnheit.)* Reason is and ought to be the slave of custom.

So, no further need for the abortive search for the principles underlying our formation of concepts, our ability to apply concepts correctly to infinite classes. We had all been looking in the wrong places – in Platonic repositories of abstract norms of conceptual rectitude, or in the inner recesses of our psyche, where a private homunculus was matching standard samples with new specimens, or in external physical, 'operationalised' touchstones. These solutions, proposed by Platonists, early empiricists and later instrumentalists respectively, were all abortive, and Wittgenstein, it seems, has shown them to be so. Look elsewhere: the sheer brute fact of consensus, if and when it occurs, does not so much engender, it constitutes, it *is* our conceptual life! As Kripke puts it (p. 96):

> if there was no general agreement in the community responses, the game of attributing concepts to individuals . . . could not exist.

No consensus (by and large, for a few deviations are allowed), no concepts. Communal consensus, being the sole matrix of concepts, must consequently be sovereign:

> The set of responses in which we agree, and the way they interweave with our activity, is our *form of life* . . . Wittgenstein stresses the importance of agreement, and of a shared form of life, for his solution to his sceptical problem. . .

(p. 96)

Remember that Wittgenstein said that 'forms of life' were a kind of ultimate datum, beyond the reach of questioning. My Form of Life, right or wrong. It is all a bit like the theory that judges are not controlled by the law, but that the law is what judges decide – and, like that theory, it is a half-truth, and can make little sense of the occasional powerful influence of statute law, though it does apply much better to customary law. Wittgenstein's notorious lack of historical interest or imagination was not just a personal idiosyncrasy: it was of the essence of his thought, and without it he could not have held the views he did hold.

Again Kripke says:

our licence to say of each that we mean addition by '+' is part of a 'language game' that sustains itself *only* because of the *brute fact* that we generally agree.

(p. 97, my italics)

A similar formulation appears on p. 109 as part of the summary:

The success of . . . practices . . . depends on the *brute fact* that we agree with each other in our responses . . . This success cannot be explained by 'the fact that we all grasp the same concepts'.

(my italics)

To call something a 'brute fact' is to say that no explanation can be given of it, and Kripke makes it plain that this is indeed intended. It is of course just a fact, brute or other, that a given style of thought contains the notion of addition at all; it is not at all a brute fact that, given that notion, answers to problems of addition are uniquely determined. Though Kripke really does at times talk as if it were a mere 'brute fact', and that the only possible explanations of 'the rough conformities in our mathematical behaviour' could occur 'on the neurophysiological level'.

All these quotations should make plain the solution which Kripke credits to Wittgenstein, though so far without the qualifications, insurances and safety nets.

There is a striking parallel (unexplored by Kripke) between this alleged demonstration by Wittgenstein of the impossibility of transcending our concepts (they are the creatures of our custom), and Bishop Berkeley's demonstration of the impossibility of transcending our *sensations*. The paths leading towards the conclusion in each case are also similar. Berkeley thought that the idea of abstraction was the snare which led people to the mistaken supposition of a substrate/matter independent of sensation, and Wittgenstein supposed that the idea of a common universal linguistic form, and it alone, led people to the supposition of a supra-customary, normative language, anchored to reality in a trans-consensual, trans-customary manner. In each case, a shared universality is denied, by each of the two thinkers, as a means towards the affirmation of a strict immanence. In one case mankind is enjoined to remain within the bounds of its sensations, and in the other, within the bounds of its customary concepts (and hence the common-sensical ordinary world they engender), on pain of committing a profound philosophical error. This is the link between his view of language and concept-formation, and his vindication of the *Lebenswelt*, of the world of common sense.

So, just as there were no sensations beyond our sensations, there are to be no concepts beyond our concepts. A crucially important implication of this apparent modesty is that there is and can be nothing whatsoever which could constitute a check on our (customary) concepts, which are thereby given a kind of left-handed, by-default absolute validation. (A curious dogmatism lurks behind the alleged scepticism.) In either case, we reach a kind of terminal wall and have to accept it, or so we are told. That is the argument.

There are of course also significant differences between the Berkeleian and Wittgensteinian cases. The divergencies between the conceptual systems of various cultures are far greater than those between their sensory perceptions. Hence, given the indisputable historical facts of interaction between societies and of radical social change, we *have* to chose between rival conceptual systems (however final they claim to be), whereas the shared sensory base of mankind we can more easily accept as terminal. We *must* seek for an extraneous norm which sits in judgement on concepts, but we are not obliged to do the same unto our sensations. (The whole point of empiricism was precisely the attempt to use *sensations* as the ultimate court of appeal for *concepts*.)

The consequence of Wittgenstein's theory (as lucidly described by Kripke) is that it assimilates the most opportunist, socially time-serving concepts, with cognitively effective, well-operationalised concepts, fit to serve as tools for a genuine and cumulative exploration of nature. *Each* is presented as simply custom-based and ineligible for any validation outside and beyond custom and contingent consensus.

Formulated thus, in the abstract, this only constitutes an oddity, an unacceptable paradox. When, however, such levelling-out, such relativism, is articulated in terms of entire cultures, it places a cognitively cumulative culture on the very same level as stagnant and self-revering ones. So the theory does constitute an implicit philosophy of history and a sociology.

In his confused, somnambulistic and ahistorical way, Wittgenstein was half aware of all this. He was taking sides in the romanticism–scientism debate, even though he did not properly understand it. Note that he *could not* be clear about it; it was an essential part of his position that false philosophy sprang from the misguided unitarian, normative theory of language, that it prejudged nothing, that it 'left everything as it is'. Hence to place his contribution explicitly in the context of the enormous debate of which in fact it *is* part would require one to believe that all those religious and intellectual movements which preached that there were indeed extra-customary norms which sat in judgement on our concepts – for instance, the Reformation or the Enlightenment – were simply by-products of a mistake about the nature of language. If only Luther and Voltaire had been told how language functioned, they would not have striven to reform the conceptual custom of their time. If you believe that you will believe anything.

Wittgenstein's appeal lies in the fact that he provides a strange kind of vindication of romanticism, of conceptual *Gemeinschaft*, of custom-based concepts rather than statute-seeking Reform, and that he does so through a very general theory of meaning, rather than from the premises habitually used for this purpose. Because there is no unique formal notation valid for all speech, each and every culture is vindicated. One never knew that could be done – and so quickly too! It is that above all which endows this philosophy with such capacity to attract and to repel. His mystique of consensual custom denies that anything can sit in judgement on our concepts, that some may be more rational and others less so. So all of them are in order and have nothing to fear from philosophy, as indeed he insists. This is a fairly mild form of irrationalism, invoking no fierce dark Gods, merely a consensual community. It is the Soft Porn of Irrationalism.

He himself half knew all this. It is a curious feature of Kripke's book that this aspect of the matter, its implications for our views of man, society, and history, which really are absolutely fundamental, are almost totally ignored. Reading Kripke, you might well suppose that all that is at stake is an abstruse problem about the nature of concept-formation, of little interest outside the philosophical trade. But though Wittgenstein is wrong, he is not quite so irrelevant. Kripke does incidentally make some interesting observations about the relationship between Wittgenstein's and Chomsky's ideas. But basically the matter is very simple. The essence of Chomsky is that he has seen how very much our linguistic competence is a *problem*, and he goes about trying to solve it. The essence of Wittgenstein is that he treats our culturally idiosyncratic shared conceptual competence as a *solution*, 'to be accepted' as something final.

It should be clear now what a striking inversion of our normal attitude this solution of Wittgenstein requires. It is curious that Wittgenstein should have made quite an impact in America. For obvious and well-known historical reasons, Americans tend to be natural Contractarians, who suppose that they bring *pre-existent* concepts and values, endowed with self-evident authority, to the formation of a national consensus. Americans like to think that they create their society in the light of their own pre-existent ideas, rather than mystically drawing their ideas from the conceptual womb of a pre-existing community. Recent trends in American political thought have revived such assumptions, or perhaps have simply reaffirmed a continuing tradition. (Conceptual inhibitions, it appears, can easily survive a 'veil of ignorance'.) It is East and Central Europeans who rather tend to be romantics/populists, seeing concepts, and above all their authority and affective charge, welling up from the depths of an idiosyncratic, non-universal communal consciousness. (*Blut, Boden und Begriff*, as you might say.) Wittgenstein was very much a part of this tradition, though he had little if any inkling of it or of historical context and implications, and the universal trans-communal idiom against which he was reacting was not French classicism or Enlightenment philosophy, but the notation of set theory...

This, then, is the overall plot of the book, without some of the small print. What are we to make of it? One must not of course identify Kripke with Wittgenstein: in his book, Kripke speaks as an expositor, rather than as one expounding his own views, though of course he allows himself many asides which convey his own opinions, and there can be no doubt about his admiration for his subject. It may be useful to discuss the two of them in turn, and to take Kripke first.

The question has initially been formulated as follows: is Kripke really the Bobby Fischer of American philosophy? This is a useful way of putting it, because it enables us to separate his opening, his middle game, and his end-game. Let me say right away that I greatly admire his middle game, but am not too impressed by either his opening or his ending.

Kripke's opening game is sadly and characteristically Wittgensteinian, and ought indeed to be called 'Ludwig's Gambit'. The reader/opponent is softened up by a barrage of repetitive examples, which hammer in a point which has a plausible aspect with others which have none, without at the same time clarifying just what it is that is being argued, thus pushing us into an unwelcome bulk purchase. The point which is being rammed home is that there is no fact, and can be none, inner or outer, which would establish what rule, what series, what concept, a given individual is applying. It is indeed true that there is no fact, inner or outer, transcendent or natural, which could do the job of identifying unambiguously the rule of selection which is being followed:

this elimination of possible principles of concept formation clears the way, as we have seen, for Wittgenstein's solution, which is that communal custom, and nothing else, can be the foundation of our conceptual world. As you might put it, there are no natural kinds, there are only social kinds – and each society makes up its own.

In expounding the paradoxical conclusion, the denial of any specifiable delimitation of or basis for our concepts (which is then to be overcome only by the Wittgensteinian invocation of social consensus, as a kind of concept-generating Black Box or *deus ex machina*), Kripke fails to make, or at any rate to press home, a number of very crucial distinctions. For instance, he does not distinguish between the very strong and highly implausible thesis that *no* concepts can really be explicated, that *all of them* emerge directly from the Black Box of a given culture or 'form of life', and are thereby, and in *no* other way, validated; and a much weaker and more plausible claim, which many people might accept, to the effect that the inexplicability paradox does instead apply to certain basic notions (either you have them or you don't), but that unambiguous instructions as to how to apply very many derivative notions *can* be formulated, for the benefit and use of all those equipped with the initial set.

This is a far more plausible position than the suggestion that *all* our concepts are directly linked to and dependent on the Black Box of Culture, that each as it were separately depends for its meaning on the convergence of verbal custom; and the distinction deserves more thorough discussion than it actually receives. Some of the space devoted to the Wittgensteinian examples-barrage might more profitably have been devoted to it. Of course, such a distinction would not serve Wittgenstein's purpose: firstly, there is the possibility (for many people, the *hope*) that those basic indefinables, which would render all *other* concepts explicitly specifiable, are *not* linked to individual cultures, but are universal amongst humankind; and secondly, such an approach might lead one to try to isolate those self-sufficient conceptual clear and distinct elements, and erect a tidy structure on them. Such a Cartesian procedure or approach is of course precisely what Wittgenstein wishes to destroy; all concepts, he tells us, are equally 'humble'; but if that approach can be demolished, one would prefer to see it done by argument, rather than by ignoring it.

Kripke's opening leaves me very far from convinced that the argument leading to the alleged sceptical paradox is indeed cogent. I for one am not at all clear that I am indeed susceptible to this newly discovered, and allegedly potent sceptical virus. But one thing is absolutely and overwhelmingly certain: the proffered cure is far, far worse than the questionably imputed illness. I am not at all sure that I have been infected: but if I were, which I do not think I am, I should find such a condition infinitely preferable to the therapy offered by Wittgenstein.

Just consider what has happened. An attempt has been made to tell us that we cannot really be sure of having grasped even a very simple and lucid rule, such as the one generating the series 2,4,6,8, etc., because however long the list, it might be exemplifying some rule other than the most obvious one, and the elimination of ambiguity is eliminated only if we already understand the rule intended. Of course, it is only a *paradox*, and we are not meant to conclude that we really don't grasp the notion of a series of even numbers: but we *are* meant to concede that we cannot explain how the trick is done, that it is much harder to explain it than we had supposed, and therefore to allow ourselves to be pushed into the one solution which is then offered – it is the Black Box of Culture, it is our shared Form of Life, what done it.

Well! Our standards of what is comprehensible have become so high that we can't really grasp the notion of adding 2 to previous even numbers, but we *are* expected to grasp, and be content with (treat as final, ultimate), without further anxiety, the sociological notion of Culture, of a Form of Life, of a kind of socio-conceptual matrix, which endows a whole population with their conceptual wealth, by methods which are not to be scrutinised further!

What has to be accepted, the given, is – so one could say – *forms of life*.

> (Lugwig Wittgenstein, *Philosophical Investigations*, Oxford, 1953, p. 225e)

The Form of Life, it appears, is a Hidden Culture, which like a Hidden God neither offers nor owes any explanations to its subjects. Its verdicts are both final and inscrutable, and there are and can be no further and higher standards in the names of which they could be challenged, for it is the ultimate and sole and only possible source of standards.

When we are taught to grasp the paradox, to be infected with the sceptical virus, we have to be so incredibly fastidious logically as to realise that we can find no warrant either in our inner consciousness or in our operational instrument, or in the heavens above, for using even the most lucid concepts which we do use. (Neither the starry heavens above nor the law within can help us, it appears.) In fact, we have to attain a standard of logical fastidiousness which had not been attained by any thinker prior to Wittgenstein, for only he, says Kripke, managed to think up this doubt, in all the two and a half odd millennia of philosophical reflection.

But having done it, having raised ourselves to this quite unprecedented altitude of doubt, we are suddenly asked to relax our logical standards, and to be content with, to rest upon, the notion of a 'Form of Life', of Culture. The bizarre Joker card of a 'Form of Life' is played, and we are to accept it without question. This really is logical anti-nomianism, the alternation of utmost severity and near-total licence, with a vengeance. Who exactly is it who has decreed these astonishing rules of the game? Note that the sociological concept of culture (the nearest equivalent in public language to Wittgenstein's private notion of a 'Form of Life') is a kind of proto-concept, useful enough as a shorthand indication of a certain cluster of phenomena, but in no way precise enough to constitute, when used on its own, any kind of serious explanation of anything. It can cover anything from the shared assumptions of a small guild to the shared assumptions of all mankind. (The looseness and pliability of this key explanatory concept of the whole system is not unconnected with its popularity.)

There is a really important difference between causation and conceptualisation, between Hume and Wittgenstein, which Kripke, so keen on the Hume–Wittgenstein parallel, does not seem to have spotted. Hume, says Kripke, showed that causation does not explain regular succession, it *is* regular succession; and Wittgenstein similarly shows that concepts do not explain consensual reactions, they *are* consensual reactions. But in the case of nature, there are only facts, and no norms. In trying to establish precisely what ultimate regularities there are in nature, we can only observe the data, and allow them to decide. It really would make no sense whatever, at any rate in our non-animist age, to say that a certain set of data are in a minority, but nevertheless possess greater normative authority than the majority, and consequently should be obeyed. There are no minority laws of nature.

It is by no means obvious to me that this is so with the laws of reason. A given concept may cogently contain implications which, through a failure of clear thought, a majority of the users of that concept has failed to perceive. At some stage, a minority, even a small minority, may spot the implication and its cogency, and its view may eventually prevail. Major events which at least look as if they fitted this description have occurred in human history: they may in fact be the most important events in all intellectual history. On Wittgenstein's theory of meaning, such an event becomes an a priori impossibility:

'false moves' can only exist as an exception. For if what we now call by that name became the rule, the game in which they were a false move would have been abrogated.

(Wittgenstein, *Philosophical
Investigations*, p. 227e)

Wittgenstein here makes plain that in his view majorities make or break concepts.

There is another distinction or difficulty which Kripke does mention (in fact it is crucial for both his opening and his end-game), but which he simply does not pursue far enough. This point can perhaps be approached best through what is the central, the most fundamental difficulty for Wittgenstein. Suppose the proffered solution to be correct: it is culture and culture alone (the 'Form of Life'), which makes our concepts, and above all, which endows them with what authority they possess. It follows immediately that, conceptually speaking, a culture can do no wrong, for after all it alone sets the standards, there being no other possible source, and so there is no standard in terms of which it in turn could ever do wrong. So every culture makes its own world, sets its own criteria or reality. Some followers of Wittgenstein have warmly, indeed ecstatically, welcomed this conclusion.

But neither Wittgenstein nor Kripke (in expounding him) wishes to go that far, or at any rate to do so consistently and all the time. The idea that each society or culture rolls its own reality as it pleases is exceedingly strong meat, and the Master shrinks from endorsing some extreme implications of it, and the expositor documents this well. Kripke is quite clear that, for instance, given the concept of addition as we know it, no society employing that concept has the power to interfere with what the sum of two given numbers happens to be. But in that case, is the role of communal cultural consensus to tell us just what concepts we happen to have, whilst the limits and authority of a concept once given spring from some *other* source? If *that* is all that is meant, then the doctrine of the ultimacy of consensus of 'forms of life' turns out to be rather tame and trivial.

My objection to Kripke's end-game (notably on and around p. 111) is that he simply does not push this central problem to a point where we could see where we stand on this absolutely crucial question. He concedes (and convincingly documents that Wittgenstein concedes) that concepts (or rather the rules governing their application) possess a kind of autonomy, a kind of authority which consensus or cultural custom cannot overrule. But in that case, what has happened to the Wittgensteinian solution to the problem of concept-formation and of the mysterious power of concepts, of their evident capacity to determine what does or does not fall under them?

As far as I can see Kripke endorses Wittgenstein's attempt to wriggle out of this (or if he does not endorse it, he certainly refrains from uttering any criticism of it). The mechanics of this wriggling in effect consist of saying that Wittgenstein is asking a new kind of question, and that this new question can legitimately replace the old one. Wittgenstein is abandoning the quest for the specification of the necessary and sufficient conditions of application of this or that concept, and replacing it by a new question, roughly – under what conditions does a given community credit its members with comprehension? We shift from objects of speech to speech users, their purposes, customs and social acceptability. This formulation then apparently does not preclude the members themselves being in possession of sufficient and necessary conditions (which thus would become more authoritative than communal consensus, and which may, or may not, be reflected in consensus).

But the matter is not clear: it would seem that those truth-conditions, if they exist, nevertheless cannot be formulated by us, for to do so would mean to break out of the circle of explications and examples, and it was shown to us that this cannot be done. So custom is not final, yet *only* custom may be invoked. When you look at Wittgenstein's philosophy as a whole, custom is King. When you focus on custom and consensus and ask whether they may err, you are reassured – yes, they may. Please make up your mind. A whole crucial passage is so wobbly in its meaning that it had better be quoted extensively (Kripke, pp. 111 and 112):

One must bear firmly in mind that Wittgenstein has no theory of truth conditions – necessary and sufficient conditions – for the correctness of one response rather than another to a new addition problem. Rather he simply points out that each of us *automatically* calculates new addition problems (without feeling the need to check with the community whether our procedure is proper): that the community feels entitled to correct a deviant calculation: that in practice such deviation is rare, and so on. Wittgenstein thinks that these observations about sufficient conditions for justified assertion are enough to illuminate the role and the utility in our lives of assertion about meaning and determination of new answers. What follows from these assertability conditions is *not* that the answer everyone gives to an addition problem is, by definition, the correct one, but rather the platitude that, if everyone agrees upon an answer, no one will feel justified in calling the answer wrong.

As a matter of important historical fact, what Kripke calls a platitude is actually a falsehood. Brave and/or demented individuals have on occasion felt justified in defying consensus; and, on even rarer occasions, they were subsequently vindicated. Wittgenstein's theory seems to have no way whatever of coping with these supremely important cases in which consensus and cogent criteria diverge. There can apparently be moral or political drop-outs, but there can never be any *conceptual* drop-outs: for if a man opts out of the conceptual consensus, his concepts drop out with him. I had always thought that Descartes had had a pretty good try at going it alone conceptually, but one must assume that he had failed. . .

But assume that what Kripke says is a platitude, really is such. It is of course true in many, many cases that mechanical consensus prevails. We are now being given a trite generalisation about what people happen to do – they do agree on uncontentious, mechanically decidable matters such as addition, and in consequence credit each other with comprehension. Where previously we had been offered a daring, fascinating (though to me incredible), and very powerful theory in answer to a fundamental problem, namely, what is it that accounts for the mysterious power of (some) concepts to elicit, compel, constrain similar responses? – we are now given a dud. The fascinating, teasing, 'priority-reversing' answer had been: it isn't that something-or-other in the concept which compelled the consensual answer, but on the contrary, it is the consensus as such (not explicable further, other than as a manifestation of a Holy Ghost named 'Form of Life') which had made, created the concept... Well, we may not have been convinced by this dramatically original theory (I certainly never was), but it sure was interesting. But now suddenly we are told that there is no theory here about what compels the answer, only a rather trite external description of what happens in cases of consensual use of mechanically applied notions...

It is all a bit as if, at some savage spectacle, we were all set to witness a terrible sacrifice, and at the very last moment a harmless, innocuous, obvious dummy were substituted for the sacrificial victim. Bathos replaces horror. We have been told that the most awe-inspiring imperatives of Reason, of logic and mathematics, are about to be devoured by Custom and Consensus, we gape with *frisson* and with shame, and then a set of obvious pastry dummies is harmlessly gobbled up instead.

But there is more to it than that. Wittgenstein's work is permeated by the suggestion that the substitution is justified, that we should not complain of it, that this is all we can have and all that we should ask, and that somehow the Ersatz-solution is as good or better than the real thing, and that if we don't see that, it is *our* fault, our understanding is defective, and we are asking for the wrong thing, because we don't understand how language really works. I for one see no reason for allowing myself to be bluffed into accepting this – all the more so since I can see the position (*and* Kripke's exposition of it) oscillating between the genuine and strong solution and the trivial 'solution'. The theories have gone into partnership, one strong and contentious, and the other trivial. They take turns at standing at the counter. The strong one explains a lot, the trivial one wards off all critics. As long as they are allowed to stand in for each other in this manner, the partnership is invulnerable.

Transcendence of custom is the most important fact in the intellectual history of mankind. Somehow or other, some cultures have succeeded in subjecting at least part of their cognitive life to external criteria, in the sphere of both formal and empirical truths. (Even if this transcendence were an illusion, that illusion would still be supremely important.) Reality is not something which shows itself *in* a language, but is rather something which arises *for* languages and separates them; some attain far more of it than others. Wittgenstein presents us with the shocking claim that such transcendence is indeed an illusion, and that custom alone is the foundation of all conceptual congruence. All customs are equal, by default, for lack of supra-customary norms. When objections are raised, when we point out that concepts constrain us, and that on occasion they do so independently of custom or even *in violation* of it, we are suddenly offered an unutterably trivial theory about routine situations which has no power to shock at all.

Of course I can see *some* good reasons for switching from a truth-condition-seeking theory of language to a social, functional one: but one reason for such a switch of vision which I will not accept is the use of it as a smoke-screen for the substitution of a trivial non-solution for a strong, contentious solution to a real problem. And what really puzzles me is why Kripke, who must see what is going on, allows Wittgenstein to get away with it all, without comment.

So we have simply abandoned the philosophically supreme question as to what endows certain concepts with authority – for instance, why certain inferences are cogent – and replaced it with an impressionistic sociology of how, in fairly consensual communities, people credit each other with the mastery of locally pervasive ideas. If consensus is lacking, well then, we just cease to attribute concepts to people, it seems, and we lose interest (p. 96). I must say that both Wittgenstein and Kripke grossly underrate the frequency, and above all the historical importance, of non-consensual situations. Interesting societies have survived without conceptual consensus. When under pressure the whole doctrine degenerates into the platitude that in consensual situations, where people by and large use the same concepts with the same results, 'mechanically' and without reconsidering fundamentals, comprehension of a concept is pretty much the same as conformity with the culture. What else is new? (But what criteria do we apply if someone says something original or shocking? – and is later applauded as being right?)

But the entire thrust of Wittgensteinism is that something far more potent and less trite is being said, and I simply cannot accept the claim which seems to constitute most of Kripke's end-game (pp. 110–13), namely, that the problem-shift (from truth-conditions to socio-conditions, in effect) in any way excuses or justifies this ambiguity. Of course the triviality of the 'solution' is itself conceded and stressed by Wittgenstein himself, but with a persistent hint that when properly understood, it is really important and profound after all.

My complaints about Kripke's opening and end-game should now be clear. He allows the Master to get away with far too much and far too easily, both in the initial formulation of the problem and in its solution. A real philosophical Bobby Fischer would have made mincemeat of this opponent both in the opening and in the end-game, if it ever came that far.

It is fair to add, however, that Kripke's middle game is excellent. His interpretations of Wittgenstein seem to me convincing (in so far as Wittgensteinian exegesis can ever be an exercise with determinate answers), and the manner in which he places Wittgenstein in the context of the history of philosophy (though not, alas, of social history) and of other thinkers is genuinely illuminating. For instance, I am fully convinced by the parallel he draws between Wittgenstein's treatment of mathematics and of sensation. *Each* of these spheres had been used by thinkers eager to anchor our concepts directly on to something trans-social and more than merely consensual; it is important for Wittgenstein to block each of these attempts, and he does it in a broadly similar way. Neither the most private sensation, nor the most formal and rigorous deduction, is to be allowed to be a Jacob's ladder which would enable us to escape from the closed circle of shared-custom-based ideas.

Leaving Kripke aside, why do Wittgenstein, and his errors, matter? The basic issue is really the authority of concepts. How do they manage to constrain our thought, speech and conduct? Is it all merely cultural, or is it at least sometimes, say in great intellectual advances, trans-social? Platonists, religious believers, rationalists, empiricists, naturalists, have all been at one in supposing that some concepts at least possess an authority which transcends culture, so that an entire community *can* be in error. The truth sometimes moulds us, and we do not always collectively invent it. These various types of thinker differed of course in just where they located the source of that authority, but they were at one in refusing to place it in communal consensus. No conceptual community could be a law unto itself.

Some concepts almost certainly are 'purely cultural'. For instance, if a given community has a list of ritually sacred objects, there may simply be no rhyme or reason concerning just why the list of these objects should be precisely what it is. An anthropologist can do no more than enumerate it, and perhaps convey its spirit and the way in which it interlocks with other institutions. Where concepts are open and admit of new instances, the matter may be more difficult. If the concept is a multi-stranded one, a syndrome rather than something rigorously defined (a set of 'family resemblances', in Wittgenstein's terms), members of the community who share its spirit may agree on the delimitation of new cases, yet be hard put to it to explain how they do it. Its many-strandedness will of course make the concept socially manipulable and opportunistic. And finally, at the other end of the spectrum, there seem to be concepts whose application seems impersonal, single-stranded, fairly unambiguous, which seldom generate dissent, which seem fairly detached from the other institutions of any one culture, and which seem to be prominent in those cognitive structures which have grown so remarkably in the last three centuries or so. Wittgenstein does not recognise the significance of these differences. Ironically, though he talks as if he had invented the diversification of linguistic function, when it comes to the validation of concepts, he unifies everything under a single, and misguided, formula.

Kripke's exegesis, though very illuminating and correct as far as it goes, does in some ways misrepresent the spirit of Wittgenstein's philosophy. It makes it sound as if Wittgenstein had thought up a new problem, and *then* found a solution to it, but also as if the two steps were separable and we could take one without the other. In fact, Wittgenstein's philosophy is far more of a unity than that. The solution is embraced for reasons other than and additional to the fact that it allegedly solves the problem highlighted by Kripke. The whole thing is not a neat two-stroke system, with one problem and one solution, but an interlocking whole in which most parts sustain and are sustained by the others. Wittgenstein's oscillation between a strong and a trivial thesis, tolerated by Kripke, is reinforced by Wittgenstein's frequently reiterated meta-theory, to the effect that there are and can be no contentious claims in philosophy:

Philosophy . . . leaves everything as it is.

If one tried to advance *theses* in philosophy it would never be possible to question them, because everyone would agree with them.

Philosophy only states what everyone admits.

(*Philosophical Investigations*,
pp. 49e, 50e and 156e)

In the light of this principle, which is central and not tangential to Wittgenstein (and intimately connected with his firmly stated doctrine that in philosophy one may describe but never explain or justify any usage), one would have to conclude that he *only* intends the 'cultural' solution to the problem of concept-formation in the most innocuous way possible, as indeed Kripke presents it when the doctrine gets into trouble. But no: as correctly presented by Kripke at other times, and indeed by himself, he *also* means the fascinating and shocking 'social' theory of concept-formation in its strong sense. And this, of course, is where we are entitled to get cross at the sleight-of-hand to which we have been subjected.

The falsity of the social theory of concepts is probably the single most important fact about the intellectual life of mankind. Somehow or other men *have* become susceptible, in their thought, to constraints other than those of mere social consensus. In recent centuries, there has been an important shift from the use of merely social to genuinely cognitive concepts: this is normally known as the Scientific Revolution. Wittgensteinianism makes it impossible to ask any questions about this event, for on its terms nothing of the kind could ever occur, could make any sense.

Wittgenstein makes his attitude to these matters plain in a remarkable passage (*Philosophical Investigations*, p. 227e) in which he compares arithmetical calculation with the ritual of a coronation. This putative analogy is the heart of the matter. In fact, the compulsiveness of a coronation ritual (for those who have deeply internalised its rules) may indeed *feel* similar to the compulsiveness of a simple arithmetical calculation; but, whatever the psychological feel of it all, the roots of the compulsiveness could hardly be more different. In recent centuries, our calculations have become incomparably more powerful than they had been, whilst our coronations have become much shakier. Cognition has expanded, whilst the social/moral order has lost its foundations. *That* is our predicament. We don't fully understand either aspect of it. Philosophy is an attempt to do so, and to seek out whatever bases may be available for either calculation-and-verification on the one hand or for coronations (and their modern equivalents) on the other. This need is *not* inspired by a misunderstanding of language, and cannot be cured by descriptions of verbal custom, as Wittgenstein claimed. Wittgenstein taught a whole generation of philosophers to ask the wrong questions. Those, however, who acclaim the gospel according to Ludwig generally do so because they love to see calculations demoted, and coronations (or equivalents) receive this unexpected, welcome – and utterly illusory – vindication.

But conceptual compulsion cannot be reduced to social control. Social control cannot be reduced to conceptual compulsion. Wittgenstein has taught the former error to philosophers and the latter to social scientists, some of whom have come to think that the world is the totality not of things but of meanings. *Hermeneutik über Alles.*

As a tool towards understanding the central and *differential* philosophical problem – why are *some* cognitive systems so much more powerful and effective than others, how do *some* concepts attain an authority far above that of the mere contingent custom of any one community, how do they manage to lock in with reality with special effectiveness? – on all this, the Wittgensteinian night, in which all conceptual cows are the same shade of communal grey, is of no use at all.

Sources

Chapter 1, not previously published; chapter 2, not previously published; chapter 3, from Barbara Lloyd and John Gay, eds., *Universals of Human Thought*, Cambridge University Press, 1981, pp. 1–20; chapter 4, © Unesco 1982. This article will appear in a collection of studies on *The Logic of Knowledge and Imperatives of Action in the Social Sciences*; chapter 5 from Colin Renfrew, Michael J. Rowlands and Barbara Seagraves-Whallon, eds., *Theory and Explanation in Archaeology*, San Francisco: Academic Press, 1981, pp. 97–123; chapter 6, from *London Review of Books*, 4, no. 16, 2–15 September 1982; chapter 7, from *American Scholar*, Spring 1984, 243–63.

Bibliography of Ernest Gellner (III)

Supplements and additions compiled by I. C. Jarvie

This bibliography continues those in *The Devil in Modern Philosophy* (London, 1974) and *Spectacles and Predicaments* (Cambridge, 1980).
Items reprinted are marked thus:
**** *Spectacles and Predicaments*
MS Muslim Society (Cambridge, 1981)
***** *Relativism and the Social Sciences*

1969
(*k*) 'O Holismo contra o Individualismas em Historia o Sociologia. Reposte a Watkins', in Patrick Gardiner, ed., *Teorias da História*, Lisbon; reprinted 1975. (Portuguese translation by Victor Matos e Sá of 1956 (*d*).)

1970
(*f*) (under the pseudonym 'Philip Peters') 'Tunisia: A System on Trial?', *New Society*, **16,** no. 408, 23 July, 144–6.

1972
(*d*) (under the pseudonym 'Philip Peters') 'Algeria After Independence', *New Society*, **20,** no. 497, 6 April, 9–11.

1977
(*o*) Foreword to Sawsan el-Messiri, *Ibn al-Balad, A Concept of Egyptian Identity*, Leiden, pp. ix–x.

(*p*) 'The Limbus Between Functionalism and Marxism', review of Philippe Sagant, *Le Paysan Limbu: sa maison et ses champs*, in *Kailash* (Kathmandu), **5,** no. 3, pp. 258–62.

1978
(*f*) 'Philosophy – The Social Contract', in Bryan Magee, ed., *Men of Ideas*, London, 1978, pp. 286–99; paperback edition, 1982.

(*m*) 'Notes Towards a Theory of Ideology', *L'Homme*, **23,** nos. 3–4, July–December, 69–82.****

(*n*) Review of Wilfred Knapp, *North West Africa*, in *Political Studies*, **26,** 162–3.

1979
(*a*) 'Plaidoyer pour une liberalisation manquée', reply to Raymond Aron, *Government and Opposition*, **14**, no. 1, Winter, 58–65.****

(*b*) 'Rulers and Tribesmen', review of Raphael Danziger, *Abd-al-Quadir and the Algerians* and Ross E. Dunn, *Resistance in the Desert*, in *Middle Eastern Studies*, **15**, no. 1, January, 106–13. (*MS*)

(*c*) Review of Alexander Vucinich, *Social Thought in Tsarist Russia*, in *Philosophy of the Social Sciences*, **9**, no. 1, March, 121–2.

(*d*) Review of B. G. Martin, *Muslim Brotherhood in Nineteenth Century Africa*, in *Middle Eastern Studies*, **15**, no. 2, May, 285–6.

(*e*) Review of Hugh Seton-Watson, *Nations and States*, in *Political Studies*, **27**, no. 2, June, 312–13.

(*f*) Review of Mervyn Matthews, *Soviet Sociology, 1964–75*, in *The Slavonic and East European Review*, **57**, no. 3, July, 473–4.

(*g*) 'State Before Class, The Soviet Treatment of African Feudalism', in Percy Cohen and William A. Shack, eds., *Politics in Leadership: A Comparative Perspective*, Oxford, pp. 193–220. (Reprint of 1977 (*n*).)

(*h*) 'The Withering Away of the Dentistry State', review of Albert O. Hirschman, *The Passions and the Interests, Political Arguments for Capitalism Before Its Triumph*, *Review*, **2**, no. 3, Winter, 461–72.****

(*i*) Foreword to José Merquior, *The Veil and the Mask, Essays on Culture and Ideology*, London, pp. ix–x.

(*j*) *Words and Things*, second edition, London. (Reprint of 1959 (*d*), with the addition of 1979 (*k*).)

(*k*) 'The Saltmines of Salzburg or Wittgensteinianism Reconsidered in Historical Context', a new introduction written specially for the second edition of 1959 (*d*). Pp. 1–37 of 1979 (*j*).

(*l*) Review of Hassan Jouad and Bernard Lortat-Jacob, *La Saison des fêtes dans une valée du Haut-Atlas*, *Middle East Journal*, **33**, no. 3, 374–5.

(*m*) Viewpoint: 'A Blobologist in Vodkobuzia', *The Times Literary Supplement*, no. 4001, 23 November, 23.

(*n*) 'The Social Roots of Egalitarianism', *Dialectics and Humanism* (Poland), **6**, no. 4, 27–43.

(*o*) 'Philosophy, the Social Contract', in Bryan Magee, ed., *Men of Ideas*, New York, pp. 286–99. (American edition of 1978 (*f*).)

(*p*) 'Felsefenin Toplumsal Icerigi', in Bryan Magee, ed., *Yen Dusun Adamlari*, Istanbul, pp. 449–69. (Turkish translation of 1978 (*f*).)

1980
(*a*) *Spectacles and Predicaments, Essays in Social Theory*, Cambridge. Pp. viii + 385. Contains: 1980 (*b*), 1976 (*e*), 1975 (*p*), 1975 (*e*), 1975 (*m*),

1977 (*i*), 1978 (*m*), 1974 (*c*), 1978 (*g*), 1976 (*h*), 1975 (*o*), 1975 (*h*), 1981 (*e*), 1978 (*c*), 1975 (*d*), 1979 (*h*), 1976 (*g*), 1979 (*a*), 1977 (*d*), 1975 (*l*).

(*b*) Introduction to 1980 (*a*), pp. 1–9.

(*c*) 'How the System Manages to go on Functioning in War-Torn Lebanon', *The Times*, 1 February, 10.

(*d*) 'In Defence of Orientalism', *Sociology*, **14**, no. 2, May, 295–300.

(*e*) 'Breaking Through the Bars of the Rubber Cage', *The Times Higher Education Supplement*, no. 394, 9 May, 11–12.

(*f*) Edited, *Soviet and Western Anthropology*, London and New York. Pp. xxv + 285.

(*g*) Preface to 1980 (*f*), pp. ix–xvii.

(*h*) Translation of Yu. I. Semenov, 'Theory of Socio-Economic Formations and World History', in 1980 (*f*), pp. 29–58.

(*i*) 'A Russian Marxist Philosophy of History', in 1980 (*f*), pp. 59–82. Also in *Theory and Society*, **9**, no. 5, September, 757–77.

(*j*) 'State and Revolution in Islam', *Millennium*, **8**, no. 3, 185–99.

(*k*) 'Actions Before Words', review of C. R. Hallpike, *The Foundations of Primitive Thought*, in *The Times Literary Supplement*, no. 4083, 15 August, 911.

(*l*) 'Recollections in Anxiety', *Government and Opposition*, **15**, nos. 3–4, Autumn, 376–88.

(*m*) Review of Terence Cox, *Rural Society in the Soviet Union*, in *Journal of Peasant Studies*, 8, no. 1, October 116–18.

(*n*) 'The LSE – A Contested Academy', *The Times Higher Education Supplement*, no. 418, 7 November, 12–13; translated into French in *Le Débat*, no. 6, November, 56–65.

(*o*) Letter, 'Soviet Anthropology', in *Royal Anthropological Institute News (RAIN)*, no. 41, December, 12.

(*p*) 'Ethnicity Between Culture, Class and Power', in Peter F. Sugar, ed., *Ethnic Diversity and Conflict in Eastern Europe*, Santa Barbara, pp. 237–77. (Edited version of 1981 (*j*).)

(*q*) Review of Haim Shaked, *The Life of the Sudanese Mahdi*, in *International Journal of Middle East Studies*, **12**, 539–56.

(*r*) 'Talking with Tamerlane', review of Ibn Khaldun, *Le Voyage d'Occident et d'Orient*, in *The Times Literary Supplement*, no. 4042, 19 September, 1041.

(*s*) 'As raizes sociais de nacionalismo e a diversidede de suas formas', in *Alternatives politicas, economicas, e sociais ato o final do secuto*, Editore Universidede do Brazilien.

(*t*) 'Les Traits Distinctifs de l'Etat Musulman'; in *Recherches et documents du Centre Thomas Moore*, Septième Année, Septembre. (French translation of 1981 (*o*).)

(*u*) Edited a special number of *The Maghreb Review*, September–December, 5, nos. 5–6 and 6, nos. 3–4, with an Introductory Note, vol. 5, p. 90.

(*v*) Review of Abdallah Mammoudi, *La Vallée de l'Azzaden*, in *L'Annaire de l'Afrique du Nord*, 1064–5.

1981

(*a*) 'How Socialism Has Made Czechoslovakia the Captive Hamlet of Europe', *The Times Higher Education Supplement*, no. 433, 20 February, 10–11.

(*b*) 'Anomalies of No Fixed Abode', review of Sevyan Vainshtein, *Nomads of South Siberia*, in *The Times Literary Supplement*, no. 4067, 13 March, 273.

(*c*) *Muslim Society*, Cambridge. Pp. x + 264. Contains: 1981 (*d*), 1975 (*b*), 1973 (*a*), 1972 (*f*), 1963 (*d*), 1974 (*h*), 1978 (*a*), 1976 (*b*), 1962 (*e*), 1976 (*c*), 1977 (*f*), 1979 (*b*); paperback edition, 1983.

(*d*) 'Flux and Reflux in the Faith of Men', in 1981 (*c*), pp. 1–85. (Greatly expanded version of 1968 (*c*).)

(*e*) 'Pragmatism and the Importance of Being Earnest', in R. J. Mulvaney and Philip M. Zeltner, eds., *Pragmatism, Its Sources and Prospects*, Columbia, SC, pp. 41–65. (Reprint of 1980 (*a*), ch. 12.)****

(*f*) 'Relativism and Universals', in Barbara Lloyd and John Gay, eds., *Universals of Human Thought: Some African Evidence*, Cambridge, pp. 1–20.)*****

(*g*) 'What is Structuralisme?', *The Times Literary Supplement*, no. 4087, 31 July, 881–3. (Longer version in Colin Renfrew, Michael J. Rowlands, Barbara Seagraves-Whallon, eds., *Theory and Explanation in Archaeology*, San Francisco, pp. 97–123.)****

(*h*) Edited *Islam, société et communauté, anthropologies du Maghreb*, Paris. Pp. 163.

(*i*) *Présentation* to 1981 (*h*), pp. 5–7.

(*j*) 'Nationalism', *Theory and Society*, 10, 753–76.

(*k*) *Nacionalismo e Democracia*. Editore Universede de Brasilia.

(*l*) Introduction to E. E. Evans-Pritchard, *A History of Anthropological Thought*, edited by André Singer, London, pp. xiii–xxxvi.

(*m*) Edited with Jean-Claude Vatin, *Islam et politique au Maghreb*, Paris. Pp. 374.

(*n*) *Présentation Générale* to 1981 (*m*), pp. 11–13.

(o) 'The Distinctiveness of the Muslim State', in 1981 (*m*), pp. 163–74. (English version of 1980 (*t*).)

(p) 'Problems Facing the Ibn Khaldum Model of Traditional Muslim Society', in Faud I. Khuri (ed.), *Leadership and Development in Arab Society*, Beirut: American University of Beirut pp. 14–29.

(q) 'Setting the Zeal on the Muslim State', *The Times Higher Education Supplement*, 20 November, 12–13.

1982

(a) 'God, Man and Nature', review of *Masterguides* by L. Kolakowsi, E. Leach and T. Hinde, in *The Sunday Times*, 28 February, 41.

(b) Review of G. Tagliacozzo, ed., *Vico and Contemporary Thought*, in *Man*, **17**, no. 1, March, 194–5.

(c) 'The Paradox in Paradigms', review of Barry Barnes, *T. S. Kuhn and Social Science*, in *The Times Literary Supplement*, no. 4125, 23 April, 451–2.

(d) Review of Christel Lane, *The Rites of Rulers*, in *Soviet Studies*, **24**, no. 2, April, 305–6.

(e) Review of Fuad Baali and Ali Wardi, *Ibn Khaldun and Islamic Thought-Styles*, in *British Journal of Sociology*, **23**, no. 2, June, 295–6.

(f) 'The Individual Division of Labour and National Cultures', *Government and Opposition*, **17**, no. 3, Summer, 268–78.

(g) 'Down with Occidentalism', review of B. Lewis, *The Muslim Discovery of Europe*, in *The New Republic*, nos. 3526–7, 16 and 23 August, 31–4.

(h) 'Accounting for the Horror', review of E. Young-Bruehl, *For Love of the World*, in *The Times Literary Supplement*, no. 4140, 6 August, 843–5.

(i) 'No Haute Cuisine in Africa', review of Jack Goody, *Cooking, Cuisine and Class*, in *London Review of Books*, **4**, no. 16, 2–15 September, 22–4.*****

(j) 'Relativism and Universals', in Martin Hollis and Steven Lukes, eds., *Rationality and Relativism*, Oxford, pp. 181–200. (Reprint of 1981 (*f*).)

(k) Review of Leo E. Rose and John T. Schatz, *Nepal: Profile of a Himalayan Kingdom*, in *Journal of Asian Studies*, **52**, no. 1, November, 202.

(l) 'The Moslem Reformation', review of Edward Mortimer, *Faith and Power: The Politics of Islam*, in *The New Republic*, no. 3540, 22 November, 25–30.

1983

(a) 'Stagnation Without Salvation', review of Stephen P. Dunn, *The Fall and Rise of the Asiatic Mode of Production*, in *The Times Literary Supplement*, no. 4163, 14 January, 27–8.

(b) 'Verbal Euthanasia', review of A. J. Ayer, *Philosophy in the Twentieth Century*, in *American Scholar*, 52, Spring, 243–58.

(c) 'Nationalism and the Two Forms of Cohesion in Complex Societies', Radcliffe-Brown Memorial Lecture, *Proceedings of the British Academy*, 58, 165–87.

(d) Review of T. W. Adorno, Hans Albert, Ralf Dahrendorf, Jürgen Habermas, Harald Pilot and Karl Popper, *The Positivist Dispute in German Sociology*, in *British Journal for the Philosophy of Science*, 34, 173–5.

(e) *Nations and Nationalism*, Oxford. pp. x + 150.

(f) 'The Tribal Society and its Enemies', in Richard Tapper, ed., *The Conflict of Tribe and State in Iran and Afghanistan*, London, pp. 436–48.

(g) 'The Social Roots of Modern Egalitarianism', in G. Andersson, ed., *Rationality in Science and Politics*, Boston, pp. 111–130. (Reprint of 1979 (*n*).).

(h) Review of John Whelpton, *Jaug Bahadur in Europe: The First Nepalese Mission to the West*, in *The Times Literary Supplement*, no. 4212, 23 December, 1438.

(i) 'Leff', *The Encyclopaedia of Islam*, new edition, ed. C. E. Bosworth, E. van Douzel, B. Lewis and Ch. Pellat, 5, Fascicules 89–90, Leiden, p. 715.

Name index

Subject index

abstract entities, 26
abstraction, 172
active inquiry, 16
Against Method, 116 n6
agro-literature societies, 113–15, 117
America, 50–1, 166, 175
amoeba, 18, 23, 46–8, 55, 61, 92, 109
anthropologists, anthropology, 77, 86,
   135–45, 158–66
Archives Européenes de Sociologie, 37n,
   66n, 122 n12, 131n
armies, ritualisation of, 80
atomism, *see* granular vision

Baconians, *see* empiricism
Big Divide, *see* coupure
binarism, 141–3, 148, 156–7, 164
   can present any finite set of
     distinctions, 144
Blue Patch problem, 138
*British Journal for the Philosophy of
   Science*, 25n, 135n, 146n
British parliament, 152
Bundle of Hypotheses, 76
bundle of sensations, 70, 76

California, 43, 56
Cambridge, 128
Cartesian views, 19, 21, 65n, 75, 76,
   108, 146, 176
causation, 130–5, 141–2, 146–7, 169–
   70, 178
   covering-law theory of, 131–5, 141–2
   emanation theory of, 130–5, 146
Cause and Meaning in the Social Sciences,
   122 n12
Chomskian theory of language, 95
Christianity, 7, 110
clarity, 39–42
   culture-bound, 41
   and simplicity, 41
Closed Society, 19, 23, 108–9
code, 73, 151, 163
   see also structuralisme

cognition, 77–82, 113, 125, 186
   cognitive capital, fixed and variable,
     77–82
   cognitive growth, 113, 125
   cognitive power, 186
   see also knowledge, progress, science
collectivism, 49
commensurability, 71, 76, 110
Communism, 128
Complete Works of Lewis Carroll, The, 116
Comtian positivism, 55
concepts, 16–17, 103–5, 155–6, 167–86
   change of, 178
   compulsiveness of, 155–6, 170, 179,
     183
   Concepts maketh community, 170
   falsity of social theory of, 185
   formation of, 174, 179
   no concepts beyond concepts, 173
conjecture, 21, 22, 24
   see also trial and error
Conjectures and Refutations, 38n
consensus, 180–1
   non-consensus, 182
Continuity Thesis (epistemological), 48–
   67, 116
   and detour, 109–10
   discontinuity, 51–9, 92
   (genetic or biological), 99–100
   see also amoeba, *coupure*
conventionalism, 103
Cooking, Cuisine and Class, 158n
Cosmic Exile, 18–19, 22, 91
coupure, 3, 25, 65n, 165
criteria
   of belief, 14ff, 45, 76, 106, 125–6
   of excellence, 28
   of positivism, 55
   of science, 106, 125–6
criticism, 37–8, 46, 56, 61
   inadequacy of for science, 36–61
Critique of Pure Reason, 154–5
culture, 117, 124–5, 135–6, 136, 140,
   147, 148, 173